D1240645

Power and the Vote

How do developing states decide who gets access to public goods such as electricity, water, and education? *Power and the Vote* breaks new ground by showing that the provision of seemingly universal public goods is intricately shaped by electoral priorities. In doing so, this book introduces new methods using high-resolution satellite imagery to study the distribution of electricity across and within the developing world. Combining cross-national evidence with detailed subnational analysis and village-level data from India, *Power and the Vote* affirms the power of electoral incentives in shaping the distribution of public goods and challenges the view that democracy is a luxury of the rich with little relevance to the world's poor.

Brian Min is assistant professor of political science at the University of Michigan. His doctoral dissertation received the 2011 Gabriel A. Almond Award for the best dissertation in comparative politics from the American Political Science Association. Dr. Min's articles have appeared in *World Politics*, *American Sociological Review*, and *Annual Review of Political Science*. He has received grants from the World Bank, the International Growth Centre, and the National Science Foundation. Min received his PhD from the University of California, Los Angeles, MPP from Harvard's Kennedy School of Government, and BA from Cornell University.

Power and the Vote

Elections and Electricity in the Developing World

BRIAN MIN
University of Michigan

CAMBRIDGE
UNIVERSITY PRESS

CAMBRIDGE
UNIVERSITY PRESS

32 Avenue of the Americas, New York, NY 10013-2473, USA

Cambridge University Press is part of the University of Cambridge.

It furthers the University's mission by disseminating knowledge in the pursuit of education, learning, and research at the highest international levels of excellence.

www.cambridge.org
Information on this title: www.cambridge.org/9781107525382

First published 2015

Printed in the United States of America

A catalog record for this publication is available from the British Library.

Library of Congress Cataloging in Publication Data
Min, Brian
Power and the vote : elections and electricity in the developing world / Brian Min.
    pages cm
Includes bibliographical references and index.
ISBN 978-1-107-10984-1 (hardback) – ISBN 978-1-107-52538-2 (paperback)
1. Elections – Developing countries. 2. Electrification – Political aspects – Developing countries. 3. Electric utilities – Political aspects – Developing countries. 4. Rural poor – Political activity – Developing countries. 5. Democracy – Developing countries. 6. Developing countries – Politics and government. I. Title.
JF60.M558 2015
324.9172'4–dc23   2015016874

ISBN 978-1-107-10984-1 Hardback
ISBN 978-1-107-52538-2 Paperback

To my family

Contents

Figures

Tables

Acknowledgments

For many across the world, whether one has access to the benefits of electricity depends largely on the choices of governments and political leaders. This book offers an account of the intricate political motivations that shape leaders' decisions about how to deliver electricity and how elections influence the provision of these seemingly universal public goods. This project began as a doctoral dissertation under the wise counsel of Miriam Golden and Daniel Posner. I am ever thankful for their encouragement and support. I also thank the other members of my committee, Ronald Rogowski, Timothy Groseclose, and Frederico Finan.

Over the years, I have benefited from helpful discussions and advice from Lisa Blaydes, Pradeep Chhibber, Gary Cox, Alberto Diaz-Cayeros, Thad Dunning, James Fowler, Francesca Jensenius, Robin Harding, Philip Keefer, Noam Lupu, Beatriz Magaloni, Rebecca Morton, David Patel, Jan Pierskalla, Alison Post, Jonathan Rodden, Audrey Sacks, Jun Saito, Susan Stokes, Erik Wibbels, and seminar participants at Berkeley, Cornell, CU Boulder, Dartmouth, ETH Zurich, Naval Postgraduate School, Rochester, Stanford, the World Bank, UC Santa Cruz, UC San Diego, and Yale. I owe special thanks to Andreas Wimmer, who shaped how I think about social science, and to Bill Clark for believing in me.

I am especially grateful for the close reading of the entire manuscript and the incisive feedback I received from Kanchan Chandra, Robert Franzese, Anna Grzymala-Busse, and Ken Kollman, and for crucial help on key parts of the book from Lars-Erik Cederman, Pauline Jones Luong, Mark Tessler, Anne Pitcher, and Nahomi Ichino. My colleagues at the University of Michigan have provided generous advice and support along the way, especially Allen Hicken, Bill Zimmerman, Bob Axelrod, Charles Shipan, Christian Davenport, Elisabeth Gerber, George Tsebelis, John Jackson, Jowei Chen, Mariah Zeisberg, Mark Dincecco, Mary Gallagher, Mika LaVaque-Manty, Nancy Burns, Nick Valentino, Rob Mickey, Rocio Titiunik, Scott Page, and Skip Lupia.

I am indebted to Gyanam Mahajan, Ashutosh Varshney, and Steven Wilkinson for their generosity and encouragement in supporting my research in India. In New Delhi and Uttar Pradesh, I received priceless insights from Anjoo and Priyankar Upadhyaya, Sanjay Kumar, Anil Kumar Verma, Ajit Kumar Singh, and Rohini Somanathan. Numerous officials at the Uttar Pradesh Power Corporation generously answered questions. I could not have succeeded in my fieldwork without the help of Devesh Tiwari, Santosh Dubey, Kamal Srivastava, Ankit Agrawal, and Shoaiv Ahmad.

In 2002, Phil Auerswald invited me to attend a workshop where he showed a slide of the earth at night. That image stayed seared into my brain until it became the answer to the question that motivated the methods of this book – How do we measure what governments do if the data we have are not reliable? The use of nighttime satellite imagery would not have been possible without the efforts of the National Oceanic and Atmospheric Administration's National Geophysical Data Center. I am especially indebted to Chris Elvidge and Kim Baugh, who have made the nighttime lights data available to the world and who generously shared time, technical assistance, and ideas. In working with these data, I have been fortunate to collaborate with Alassane Agalassou in Mali, Ousmane Fall Sarr in Senegal, Tuan Nguyen in Vietnam, Kwawu Mensan Gaba at the World Bank, as well as Thushyanthan Baskaran, Tom Gillespie, Raj Rao Nadakuditi, and Yogesh Uppal.

Thank you to my excellent research assistants: Young Chang, Cory Honeyman, Nicole Gibson, Diana Greenwald, Shangyayi Liu, Ephraim Love, Zachary O'Keeffe, Emily Samuelson, Jessica Steinberg, Lingao Tong, Priyamvada Trivedi, and Brendan Wu. I benefited from the talents of Danielle Lavaque-Manty, who capably edited the manuscript. At Cambridge University Press, I am grateful for the enthusiastic support of Robert Dreesen, two anonymous referees for their constructive suggestions, and Liz Janetschek, Brianda Reyes, and Vincent Rajan for shepherding this project through to the end.

I acknowledge the generous financial support of the World Bank, the International Growth Centre, the National Science Foundation (SES-0921531), the UC Institute on Global Conflict & Cooperation, UCLA, and the University of Michigan. I received invaluable support from the team at UM's Center for Political Studies, especially David Howell and Lori Maddix. Many others have helped me along the way. As a graduate student at UCLA, I learned so much from Kathy Bawn, Michael Chwe, James Honaker, Jeff Lewis, and Michael Ross, and from my classmates, Elizabeth Carlson, Kim Dionne, Ryan Enos, Kyung-Joon Han, Seth Hill, Wooyeal Paik, Jessica Preece, Tyson Roberts, and Anoop Sarbahi. Before that, I was fortunate to be inspired at the Kennedy School by John Holdren, Joseph Kalt, John Donahue, and at Cornell by Trevor Pinch, Sheila Jasanoff, Michael Dennis, and Stephen Hilgartner.

I have been cheered on by many friends over the years of this project. Thank you to Erwin Cho, Dan Braga, JunSoo Lee, Brian Jonason, Matt and Ben Redelings, and Will and Sandy Bredberg. My *fidus Achates*, Antony Moon, passed away before he could see this book in print. Always upbeat, he was encouraging me to finish even as he fought valiantly against illness. In Ann Arbor, I was fortunate to be reminded that there is life outside of work by Chinedum, Towela, Noeleen, Marie, Jong, Annette, Vance, Joseph, and Lauretta.

Thank you to the far-flung members of my family: Benny, Shannon, Lillian, Chi, William, Tori, David, and Juliana. John and Florence Chiang have been wonderful and tireless supporters, and I am more than fortunate to have them as my parents-in-law.

My parents, James Young-Key Min and Hester Soon-Hee Min, grew up in the rubble of postwar Korea and lived their fair share of nights without electricity. I thank them for teaching me to be grateful for all I have and the many quiet sacrifices they made for me. This book is the direct result of their love and faith.

I am so thankful for my two children. Ezra (age nine) inspires me with his wonder and curiosity about everything in the universe. I appreciate both his determination and his kindness, and that he occasionally lets me beat him at chess. Ellie (age six) helped me finish the book, showing me how to combine laughter with a hard-nosed work ethic. When we were daunted by blank pages and pondered how we would ever fill them, she often reminded me that the important thing is to "just start."

Finally, to my precious wife, Lillian. She is amazing at all she does, but especially in how she loves me and brings joy into our lives. I am thankful for the many nights she stayed up working with me, the countless puzzles she helped me solve, and the way she has championed me and my work. Nothing in my life would be possible without her.

I

Introduction

At one o'clock as the sweltering sun beat down on India, a load protection circuit tripped on a transmission line near Agra, not far from the Taj Mahal. Instantly, all the power on that line rushed to neighboring lines that quickly overheated, triggering other parts of the network to shut down. As current surged across the crippled grid, load protection circuits flipped like dominoes, cascading across the vast state of Uttar Pradesh, into the Delhi capital region, and soon across all of northern India. Just three minutes later, a final circuit breaker tripped along the Kankroli–Debari corridor in Rajasthan and most of India went dark. On that day, July 31, 2012, some 620 million people lost power. It would be the largest blackout in history.

The outage stretched across nearly 2,000 miles, from India's western border with Pakistan to the Naga Hills it shares with Myanmar. India's vaunted rail system ground to a halt, stranding hundreds of thousands of passengers. In Delhi, traffic signals went out, leading to traffic jams stretching as far as the eye could see.

Indians fumed in frustration as government officials scrambled to restore power and resolve the massive breakdown. The catastrophic failure highlighted an uneasy reality in India. Electricity is a critical public good, undergirding economic production and social welfare. Yet access to the benefits of electricity is anything but universal or assured. Its distribution is an uneven patchwork, connecting fortunate areas to the grid but also passing over millions, leaving more people without power than in any other country in the world. For those with electrical connections, service can be irregular, gone in a moment because of rolling blackouts whose incidence and timing are controlled by bureaucrats and public officials. In ways large and small, access to electricity depends on the state and is shaped by the preferences, strategies, and interactions of a moving cast of political actors. The official explanation for that day's massive power failure was mundane, if paradoxical. Everyone *lost* power because everyone *wanted* power. With demand swelling to perilously high levels, no state wanted to be the first to turn off the power to its residents. In India, the "grid" is composed of interconnected regional power networks, allowing states to borrow from areas with surplus capacity as necessary. Yet even as demand mounted, individual state utilities continued to allow their users to draw on the stressed grid, betting that others would reduce their demand first.

To many observers, the catastrophic failure was an inevitable outcome of a system governed by political actors beholden to political interests. As in much of the developing world, India's power sector is publicly owned and managed. Its 600,000 public servants are overseen by senior political appointees who serve at the pleasure of elected political leaders. For India's politicians and their agents, the drive to keep the power flowing to their constituents can be irresistible. Blackouts antagonize farmers who cannot pump water, frustrate teachers trying to get through lesson plans, anger business owners in darkened shops, and annoy families unable to turn on their lights and fans. Indians frequently rank electricity problems as one of the most important challenges facing the country, and vexation over outages is a prominent issue at election time. On that July day, India's battered grid simply could not sustain the relentless pressure to keep electricity flowing.

Electricity is the lifeblood of the modern economy. It enables production, keeps factories humming, illuminates streets, and lights up homes. In every corner of the globe, people rely on electricity to power fans, mobile phones, and televisions. It enables refrigeration of food and medicines. More than simply a modern convenience, access to electricity is a life-altering transformation that improves welfare and promotes economic development. Electric light extends a day's hours, enabling workers to continue producing into the night, allowing children to study after the sun has set, and enhancing public safety in the darkness. Electric stoves save cooking time and eliminate the labor and time needed to gather wood and other biomass fuels. Electricity improves agricultural productivity by powering water pumps and encourages industrial development and the use of more efficient power tools and machinery.

Yet more than a century after the introduction of electric power transmission, some 1.3 billion people – a fifth of the world's population – still live without electricity (International Energy Agency 2013). Predictably, most of those lacking access reside in poorer countries. Yet even in these states, access to electricity is uneven, marking a bright line separating those on the road to modernity from those mired in persistent poverty. In India, nine in ten city homes have electric power. Yet in the villages where most Indians live, half the population still have no electricity at home. In rural Mali, access to electricity is almost nonexistent. In Indonesia, one in four people lack electricity while electrification is nearly universal in neighboring Malaysia.

The unevenness of electricity access in many countries indicates the severity of the challenge facing governments. Across most of the world, governments are the primary purveyors of electricity because public goods such as power grids, roads, education, and public health are so important to social welfare and because markets often fail to provide them, especially in the poorest parts of a country.

Who gets electricity and why? How do governments decide who gets vital public goods such as access to electricity, clean drinking water, and education? These are important questions anywhere but absolutely critical ones in the developing world, where such services are key building blocks of development. For the poor who can afford few other alternatives, access to electricity and other basic services provided by the state can mean the difference between opportunity and destitution, and sometimes even life and death.

This book seeks to explain how political institutions shape access to public goods, particularly among the poor. Put simply, do democracies provide greater access to electricity than nondemocracies? And if so, do these benefits flow to the rural poor? Prevailing theory expects that democracies will deliver more public goods because of pressures induced by electoral competition under the gaze of a free press (Sen 1999), an institutional apparatus that privileges the interests of the poorer median voter (Meltzer and Richard 1981), the efficiency by which public goods can secure the support of a large coalition (Bueno de Mesquita et al. 2003), or a normative preference toward equality. But a growing body of empirical evidence has cast doubt on this expectation. International development experts Keefer and Khemani (2005, 2) observe that "policymakers in poor democracies regularly divert spending away from areas that most benefit the poor or fail to implement policies that improve the services that are known to disproportionately benefit poor people." Others have argued that electoral democracies are vulnerable to several types of "political failures" since candidates are motivated more by the pursuit of reelection than the welfare of their citizens (Besley and Coate 1998). Besley and Burgess (2002, 1415) also suggest that because of lower voter participation rates, "the poor and vulnerable may not obtain the full attention of politicians even in a democracy where they have numerical strength." Moreover, a vast literature shows the ways in which ethnic identities, clientelism, special interest groups, and corruption can reduce the incentives to provide public goods by vote-seeking politicians who prefer goods that can be more easily targeted and withdrawn (for reviews, see Hicken 2011 and Golden and Min 2013).

When it comes to electricity, anecdotal evidence suggests that democracies may be no better at providing access to this critical service than nondemocracies. According to official estimates in 2001, 57 percent of Indian citizens lacked basic household electricity compared to fewer than 2 percent in China, despite similarly massive populations, large territories, and expanding but impoverished rural economies (International Energy Agency 2002). These statistics are notable given India's history of vibrant democratic rule and China's long surviving single-party government. For theories that expect democracies to provide more public goods (Lake and Baum 2001; Bueno de Mesquita et al. 2003) and to distribute them more efficiently (Wittman 1989; Gradstein 1993) and equitably (Weingast, Shepsle, and Johnsen 1981; Collie 1988), the track records of the world's most populous democracy and autocracy indicate a limitation of our theories, represent an exceptional anomaly, or suggest that the data underlying this paradox are unreliable.

Each of these explanations represents strands of the story I weave in this book. By relying on new and objective data measures derived from satellite imagery, this book presents new theory and evidence from across the developing world to show that democracies systematically favor the provision of public goods because of their unique political properties.

The Argument

This book argues that democratic governments provide greater access to public goods, particularly among the rural poor, than do nondemocratic rulers.[1] Building on prominent theories of democracy, I argue that public goods are valuable to democratic leaders not only because they reach many voters and are valued by the masses, but also because of the *political externalities* they generate for electorally minded politicians. Since the seminal work of Samuelson (1954), scholars have understood that many public goods will be underprovided by markets that do not appropriately value the *economic externalities* that accrue beyond the individuals who directly benefit from a good. As a result of these economic spillovers, firms lack the incentive to provide even those goods that are in high demand and of great social benefit. Thus it is often argued that valuable societal goods such as national defense and power grids require collective provision by the state.

But although economic externalities legitimize government provision, they do not explain the varying efforts by which states seek to provide public goods. Political externalities motivate state leaders to deliver public goods. By political externalities, I mean the political benefits and costs that accrue in the political arena to politicians beyond the citizens who benefit from public goods and the state that funds them. Under democracy, political externalities are of great value, mapping tightly onto the reelection incentives of incumbents and spurring strategic efforts to deliver the benefits of public goods to pivotal areas at critical times. As a result of electoral incentives, democratic leaders will provide public goods in ways that maximize political benefits that are markedly different than the distributional strategies adopted under autocratic rule. If free market capitalism devotes itself to the capture of economic profits, democracy is a system that prioritizes the capture of political profits.

The argument, described more fully in Chapter 2, is built on two pillars. First, I argue that seemingly universal public goods can be distributed and

---

[1] Following Przeworski et al. (2000), I conceive of democracies as regimes in which electoral competition can result in turnover. That is, election outcomes are characterized by both ex ante uncertainty (anyone can win) and by ex post irreversibility (results cannot be reversed by losers).

targeted in ways that are intricately shaped by political priorities. At first blush, this statement seems self-contradictory: How can the benefits of public goods be targetable if, by definition, public goods are nonrival and nonexcludable? The answer lies in the mixed nature of many government schemes. Public goods schemes may offer universal benefits to a country as a whole, but in their implementation and delivery, the individual fragments that make up these schemes have many of the characteristics of private goods.

Because public goods are so highly valued by citizens and come wrapped in a veneer of universalism, they are easy for political leaders to champion and promote. But beneath that veneer, public goods schemes are rife with opportunities for political influence and manipulation. Any effort to deliver public goods entails a set of discrete actions, siting decisions, and locally concentrated expenditures. When it comes to electricity, the presence of a power grid and the promise of electrical power may appear as a public good for the country as a whole, but in the way it is delivered, electricity is also a private good that can be targeted, rationed, and withdrawn. The coexistence of these public facing universal benefits with the presence of finely targetable benefits under the umbrella of the same "public goods" scheme generates political externalities of great value to political leaders.

Second, because of the influence political actors have over the provision of public goods, political incentives will shape the distribution of public goods and the benefits that flow from them. For democratically elected leaders, public goods projects are highly appealing because of the opportunities they provide for legislators to shape their delivery and oversee their implementation. Each of these opportunities results in political externalities that are of great value to election-minded incumbents. As a result, democratic leaders will have a stronger preference for public goods provision than nondemocratic rulers who cannot directly capitalize on these political externalities in the absence of elections.

Although both selectorate theory (Bueno de Mesquita et al. 2003) and theories of redistribution (Meltzer and Richard 1981; Boix 2003; Acemoglu and Robinson 2006b) agree that democracies will have larger governments and higher levels of spending on public goods, they do not explicitly model the geographic distribution of these benefits. It is the political externalities of public goods, far more than their economic externalities, that shape their distribution. Under democracy, the need to win a large base of support leads to broader competition, encompassing a more expansive set of communities than in settings without elections. As democratic politicians seek to maximize the political benefits that flow from public goods projects, their catchment area will encompass spaces that would not be targeted on purely economic and technical grounds – rural regions and villages whose geographic remoteness, economic frailty, and historical exclusion make them otherwise improbable project sites. Indeed, these weaknesses make them particularly attractive opportunities for political targeting because it is here where the effort of legislators is most obvious to voters. Meanwhile, in autocratic settings, there are no electoral incentives for leaders to direct public goods to the rural periphery, though they may do so for other reasons. Because of the political consequences that flow from the provision of public goods, the spatial configuration of these public goods will differ markedly across regime types, with especially important repercussions among the rural poor.

Why Electricity Matters

Electricity provision is not a widely studied topic in political science.[2] Yet the flow and distribution of electrical power provides an unusually clear window into how political institutions work. Consider a national village electrification program in a developing country. Owing to budget constraints, only a small portion of unelectrified villages can be electrified at a time. Which villages should be selected? Imagine two scenarios. In the first, the selection of villages is based on a technical evaluation of project costs and benefits. Such a process might prioritize villages with the largest number of potential residential and business customers. A more sophisticated assessment could even take into account potential network and scale externalities – it may be more cost-effective to electrify villages that are proximate to preexisting supply lines, or where the new connected load would be particularly beneficial in balancing load to a nearby power station.

Now imagine that an elected leader can influence the choice of which villages will be electrified. The political opportunities tied to this undertaking are lucrative.[3] A successful electrification project is highly visible, with ribbon-cutting ceremonies, project plaques, and lights that turn on every night to remind voters of who helped bring power to the village. By negotiating with village leaders, promises of loyalty and support can be sought. Perhaps village chiefs can even be pitted against one another as they compete for the legislator's attention. The ability to influence the rollout of the electrification program is thus a lucrative opportunity for electorally minded leaders.

Under democracy, public goods have valuable political externalities that politicians can capture and benefit from at the polling station. Promises to bring the benefits of public goods to individual communities are an especially powerful campaign tactic in the developing world because such goods are

---

[2] There are some notable exceptions, especially Brown and Mobarak (2009), who examine the effect of democracy on the sectoral distribution of electrical power. Briggs (2012) is among the few studies to explicitly consider political motivations to target electrification projects, in this case in Ghana. Kale (2014) provides a detailed political history of electrification across three Indian states with divergent outcomes. Another broader literature has focused on the politics of regulatory reform and privatization in the power sector (Levi-Faur 2003; Murillo 2009; Wengle 2015).

[3] In fact, such a scenario is not farfetched. In India, village electrification initiatives provide a wide range of opportunities for elected leaders to intervene in the selection of villages. Some programs explicitly enumerate the number of villages a legislator can select in each period.

highly valued by the poor, provide broad benefits to large numbers of voters at once, and serve as a visible accomplishment for which politicians can claim credit in campaigns (Mani and Mukand 2007; Harding and Stasavage 2014). As Kale (2014, 4) describes, "the process of electrification, while highly technical, is never neutral. In every instance, social and political contexts shape the way that electricity becomes embedded in a given place."

As mentioned previously, electricity is important because it is critical to social welfare and economic prosperity. It is also important because governments remain the primary providers of electricity in much of the developing world. This combination makes electricity a highly salient political issue in many countries. In 2011 alone, citizens engaged in protests and riots in fifty countries in response to power outages, fuel shortages, and price spikes. In 2008, unprecedented blackouts in South Africa weakened the legitimacy of President Thabo Mbeki, who eventually resigned. In the winter of 2010, power and fuel shortages in Kyrgyzstan sparked riots and the eventual ouster of President Kurmanbek Bakiyev. In 2011, violent protests over protracted outages shook once tranquil streets in Senegal, culminating in the electoral defeat of President Abdoulaye Wade. And in India, the state of the nation's power grid is a dominant theme in state and national-level elections.

Electricity is a common campaign issue because so many rely on it for their well-being and no one prefers fewer hours of electricity, less reliable supply, or higher rates. These valence-like qualities are characteristic of electoral discourse around many public goods. Their high value to citizens makes them easy to champion from the campaign podium, even when states lack the capacity to provide them uniformly or universally. As states are often the only providers of many public services, politicians serve as influential middlemen, securing funds for their delivery while also influencing how those funds are spent and directed. When it comes to electrical power, its provision requires both an initial investment in electrical infrastructure "stock" as well as an ongoing commitment to maintain the "flow" of electricity. As electricity is distributed through centralized power grids, politicians can influence access to power by manipulating the incidence and severity of power cuts and even withdraw its provision to maintain oversight over voters. These characteristics make electricity provision an especially attractive target for political manipulation in the developing world.

In the developing world, where limited budgets are a perpetual constraint, political actors must prioritize who, what, and where to focus on first. The key political reality is that public services must be delivered in a sequence of practical steps, and each step is shaped by opportunities for political influence. To borrow a phrase from Scott (1969), "Between the passage of legislation and its actual implementation lies an entirely different political arena" (1142). Within the gap between policy goals and policy implementation lie lucrative political externalities that are contested, exploited, and captured by political actors, driven not only by policy goals but also by their own political incentives. This drama of political arbitrage, in which the benefits of public goods schemes are sundered, repackaged, and strategically disbursed to maximize political profits, results in patterns of provision that differ sharply around the world.

Implications

Given the political externalities associated with public goods provision, I argue that electoral competition will shape the incentives of governments regarding the level of public goods to provide, where to provide them, and when. This proposition results in three empirical implications that are tested in this book.

Hypothesis One: Electricity Is Provided More Broadly by Democratic Governments

Democratic leaders must court and win the support of large numbers of voters, resulting in an institutional incentive to invest heavily in services that deliver wide-ranging impacts to large groups of voters. Provision of public goods is an appealing policy option because they efficiently deliver benefits at a low per capita cost, they are valued by voters, and because they result in clearly visible manifestations of political effort.

To the nation, the promise of better schools, roads, and electricity is widely appealing. Such universalistic commitments are the core of many stump speeches and campaign platforms. Yet the process of implementing such broad policies yields wide opportunities for crafty politicians to target, favor, and manipulate resources. To local communities, the commitment of better education is transformed into promises of teaching jobs, the construction of school buildings, and the provision of supplies. Similarly, commitments to provide better electricity in the countryside become an exercise in selectively doling out contracts and prioritizing the electrification of favored villages. For democratic politicians, the presence of these valuable political externalities associated with public goods provision increase their value and salience. Because of the way competitive elections enhance the political value of public goods provision, electricity should be more broadly distributed and reach a greater proportion of citizens in democratic countries than in their nondemocratic counterparts.

Hypothesis Two: Democracies Will Deliver More Electricity to the Rural Periphery than Will Nondemocracies

While competitive elections make public goods especially important to democratic politicians, where should the benefits of these public goods be targeted? In democratic settings, the *political* benefits of public goods provision are often highest in areas where the *nonpolitical* justification for them is least obvious. Compared to cities, rural areas have fewer beneficiaries spread out over larger distances, have fewer profit-generating customers, and are physically more challenging and financially expensive to connect to services. Thus reaching out to the rural poor is difficult for cash-strapped governments to justify on economic grounds. But in electoral democracies, the rural poor make up a large part of the citizenry and are difficult to ignore from a political perspective. Moreover, public goods are especially valued by the rural poor who can afford few alternatives. Thus, democratic leaders can win large numbers of votes among the rural poor through the promise and delivery of public goods. Meanwhile, autocrats have no electoral incentives to invest in their rural hinterlands, though they are clearly motivated by other concerns. Ultimately, the expectation is that repeated electoral competition should induce higher levels of electricity provision to the rural poor in democracies than in nondemocratic settings.

Hypothesis Three: Efforts to Target Electricity Will Be Heightened during Election Periods

If public goods provision generates political externalities of higher value to democratic leaders, then evidence of these efforts should be most evident in electorally critical periods. This is because voter attention to the efforts of their political leaders is naturally limited. At the same time, politicians are constrained in how meaningfully they can influence policy and outcomes, both because of their own finite political influence, as well as systemic constraints on capacity. In the context of limited political and fiscal capacity (Chhibber and Nooruddin 2004; Wibbels 2008), efforts to manage public goods provision are thus most valuable when they have the highest opportunity to influence voters. Thus targeting of electricity provision should be highest in election periods when voter attention is highest and where the political opportunity and capacity for change is highest.

To be clear, these propositions do not imply that democracy is necessarily *better* for the poor or that service provision is of *higher quality* in democratic settings. Indeed, newspapers and journals are filled with accounts of corruption, inefficiency, and dysfunction in many democratic settings. There is no doubt that the benefits of many public services and goods seem to pass over the poor, even in countries with elections. What this book seeks to contribute is theory and evidence that describe how public goods provision is shaped by political institutions in the real world. In so doing, it offers some help in explaining the paradox of why democracies face such strong incentives to deliver public goods and yet fail so regularly at improving the welfare of their citizens. Elections generate political incentives that privilege the *delivery* of public goods projects, more so than improving the *quality* of such projects. One reason is that improving quality is hard and expensive. For politicians, the impact of such investments is more difficult to observe at the polls. Increased spending on educational curricula is less compelling to local voters than construction of a new school building. Extensions of the electrical grid into dark villages are more dramatic than sober maintenance budgets that promise regular inspection and replacement of burned out streetlights. And thus election-minded politicians prioritize the visible components of public goods projects over the less visible efforts required to maintain and improve the quality of services.

Empirical Approach

The study of distributional questions in public service provision has long been hampered by an absence of reliable subnational data. Collecting data on the welfare of citizens in poor countries is arduous, time consuming, and expensive, making it difficult to record data and collect the repeated measurements necessary to monitor temporal trends. Even data on important indicators such as gross domestic product are subject to quality concerns, such as the long-standing debate on estimating the true size of the Chinese economy (Maddison 1998; Holz 2006). An article in *The Economist* once quipped, "Africa's GDP data are notoriously bad … According to the latest version of the [Penn World Table], Equatorial Guinea grew by 4% a year over 1975–99. But the data in the 2002 version suggest an annual rate of –2.7%. So Equatorial Guinea may therefore have had the second-fastest growing economy in Africa. Or the slowest."[4]

Due to the lack of good data, we know "surprisingly little about what types of governments tend to improve the welfare of the poor" (Ross 2006, 871). Without reliable indicators that track the well-being of the poorest citizens, scholars tend to rely on indirect measures such as country-level averages or on survey samples that are often limited in size or frequency of observation. Thus scholars resort to asking whether democracy raises average income levels, lengthens life expectancy, increases calorie consumption, improves literacy, or reduces infant mortality. No doubt improvements on these indicators indicate some benefit to the poor, but the link leans heavily on assumption and extrapolation and not on direct data.

This book will not overcome all of these challenges. But by focusing closely on a single type of public good and studying it at multiple scales from the global level down to the local, it will show how a new empirical approach can illuminate the importance of political institutions in shaping access to public goods across the developing world. The data underlying this book do not rely on human agents or survey collectors. Rather, it exploits technologies of earth observation from space, which for decades have enabled monitoring of weather patterns, ice formations, fire onsets, and other terrestrial and atmospheric phenomena. In the 1970s, the US Air Force deployed a series of weather satellites to track cloud patterns at night, using visible and thermal band sensors to record the brightness and temperature of moonlit cloudtops during the evening hours. While it was not the original operational goal of the instrument, analysts realized that on clear nights, the pictures that came back

---

4 "How Is Africa actually doing?" *The Economist*, March 12, 2010.

from the satellites revealed a tapestry of twinkling lights from illuminated cities and towns below.

Beginning in the early 1990s, scientists at the National Oceanic and Atmospheric Administration (NOAA) began to digitally archive and process the nighttime lights imagery. This data stream represents an unusually detailed record of the distribution of outdoor lighting, covering every corner of the globe and captured on every single night since 1992. Using image processing algorithms to distinguish areas with stable light signatures from those that are irregularly lit by fires and other ephemera, NOAA scientists produced a set of remarkable annual composite images of time-stable lights across the globe (Elvidge et al. 1997a, 1997b, 2001).

I exploit this unique set of nighttime satellite imagery to generate new estimates of electricity access across the world and over time. The basic premise is simple: areas of human settlement that appear brightly lit on clear nights indicate the flow of electrical power. Certainly, illumination can be generated from many sources, but kerosene lamps, candles, small fires, and battery-powered lanterns are not bright enough to be detected by these satellites. Moreover, most artificial illumination is used indoors, and exterior lighting is only possible in contexts with plentiful energy. To be sure, electricity can come in small amounts from solar panels or diesel generators, but due to the need for batteries and fuel, self-generated power can be up to ten times more expensive than grid-based power (Eberhard et al. 2011, 13), discouraging their use for public goods like widespread outdoor lighting. Almost everywhere in the developing world, the only cost-effective way to persistently illuminate outdoor areas comes from grid-based electricity, implying that areas with consistent light output are likely to be electrified and receiving regular flows of electrical power.

In the foundational studies of nighttime lights satellite imagery, Christopher Elvidge and his colleagues demonstrated that total nighttime illumination in a country is correlated with total electricity consumption (Elvidge et al. 1997a, 1997b, 2001). Extending these findings, the results in this book show that nighttime lighting patterns can reliably identify electricity use at the country level, at the subnational state level, and in areas as small as a village, even in settings with rudimentary electrical infrastructure (Min et al. 2013; Min and Gaba 2014).

Due to the high spatial resolution of the data, we can observe levels of light output for areas as small as a few square kilometers. By comparing the light data against high-resolution population distribution maps, I construct electricity access rates at multiple geographic scales. Since the national, subnational, regional, and local estimates are all generated from the same underlying disaggregated data sources, the procedure results in measures that are resistant to concerns about aggregation bias that afflict many other development indicators. Compared to traditional survey and administrative data, these satellite-based measures of electricity access are unbiased by political factors, consistent in their measurement across all countries, and complete in their geographic coverage over a substantial two-decade timespan.[5] As a result, the data allow for a more rigorous and credible analysis of how governments differ in the provision of electricity, even to the poorest areas where traditional data sources are unreliable or may not exist.

Drawing on the satellite-derived data of electrified areas, I examine the claim that democratic governments provide more public goods and distribute them to more rural poor areas than do autocratic rulers. The findings reveal a large and significant positive effect of democracy on the provision of electricity that is unlikely to have been produced by chance or by differences in country incomes, demographics, or geography. Across all levels of wealth, democracies consistently provide electricity to a broader share of their citizens than do non-democracies. Moreover, democratic governments deliver more electricity to their poorest and most marginal citizens. Complementing global statistical analysis at the national and subnational levels, I also investigate the power of elections in India and show that governments increase the supply of electricity around elections, especially when led by parties whose platforms and ideological commitments are credibly served by targeting public services to poor and rural areas.

A Roadmap

Chapter 2 presents a theoretical overview of the way political institutions shape the incentives for public goods provision. I highlight how conflicting empirical results on the effect of democracy can be explained by inconsistency in the way public goods are conceptualized in theory and measured in practice. I then explain how a focus on the political externalities of public goods provision can help explain the incentives that drive democratic leaders to deliver public goods to the rural poor.

In Chapter 3, I describe the key role states play in the provision of electricity, especially to rural areas. Because of its great value to citizens and the way states can influence its delivery, electricity distribution provides a unique window into the revealed preferences of regimes and their associated political actors.

Chapter 4 introduces the use of nighttime satellite imagery as a measure of electricity provision at an unprecedented level of geographic resolution and temporal frequency. By comparing satellite-derived measures of nighttime light output against a range of data on electrical infrastructure and consumption, I show that the satellite-derived measures are a valid and reliable indicator of the configuration of the electrical grid and the flow of electrical power through its lines.

In Chapter 5, I ask, Do democracies provide more public goods than autocracies? Clear answers to this question have been hampered by inconsistent,

---

[5] There are, of course, many data quality and consistency issues with the satellite data. Chapter 4 provides a detailed discussion.

unreliable, or missing data. To address the shortcomings of self-reported government data, I propose a new method that more directly observes the provision of electricity across the globe using satellite imagery of nighttime lights. I show that democratization is associated with a substantial increase in access to electricity, even after controlling for differences in per capita income, population density, and state capacity. The results affirm the power of electoral incentives in inducing democratic leaders to provide higher levels of public goods than in autocracies where leaders do not need to win elections.

Although democracy leads to greater electricity provision in *poor countries*, does democracy actually benefit *poor people*? Chapter 6 evaluates this question by comparing electricity provision in the poorest areas of countries in the developing world. Drawing on a new subnational dataset constructed at the 1-degree latitude by 1-degree longitude level and identifying poor areas using subnational infant mortality and disaggregated economic data, I find that democracies provide consistently higher rates of electrification to their poorest citizens than do autocratic governments. Moreover, the spatial distribution of electricity in poor parts of developing democracies appears to reflect a conscious effort to target areas with many voters. By contrast, the spatial distribution of citizens has no effect on the provision of services by autocratic leaders.

Chapter 7 explains how the effort to win elections influences the distribution of electricity in Uttar Pradesh, India's most populous state. By observing temporal variations in nighttime light output for all 98,000 villages over four election cycles from 1992 to 2010, I show that electricity service provision increases around elections, especially in areas represented by a low-caste party aligned with the interests of the poor. The book concludes by underscoring how access to public goods is shaped by political institutions and what this implies for how we think about the energy challenge facing the world's poor and the broader implications for climate change.

2

Public Goods, Elections, and the Poor

> The legitimate object of government is to do for a community of people whatever they need to have done, but cannot do at all or cannot so well do, for themselves, in their separate, and individual capacities.
>
> Abraham Lincoln, 1854

Introduction

Long before Paul Samuelson formalized the economic theory of public goods in the 1950s, Abraham Lincoln recognized that many of society's most critical needs would go unprovided by individuals left to their own devices. President Lincoln argued that it was government's role to supply "all which, in its nature, and without wrong, requires combined action, as public roads and highways, public schools, charities, pauperism, orphanage, estates of the deceased, and the machinery of government itself."

Even well intentioned and highly motivated groups of individuals will find it a struggle to provide public goods. Theories of collective action show that when the benefits of such services are broad, the incentives for individuals to contribute to their costs are low (Olson 1965). As group size increases, the aggregate costs of provision scale up just as the individual impetus to contribute scales down. Free-riding problems in an open market undermine the incentive to engage in voluntary collective action to create infrastructure and provide basic public services. Thus societies look to their governments to help resolve the collective action obstacles that impede public goods provision. As Olson (1965) puts it, "the state is first of all an organization that provides public goods for its members, the citizens" (15). When governments do a good job of providing public goods, they gain legitimacy, while helping their countries grow and prosper. Yet, the degree of success with which states deliver public goods varies dramatically around the world. Why do some governments produce ample public goods and services while others struggle to do so? Does democracy increase the will of states to supply public goods? And after public goods are promised, how are they distributed, and who actually benefits? Although these are important questions for any citizen, they are life-defining concerns for the poor, for whom access to basic public services can mean the difference between well-being and despair. The better off can afford other solutions, but the poor often have no choice but to depend on governments for access to electricity, clean water, roads, education, and medical care.

In economics, public goods theory emphasizes the difficulty markets face in providing goods that are nonrivalrous and nonexcludable in consumption (Samuelson 1954, 1955). Because firms have little motive to produce goods that consumers can enjoy without cost or limit, markets will undersupply these goods, even if they are highly valued by society. As a result, governments are deemed necessary for the provision of many public goods. Yet, even if economic factors favor government supply of public goods, they do not explain why some governments are more motivated than others to make them available. Clean air, to take one example, is highly valued but many governments do little to enforce regulations that would protect it.

In this book, I emphasize the role of electoral incentives in driving politicians and ruling governments to embrace public goods, champion their provision, and manage their delivery. The claim that politics shapes the distribution of valuable state resources is of course an old one. In the 1920s, the celebrated political scientist Harold Lasswell defined politics as the study of who gets what, when, and how. His own arguments focused heavily on the personal influence of leaders in shaping outcomes. Since then, political scientists have emphasized the role of institutions in establishing the incentives for different distributional strategies. In particular, scholars have argued that democracy induces higher levels of public goods provision because elections privilege the interests of the median voter (Meltzer and Richard 1981), because leaders have less ability to capture rents when facing competition (Lake and Baum 2001), or because of the need to win over large numbers of supporters efficiently (Bueno de Mesquita et al. 2003).

This book breaks new ground by showing that democracies prioritize the provision of public goods for reasons that go well beyond these explanations. Drawing on institutional theories of the state, I argue that democracy favors the delivery of public goods because of the lucrative *political externalities* generated by their provision. Because public goods are funded through the state purse, political actors can influence every aspect of the timing, siting, and modes of delivery of public goods projects. Every decision generates political externalities – political benefits and costs – that accrue in the political arena to decision makers who are motivated not only by a project's goals, but also by their own political objectives. Under democracy, public goods provision is especially valuable because it generates electoral payoffs to the politicians who define who benefits and who loses from the implementation of seemingly universal public goods schemes.

In constructing the argument of this book, I make two related claims about the representation of public goods in theory and in empirical research. First, despite a now vast literature on public goods provision, theoretical definitions of "public goods" are inconsistent, leading to incompatible claims about their properties and political value. Second, flowing from the first inconsistency, there is no agreement in empirical research on what kinds of state-provided goods, services, or policy outputs merit designation as "public goods." The result of these compounding inconsistencies is lingering uncertainty on the fundamental question of whether democracies provide more public goods and whether they benefit the poor.

The Problem of Defining Public Goods
The first claim is that goods often casually labeled as "public goods" are more mixed in their characteristics than they may first appear. The result is that "public goods" are inconsistently defined, and the term is used in incompatible ways, resulting in contradictory theoretical expectations about their properties.

Many theoretical models assume that public goods cannot be targeted since they provide the same utility to all citizens. For example, Bueno de Mesquita et al. (2003) say, "Everyone receives the benefits derived from the public goods provided by the government" (79). In the theoretical model of Lizzeri and Persico (2001), "The public good yields a utility of G to each voter" (228). Similarly, in the classic public goods game from experimental economics, all participants receive an equal share of the common pot (Palfrey and Prisbrey 1997; Fehr and Gächter 2000). Yet finding goods that meet such a definition in the real world is far from straightforward.

Consider education, often cited as being among the most important public goods states provide, especially in the developing world (Ansell 2010). To some, education is a (pure) public good, as it delivers broad-based utility to an entire population, raises a nation's human capital, and generates positive economic externalities. Yet how governments go about shaping access to education is a matter of policy choice. Some strategies reflect a concern for social groups, such as the eradication of school fees to benefit the poor in new African democracies (Harding and Stasavage 2014). In such a case, policy treats education as a club good that can be shaped to benefit specific groups. But when attention is paid to variations in funding and school quality across a country, education is conceptualized as a local public good (Hoxby 1999; Miguel and Gugerty 2005), offering geographically targeted benefits that are more abundant in some areas than in others. When political motivations influence the geographic allocation of education's benefits, these efforts are often labeled pork.

Like education, many textbook examples of public goods share these ambiguous qualities. National defense benefits the entire country but also privileges defense contractors and the regional economies surrounding military bases. According to one report, "Pork barrel considerations are still behind 85 percent of [US] procurement decisions" (Kitfield 1991), and half of all defense spending is concentrated in only ten states (Levinson, Shah, and Connor 2011). Law and order should be universally beneficial, yet are variable in their provision, and some receive better protection from the law than others (Wilkinson 2004; Holland 2014). National parks are another frequently cited exemplar of a public good that offers broad communal benefit to everyone in a country. Yet parks are geographically located in ways that deliver disproportionate benefits to some over others and their placement and funding reflect the outcome of pragmatic politics. In a critical report targeting inefficient spending in the parks system, Senator Tom Coburn argued, "Congress has turned the National Park Service into its own national 'pork' service, with Washington politicians earmarking new parks for purely political and parochial purposes" (p. 8).[1]

In perhaps the most prominent academic debate on what is a public good, economists have wrestled with whether lighthouses fit the designation. John Stuart Mill famously argued that a lighthouse required public provision because there was no way to exclude free-riding ships from benefiting from its illumination.[2] America's first public works law passed in 1789 stated that "the necessary support, maintenance, and repairs of all lighthouses, beacons, buoys, and public piers ... shall be defrayed by the Treasury of the United States." But Coase (1974) famously demonstrated that there were many lighthouses in nineteenth century England that were privately funded through the collection of port fees, demonstrating that "public goods" need not be provided by the state. Disagreeing with Coase's conclusion, Van Zandt (1993), Kuran (2001), and Bertrand (2006) argued that the state provided the essential role of coordination and enforcement, without which lighthouses would not have been able to operate.

These examples illustrate the critical challenge of defining the relevant group associated with any public good. The standard economic definition emphasizing nonrivalrous and nonexcludable consumption is useful only when the relevant group of consumers is specified. As Mancur Olson illustrates, a parade may be a public good to those watching from tall buildings along the route, but it is a private good to those who must purchase tickets to sit in stands along the way (Olson 1965, footnotes 21 and 22). But specifying the relevant group that benefits from a public good is far from trivial. Governments can promote national electrification as a universal benefit for the entire country. Yet if the work is focused on the countryside where access is most lacking, then rural

---

[1] Coburn, Tom A. "Parked! How Congress misplaced priorities are trashing our national treasures." October 2013. http://hdl.loc.gov/loc.gdc/coburn.2014500005

[2] Mill makes the argument in the final chapter of his *Principles of Political Economy* (1848):

"It is a proper office of government to build and maintain lighthouses, establish buoys, etc. for the security of navigation: for since it is impossible that the ships at sea which are benefited by a lighthouse, should be made to pay a toll on the occasion of its use, no one would build lighthouses from motives of personal interest, unless indemnified and rewarded from a compulsory levy made by the state."

citizens benefit more than city dwellers. As decisions are made about where to extend the power grid, some villages will benefit first from electrification, while others are inevitably passed over. Even within a newly electrified village, not everyone may be so fortunate to get a household connection. Electricity thus benefits the country as a whole at the same time as it only benefits some and not others. Electricity can be conceived of as a public good whose universality depends on whether the relevant group of interest is the nation, the country-side, residents of specific villages, or individual households.

Critically, from the perspective of the political leader, there is no reason why only one of these groups must be the singular focus of an electrification effort. Indeed, political leaders can serve multiple audiences simultaneously, addressing the whole nation in the writing of party platforms, advocating for electricity to specific villages in campaign speeches, and promising household connections in efforts to win individual voters.

Mertha (2008) nicely documents how the very same hydroelectric dam projects held different political meanings for different actors in China:

Hydropower engineers argued convincingly that they were helping the country in its constant quest for energy sources. Local political leaders in favor of the projects understood them as ways to bring their own constituents out of desperate poverty. National-level officials ... felt an obligation to allow interior provinces to share in the dramatic wealth that has made coastal China one of the most dynamic places on earth. (xxiv)

In each case, different political actors embraced different sets of benefits flowing from the same dams, some focused on their local properties and others on their national contributions, depending on the political context in which the actors were situated.

It is worth fully citing Head and Shoup (1969), who note that whether a good is public or private is almost always ambiguous:

If, for example, a certain stretch of highway can be made either a toll road or a free road is it a public good or a private good? If a lighthouse beam can be scrambled so that only ships that purchase an unscrambler can receive the beam, how shall the service rendered by the lighthouse be classified? If an increment of protection against crime can be produced, either by increasing the police patrol or by installing additional locks and burglar alarms, is that service, with respect to that increment, a public or a private good? To base the classification on whether the service is in fact being rendered in the marketing mode is to suggest no general principle for distinguishing public goods from private goods.

For Head and Shoup, what makes something a public good depends on whether it is more economically efficient to deliver a good in a mode in which users can be excluded or in a nonmarketing mode in which no exclusion is possible. If it is more cost effective to not exclude users, then it is a public good. The key insight here is that a service *becomes* a public good or a private good depending on choices about how it is delivered and provided. Decisions about adding tolls or scramblers to light beams are not inherently tied to the physical nature of roads or lighthouses. Rather, they are negotiated by actors who are likely to consider the spillover benefits and costs accruing not only to users but also to the decision makers themselves.[3]

Thus whether or not a state-provided service is a public good or not cannot be determined based only on an evaluation of a good's physical or economic characteristics. It is also critical to acknowledge the political context in which public goods schemes are implemented, policy goals are established, services are funded, and benefits are delivered.

The Problem of Measuring Public Goods

The second claim is that public goods are inconsistently measured in empirical research, resulting in incompatible conclusions about whether democracies provide broader levels of public goods.

In most empirical research, scholars tend to starkly distinguish goods provided by the state as either public goods or private goods. This simple dichotomization is not only imprecise but also misleading: many state goods have distinctly dual characteristics, reflecting public good characteristics at the same time as providing private good benefits.

Aaron and McGuire (1970) lay out the practical challenge for empirical research this way: "In particular, the necessity arises to distinguish between government expenditures on commonly shared 'public goods,' and government expenditures on private or specific goods which are apportioned and exhausted among individuals" (908). Yet how to distinguish between these categories depends too often on "arbitrary rules of thumb." Some scholars think of public goods as policy outputs that are not easily targetable to geographic areas or groups. Bueno de Mesquita et al. (2003) offer as examples of public goods "rule of law, transparency and accountability, even-handed police services, general access to education, a level commercial playing field, antipollution legislation, parkland preservation, communication and transportation infrastructure, and the like" (29). Similarly, in "Public Goods under Alternative Electoral Incentives," Lizzeri and Persico (2001) define public goods as goods that accrue to all citizens equally and cannot be geographically targeted. This therefore excludes things like education, roads, and sewers, which to them represent pork-barrel spending and not public goods.

Yet other scholars employ a different rule of thumb. For Alesina, Baqir, and Easterly (1999), education, roads, and sewers are precisely the objects of interest when they study spending on public goods. The same emphasis on local

---

[3] Along similar lines, Weitz-Shapiro (2012) argues that there is nothing inherent about goods like foodstuffs that make them clientelistic goods. Rather, politicians determine whether to use them for clientelistic purposes. Cox and McCubbins (2001) describe compellingly how public policies, no matter how broadly conceived, can be "morselized" into discrete packages of distributive benefits.

service delivery is made by Milesi-Ferretti, Perotti, and Rostagno (2002), for whom public goods are purchases of goods and services that can be targeted geographically. They say: "there are two types of government spending: [first] transfers and [second] purchases of goods and services, or 'public goods'" (612). These purchases are public goods because spending on goods and services is "local in nature" and benefits everyone in the region.[4]

Each of these purported measures of public goods is quite different, implying divergent sets of beneficiaries and externalities. Several refinements have aimed to sharpen the way in which public goods are conceptualized and identified. Club goods are public goods available only to members of specific groups (Buchanan 1965; Cornes 1996). Local public goods are those that are available to all in the local service area (Tiebout 1956). Besley et al. (2004) distinguish between high-spillover public goods (roads, drains, street lights, and water sources) and low-spillover public goods (houses or toilets built by a government scheme). Besley and Ghatak (2006) also offer a helpful distinction between market-supporting public goods, such as law and order, and market-augmenting public goods such as health and education.

Yet even these characterizations belie the pliancy with which access to the benefits of any public good can be shaped by policy and design choices. Indeed the delivery of public goods always requires choices to select the relevant sets of beneficiaries and determine the timing and siting of projects. These are exquisitely political opportunities.

Democracy and the Political Externalities of Public Goods

Building on these observations about the inconsistency with which public goods are defined and measured, I argue that the difficulty scholars face in consistently identifying and measuring public goods reflects the reality that many public goods schemes have mixed characteristics in the real world, combining attributes of both pure public goods and pure private goods. This ambiguity is fully exploited within democratic settings, where politicians promise broad public goods on the one hand while using their influence to shape specifically how, where, and when these public goods are distributed.

Electricity provision reflects both public good properties, given the universal and indivisible benefits it provides to a country's welfare and development, and also private good properties, given the way in which electrical power can be selectively provided, redirected, and withdrawn. As I argue in the text that follows, this duality creates unique opportunities for skilled politicians who can champion universalist goals on the national stage while also managing the delivery of discrete benefits to key constituents. Politicians may thus be guided

---

[4] The actual measure of public goods in the dataset of Milesi-Ferretti, Perotti, and Rostagno (2002) is defined this way: "Public goods are defined as the sum of current and capital spending on goods and services, i.e., the sum of government consumption and of capital spending."

as much by the pursuit of political externalities to further their careers as they are by the economic gains and social welfare benefits that flow from the delivery of public goods.

Public Goods and Their Political Externalities

Whereas economic factors justify the need for public goods provision, *political* factors motivate governments to provide public goods and shape the strategies they use to do so. Because public goods are highly valued by voters, delivering them creates electoral payoffs to the political actors who influence their provision. In the presence of competitive elections, the need to win votes is a powerful objective that drives politicians to pursue provision of public goods more vigorously and to distribute them more strategically than politicians in nondemocratic regimes. As we will see in future chapters, this theory helps explain not only the higher level of public goods provision under democracy but also why new beneficiaries are often concentrated in the poorest parts of democratic states.

In his landmark economics textbook, Samuelson (1964) argues that governments have the critical role of providing public goods that will not be provided by private firms. More than simply taking care of the material needs of individuals, "Government provides certain indispensable *public* services without which community life would be unthinkable and which by their nature cannot appropriately be left to private enterprise ... Government came into existence once people realized, 'Everybody's business is nobody's business'" (45). This standard economic account thus emphasizes the role of governments in addressing market failures and supplying public goods by collecting taxes and overcoming free rider and collective action problems. As a result, an influential view holds that governments are responsible for providing public goods such as national defense, law and order, and basic infrastructure (Samuelson 1958; World Bank 1994). However, the economic justification for government provision of public goods fails to explain why governments differ in their *willingness* to actually deliver public goods. The incentives for provision and the benefits that accrue to leaders who provide them depend not only on their economic externalities but also on political spillovers.

Public goods are favored in democracies because of their political externalities – nonmonetary rewards that accrue to the political figures who broker the implementation of public good schemes and influence decisions about how such schemes get delivered in practice. Public goods projects such as electrification, road construction, and irrigation are costly and complex, with numerous opportunities for politicians to influence the delivery process, including selecting project sites, awarding procurement and operations contracts, and appointing officials to key bureaucratic posts.[5] Commitments to provide public

---

[5] Public goods provision can also be an appealing source of rents to officeholders, which may be a countervailing weight on the positive effect of democracy presented here. Because contracts are often large, projects are unique, and excess costs are difficult to prove, power over the

goods are particularly effective electioneering tools because they speak to the vital needs of so many voters. Services such as electricity, clean water, and education are particularly valued among the poor, who are electorally numerous and whose votes may be more easily swayed by delivery of these scarcities. Public goods schemes promise broad benefits to large numbers of voters at once and serve as a visible accomplishment for which politicians can claim credit in campaigns (Mani and Mukand 2007; Harding and Stasavage 2014). Their delivery is consistent with pro-poor and pro-development agendas and their costs are justified along these lines. Bueno de Mesquita et al. (2003) argue, "Public goods that enhance social welfare are especially emphasized by leaders who depend on a large coalition. Such goods are much less likely to be provided by those who rule with the support of a small group of cronies" (214).

Commitments to provide public goods also serve politicians' interests by giving them the opportunity to earn the support of a broader set of beneficiaries than would be possible in any individual-based quid pro quo. In his study of politics in post-independence India, Weiner (1962) noted that leaders learn to pursue their own interests by speaking of the general good: "The politician concerned with his own advancement and with the advancement of his own special interest has learned that this can best be achieved by couching his demands in terms of the public interest ..." (219). Indeed, successful politicians in the electoral marketplace are rewarded for promising and delivering things that appeal to critical constituencies. Weiner continues: "As in an economic market, the politician will assess his market and produce those commodities (appeals) that yield the maximum return ..."

Beneath their universalist veneer, public goods schemes provide numerous opportunities for politicians to shape how projects are implemented and services are delivered. Berenschot (2010) documents how "politicians arrange not only water connections or drainage lines, but also government jobs, roads, electricity connections, irrigation, government contracts etc. for those groups of voters who are considered to be useful in securing (re-)election." For many citizens, access to public services is fundamentally shaped by their relationships with these political brokers. According to Bardhan (1984), elected officials embrace the influence they have to mediate access to the state: "These are gangs led by a large number of MLAs and MPs, political middlemen who over the years have specialized in the profession of brokerage services" (66).

procurement process invites opportunism and rent-seeking. Bardhan (1984) laments that the "plundering of public-sector-produced goods by agents of influential politicians in collaboration with public enterprise staff, private contractors and the criminal underworld is far too common" (70). When India spent more than $11 US billion on the massive Golden Quadrilateral highway project to connect its four largest cities, many were convinced that a large portion of funds was lost to corruption. Wilkinson (2006) notes, "State level audit reports make clear that much of the money spent is being 'diverted' to non-infrastructure uses, that investments are often directed to people and places that appear not to fit the declared criteria for the program, and that in many cases only a small proportion of the targeted infrastructure has actually been built" (4).

Another way politicians influence public goods provision is through their oversight of the bureaucracy. Senior bureaucrats serve according to the favor of politicians and thus postings to the top leadership positions can be used as political currency. Bardhan (1984) explains that in the Indian context,

Headships of public sector units, particularly under the State Governments, are indiscriminately used as political sinecures. Efficient managers who fail to satisfy the Minister's political clients are often arbitrarily transferred. Expensive projects are hastily initiated on grounds of political expediency or regional favoritism... (69–70)

Moreover, politicians are often intricately involved in the day-to-day supervision or management of public service agencies. In Madhya Pradesh in 1983, the ruling party comprised 232 members of the legislative assembly (MLAs). Of these, a substantial fraction had oversight responsibilities: 42 held cabinet posts, 74 headed government or quasi-official bodies, and another 100 were nominated by the chief minister to serve on the boards of various public sector entities (Bardhan 1984).

Claiming that public goods are pliable and susceptible to distortion seems to belie their universal nature. Indeed, many accounts assume as given that public goods are nontargetable and resistant to political manipulation. According to Diaz-Cayeros, Magaloni, and Estévez (forthcoming), public goods are a potentially risky political investment because everyone, even a party's opponents, benefits from their provision:

Public goods, once realized, cannot be easily withdrawn. Infrastructure projects such as roads and highways, bridges and dams, power plants and sewer systems, are fixed investments, meaning that they are more vulnerable to voter opportunism – that is, a party cannot withdraw the benefits should the benefited voter support its rival at the polls. (20)

Yet providing public goods need not be so risky. After all, the benefits that flow from public goods require more than just physical infrastructure. Paxson and Schady (2002) describe how efforts to improve education in Peru prioritized spending on school construction projects, but also entailed significant funds for the purchase of textbooks, school breakfast programs, and the provision of school uniforms – all elements that were both targetable and whose flow could be cut off midstream. For any public goods scheme, service delivery protocols must be defined, staff must be put in place, maintenance must be provided, and effort must be made to ensure that services reach their intended beneficiaries. All these activities require funding. Across this lengthy supply chain connecting citizens to state-provided goods lie opportunities for political oversight and intervention.

In the end, citizens care whether they benefit from public services, not whether physical infrastructure exists or not. As Fox and Smith (1990) note, "Consumers and businesses are typically more concerned with the infrastructure services they receive than with the facilities themselves. In other words, consumers and businesses view public infrastructure as the electricity they use, not the power plant that produces it" (56).

When it comes to electricity, there are many ways in which access to its benefits can be regulated. Even after power lines and transformers connect a village to the power grid, the benefits of electricity still depend on whether you are provided a household connection, the affordability of fees you are expected to pay, and crucially, whether electrical power is flowing to your home when you need it. Political actors can affect all of these pieces. They can hasten the often lengthy time it can take to get an official connection, help secure reductions in connection fees, and grant lucrative designations to allow a consumer to qualify for subsidized programs and rates. Politicians can also exercise discretion over enforcement of penalties and the provision of "forbearance" for the theft of power and other legal violations (Holland 2014). Indeed, politicians may even increase the supply of illegal or unmetered electricity at election time in order to improve their re-election prospects. (Min and Golden 2014).

Public goods schemes are thus highly attractive to democratic leaders because, on the one hand, they enable politicians to build goodwill by making universalistic promises, while on the other hand, they retain influence over their benefits by affecting project siting, contracts, jobs, and service delivery protocols.

The Rural Poor

> It's very simple. In a democracy, the poor have a veto.
>
> Rahul Gandhi

Electoral competition pushes politicians to prioritize the delivery of public goods. But who are the beneficiaries of such efforts? In democratic settings, the need for politicians to secure and maintain broad bases of support precipitates a scramble to promise public goods to communities that would otherwise be overlooked. Over time, these efforts stretch out to encompass new sets of potential supporters, especially among the rural poor. There are several reasons.

The first is structural: since the dawn of civilization, the majority of the world's people have lived in rural areas.[6] In democratic settings, the sheer volume of voters who live in the countryside requires governments to be attuned to their preferences and needs. Because democratic governments have incentives to attend to rural voters, there is at least some evidence that people are more likely to stay in rural areas under democracy than in nondemocracy. Ades and Glaeser (1995) find that democracy is associated with smaller primary urban cities. Davis and Henderson (2003) argue, "Hinterland regions may have greater chance for representation in design of national policies under democratic governance with regional representation ... Hinterland states and

---

[6] According to the most recent United Nations estimates, the majority of those in developing countries still reside in rural areas. Globally, the urban population surpassed the rural population for the first time only in 2007.

cities have more autonomy to provide their own services and infrastructure investments so as to attract firms and workers from primate cities" (103).

Second, most citizens across the developing world are poor. Thus in developing democracies, the median voter is almost certainly low income and living in the countryside. Indeed, many countries fit this profile. In India, the median household earned about $US 600 per year in 2004 and lived in a village. With 70 percent of the Indian population residing in rural areas, the sheer size of the rural poor commands the attention of politicians (Varshney 1995). As India's Congress party leader Rahul Gandhi explained in the speech quoted earlier, the poor are simply too significant a portion of the electorate to ignore in a democracy.

Third, rural areas are often advantaged in democratic settings as a result of electoral geography and malapportionment of seats in favor of rural constituencies (Erikson 1972; Powell and Vanberg 2000; Samuels and Snyder 2001; Rodden 2010; Chen and Rodden 2013). Even if rural and urban voters participate at equivalent levels, rural interests are likely to be advantaged in majoritarian systems that tend to overweight the representation of rural voters in the legislature (Thies 1998; Broz and Maliniak 2011). By the 1990s, more than 40 percent of India's parliament came from rural backgrounds, compared to about 20 percent in the 1950s (Varshney 1995, 3).

In addition to these structural conditions, a powerful electoral motivation drives democratic leaders to court the rural poor (Krishna 2008). The political economist Myrdal (1957) observed:

> The poor are the many and even the relatively poor are the great majority, wherever the voting line is drawn. In order to gain power political parties had to sponsor reforms in the interest of greater regional equality; this became the more necessary as later the electorate was gradually enlarged. (45)

As suffrage expands to the rural poor, these new voters are vigorously courted because they lack the political ties that may lock in voters with longer histories of participation. Lizzeri and Persico (2004) argue that extending suffrage changes the political equilibrium from one of redistribution to one favoring the provision of public goods preferred by the newly enfranchised poor: "The extension of the franchise caused a shift away from special-interest politicking toward a more public-oriented legislative activity" (709). In Britain, the expansion of suffrage was associated with a dramatic increase in local government spending, from 17 percent of total spending in 1790 to 41 percent in 1890, most of it targeted to public infrastructure such as sewerage, filtered water, and paved roads. Evaluating education policies in democratizing states, Stasavage (2005) describes how newly elected rulers become reliant on the voting mass in rural areas and thus shifted their policy focus to primary education and away from the tertiary education that is more valued in cities. A series of papers by Toke Aidt and coauthors also affirm a general relationship between extension of the voting franchise to previously excluded groups and overall levels of government spending (Aidt and Dallal 2008; Aidt and Eterovic 2011; Aidt and Jensen 2013).

Thus, the rural poor are a highly attractive constituency in the competitive pursuit of electoral support. Indeed, recent evidence suggests that swing voters in the developing world are very likely to be situated among the poor. Drawing on a survey of 1,600 voters in Ghana, Weghorst and Lindberg (2013) report that the persuadability of voters is systematically highest among the poor.[7] Thus, expanding the political base of support by targeting the rural poor is often a compelling strategy in developing democracies.

In the late nineteenth century, postal service in the United States was transformed into a broad public service through the establishment of Rural Free Delivery (RFD), which promised direct delivery of the post to farms across the country. Rural Americans embraced the proposal to make postal delivery a universal benefit for all Americans, not only those in its cities (Fuller 1964). As Kernell and McDonald (1999) document,

> From its inception, RFD was wildly popular ... In an era of slow transportation and poor communication, when other federal services – such as rural electrification, farm price supports, and social security – were only a gleam in some visionary's eye, rural free delivery represented a major advance in federal services for the nation's large farm population. (794–795)

Yet the creation of this universal public service did not happen overnight. From decisions about how many routes to fund to where each route would be placed, members of Congress exerted great influence over the implementation of RFD.

> If a community wanted a route, it had formally to petition its congressman who then ranked and forwarded the approved request to the [postal] department... This procedure allowed representatives to claim credit for new placements, blame the department for rejected petitions, and, if they so desired, block entry of RFD into their communities by refusing to endorse petitions. (799)

A decade into its implementation, stark partisan differences in the allocation of routes were evident. One politician complained in 1906 that Republican Kansas had received 1,555 routes compared to only 532 in Democratic South Carolina (Fuller 1964). The pattern reflected greater commitment and effort by Republicans to secure postal routes: "As national policy, RFD offered the Republican party an opportunity to steal a Populist issue," securing a toehold in rural areas where it had struggled to win votes. Examining the placement of 2,136 rural routes from 1895 to 1900, Kernell and McDonald (1999) concluded

---

[7] Weghorst and Lindberg explain: "A Ghanaian who views his or her economic status as 'much worse' than other Ghanaians has a 23% higher swing count compared to a Ghanaian whose status is 'much better'... Given the received wisdom from the literature on partisanship and voting behavior, it is interesting to find that voters in Africa behave just like voters in established democracies in this respect" (2013, 11).

that the creation of RFD – although motivated by a broad commitment to serve its rural citizens – nevertheless manifested itself in electorally motivated ways: "Overall, these numbers reveal that routes were distributed as though keenly strategic actors were at the throttle – a throttle that appears to have been shared by [Republican] leaders and individual members" (808).

The claim that the poor command attention in democracies goes against some commonly held beliefs. Many argue that the poor are an ineffective constituency under democracy because they are less likely to vote and, in turn, to impact election outcomes. Powell (1986) notes that in many American and European studies, higher socioeconomic status is strongly correlated with greater political participation. However, there is at least some evidence that in the developing world, the poor participate at *higher* levels and with greater impact than widely assumed in the West.[8] In India, the recent surge in democratic participation among the poor and low castes has been especially notable (Yadav 2000). In India's 2009 national election, 59 percent of Scheduled Castes voted compared to 56 percent of upper castes.[9] In the 2004 Indian election, 59 percent of rural citizens voted compared to 54 percent of urban voters (Rana 2006). In African electoral democracies, recent voter turnout in presidential elections has been the same as turnout in the United States, about two out of three.[10] Moreover, in Africa turnout appears to be higher in countries with larger rural populations. This is probably due to a confluence of political and demographic factors:

Africa's ruling parties often receive a great deal of support in rural areas and thus focus their mobilization efforts outside the urban areas. The ability of African parties to mobilize voters may also be easier in rural Africa, where the threat of sanctions for not voting may be more effective and resource scarcity increases the impact of party efforts to buy votes. (Kuenzi and Lambright 2007, 680)

Scholars have also argued that the poor are less responsive to promises of public goods and are more interested in private transfers (Dixit and Londregan 1996; Stokes 2005). However this assumes that public goods such as electricity are not perceived to directly improve the welfare of the poor. Weghorst and Lindberg (2013) show that the poor do in fact respond to collective goods, and not just promises of private transfers, in their vote choice. They conclude, "Evidence in this article suggests that even in highly clientelistic environments, incumbents who wish to get reelected should seek to meet voter demands, including delivering collective goods" (730).

---

[8] Even in the United States, turnout patterns among historically poorer or marginalized groups may be higher than once thought. Many newspaper headlines reported that in the 2012 presidential election, African Americans had higher turnout rates than Whites for the first time (Associated Press, "In a first, black voter turnout rate passes whites," April 28, 2013).

[9] Center for the Study of Democratic Societies, 2009 National Election Study.

[10] Dionne, Kim. "Five things you probably didn't know about African politics today." The Monkey Cage, March 11, 2013, washingtonpost.com

Another reason many believe the rural poor will be overlooked is that they are difficult to reach. Many lack identification documents or formal relationships with the state. In India, only 40 percent of children younger than five had been registered at birth or held a birth certificate. The rates are similarly low in many other countries: 60 percent in Kenya, 53 percent in Indonesia, 21 percent in Uganda, and 35 percent in Nepal.[11] Yet this constraint may represent an opportunity for officeholders. Elected leaders have the authority and capacity to register citizens for government programs, thus gaining appreciation and building relationships with new potential voters (Berenschot 2010).

Does Democracy Help the Poor?

Both in theory and in popular belief, many claim that democracies provide more public goods to their citizens. Democratic leaders differ from dictators because they are held accountable by voters for their performance in office. Lipset (1959, 71) defines democracy "as a political system which supplies regular constitutional opportunities for changing the governing officials, and a social mechanism which permits the largest possible part of the population to influence major decisions by choosing among contenders for political office." Elections provide voters with the power to replace leaders when they do not serve the best interests of the public. Similarly, Schmitter and Karl (1991, 76) argue that "modern political democracy is a system of governance in which rulers are held accountable for their actions in the public realm by citizens."

An additional key feature of democracy is the responsiveness of elected leaders to the preferences of voters (Dahl 1971). In their seminal paper, Meltzer and Richard (1981) outline an elegant model describing why democracy should induce policies that favor the poor. In the model, policy outcomes reflect the preferences of the decisive voter. In democracies with universal suffrage, that decisive voter is most likely to have a below-average income. Indeed, in any economy where income is unequally distributed and concentrated among an elite, the median voter will have a lower income than the mean income earner. Democracy should therefore favor the policy preferences of the poor, who will prefer a higher tax rate and greater income redistribution away from the rich and toward the needs of the poor.

Democratic politicians must convince their constituents that they are better able to serve their needs than any challenger could. Because democratic politicians are likely to be evaluated on their ability to provide basic benefits, they should provide higher levels of local public goods than dictators (Lake and Baum 2001). Elections also invite a larger portion of the citizenry to participate in the selection of their leaders than are able to participate in nonelectoral

---

[11] World Bank World Development Indicators, Completeness of birth registration (%) (SP.REG. BRTH.ZS). Figures reflect most recent year available.

systems. Thus, Diamond (1990) explains that democratic leaders must secure a much broader base of political support than autocrats: "Democracy implies an unwillingness to concentrate power in the hands of a few, and so subjects leaders and policies to mechanisms of popular representation and accountability" (49). According to Bueno de Mesquita et al. (2003), the most cost-effective means of securing such broad political support is to invest a disproportionate share into the provision of public goods rather than in targeted private transfers: "when the [winning] coalition is large, leaders have insufficient resources to reward their supporters with high levels of private goods and so must switch to policies with a public focus if they want to survive" (104). As Fearon (2011) summarizes, "The standard justification for electoral democracy is that competitive elections give leaders an incentive to provide public goods and more generally to align public policy with citizens preferences" (1661).

In nondemocratic settings, dictators face no direct electoral pressures to respond to the poor, though they may do so for other strategic reasons (see, e.g., Padró i Miquel 2007; Tsai 2007; Kudamatsu and Besley 2008; Gehlbach and Keefer 2011; Blaydes 2013). As Gandhi and Przeworski (2006, 2) state, "dictators are dictators because they cannot win elections." A similar theme is echoed by Acemoglu and Robinson (2006b, 18):

> We argue that democracy, which is generally a situation of political equality, looks after the interests of the majority more than nondemocracy, which is generally dominated by an elite and is more likely to look after its interests. Stated simply and extremely, nondemocracy is generally a regime for the elite and the privileged; comparatively, democracy is a regime more beneficial to the majority of the populace, resulting in policies relatively more favorable to the majority.

In support of these theoretical expectations regarding the positive effects of democracy, many studies find important evidence of democracy's salubrious impacts. Boix (2001) uses general government current receipts to demonstrate that democracies have larger public sectors, especially when voter turnout is higher. Lake and Baum (2001) find that democracies deliver better education and public health to their citizens. Examining infant mortality rates, Przeworski et al. (2000) find that democracies have lower rates of early childhood death than nondemocracies, and Besley (2006) argues that democracy lengthens life expectancy. Blaydes and Kayser (2011) show that calorie intake is higher in democracies. The process of democratization has also been linked to improved outcomes, as in Stasavage (2005), which finds higher spending on primary education after the move to multiparty elections in Africa.

Yet in spite of these theories and empirical results, many remain sceptical about the impact of elections on the welfare of the poor. First, arguments dating back to Weber argue that *state capacity* is more important than regime type in determining whether a government will respond to the needs of its citizens. In perhaps the best-known statement of the argument, Huntington (1968) claimed that a state's capacity to govern is more important than the way it is organized:

The most important political distinction among countries concerns not their form of government but their degree of government. The differences between democracy and dictatorship are less than the differences between those countries whose politics embodies consensus, community, legitimacy, organization, effectiveness, stability, and those countries whose politics is deficient in these qualities. (1)

Thus many states with low institutional capacity may not have the ability to meet the needs of the poor, even if they conduct elections. Herbst (2000) highlights, how even many democratic African regimes have struggled to broadcast their authority to rural areas and have failed to build roads to many areas.

Second, democratic politics is susceptible to *political capture* by narrow interests whose preferences may differ from those of the majority (Olson 1965; Grossman and Helpman 1996; Bardhan and Mookherjee 2000). Lindert (2004) and others have observed that redistributive policies tend to be weakest in the most unequal societies such as the United States, while finding the highest support in more economically equal societies such as those in Scandinavia. In other words, the political influence of the poor in many democracies may not correlate with their actual numbers. Another mode of political capture may result in an *urban bias* that prioritizes the developmental and political interests of cities and their residents away from the rural poor. Urban bias can result from two reinforcing dynamics: the favoring of industrial interests over rural needs (Myrdal 1957; Lipton 1977; Bairoch 1988) and greater political concern about satisfying the urban masses that are both more proximate and densely concentrated (Bates 1981). Similarly, the logic of majority rule can lead to the persistent deprivation of minority groups that are too electorally marginal to shape electoral outcomes (Guinier 1994; Hajnal 2009; Wimmer, Cederman, and Min 2009).

Third, persistent pressure to campaign and win reelection can decrease the appeal of costly, long-term investments in capital projects and other services needed by the poor. Touting the success of Singapore's state-planned economy, Lee Kuan Yew notes, "Our job was to plan the broad economic objectives and the target periods within which to achieve them. Infrastructure and the training and education of workers to meet the needs of employers had to be planned years in advance" (Lee 2000, 66). Democratic leaders may not be able to afford the luxury of investing for the future when voters are keener on evaluating them on what they have done for them lately (Kramer 1971; Mayhew 1974; Kinder and Kiewiet 1979).

Fourth, a bevy of country studies has observed many pathologies in otherwise democratic settings. In her study of political machines in Argentina, Stokes (2005) suggests that when democratic leaders have the ability to monitor constituents' votes, a "perverse" accountability takes over, and rather than practicing oversight, citizens use their votes to avoid punishment and seek out rewards. Clientelistic and patrimonial practices are also said to undermine the supposed virtues of electoral accountability across the developing world (see, e.g., Bratton and van de Walle 1994; Chandra 2004; Kitschelt and Wilkinson 2007; Thachil 2014) as well as in the industrialized world (see, e.g., Scheiner 2006).

Consistent with these theoretical concerns about democracy, many studies have now challenged whether democracies provide more public goods to their poor. After a generation of research, it is still unclear whether democracy improves economic growth (Przeworski and Limongi 1993; Helliwell 1994; Barro 1996; Perotti 1996; Doucouliagos and Ulubasoglu 2008). Democratization does not consistently reduce infant mortality rates, if at all (Ross 2006; Ramos 2014). Democracies may provide fewer roads to marginalized areas (Blimpo, Harding, and Wantchekon 2013). They seem to be not much better than robust autocracies at averting civil war and violent domestic unrest (Hegre and Sambanis 2006). Moreover, evidence from nondemocratic settings suggests that at least some autocracies provide high levels of public goods and distribute them more broadly to their needy because of socialist ideology or other domestic pressures (Magaloni 2006; Tsai 2007; Wright 2008; Svolik 2012).

Empirical research on the impact of democracy on public goods provision is hampered by data measurement problems. Indeed, there are numerous weaknesses in the data sources that underlie many cross-national datasets, including missing data, measurement error, inconsistency in definitions, and incomparability of data across time. Ross (2006), for example, notes that many studies of the effects of regime type may be biased because they exclude many high-performing autocracies from their samples, notably from the Gulf region. Data problems may be especially severe in large databases compiled from a variety of sources and are probably worst where the questions matter most – in the poorest, most remote, and least stable corners of the developing world. For instance, the World Bank's *Social Indicators of Development*, the primary data source used by Lake and Baum (2001), carries this warning:

Users should bear in mind that the concepts, definitions and methodology underlying indicators vary, sometimes significantly, from country to country and over time within countries. The data also reflect differences in the way information is collected and how perceptions change. While indicators reported are considered useful for identifying broad trends and differences, little significance should be attached to minor differences among indicators.

Even variables that have been intensely studied, such as literacy rates, can be problematic. Neatly organized data tables produced by agencies such as UNESCO gloss over great variations in how literacy is measured around the world and over time. In Azerbaijan, the literacy measure is based on responses to a brief test in which a respondent is asked to "read, understand and write a short story regarding his/her routine life." But in Belarus, literacy depends entirely on a yes-or-no self-declaration of whether respondents believe they can read and write. In China, the official literacy rate of 93 percent in 2000 is based on a census question asking whether the respondent can read. Yet in a 1996 literacy test administered to 6,000 Chinese adults, the average respondent could identify only 3.6 characters out of 10. Fewer than 30 percent could identify more than five characters, and 19 percent could not identify even a single character (Treiman 2007).

Measuring changes over time can be even more problematic. In India, the best literacy estimates come from its National Family Health Survey (NFHS) of 100,000 households. In its second round report in 1999, the NFHS celebrated a "substantial decline in illiteracy in only six and one-half years," to 49 percent for women and 23 percent for men. Yet in the next survey round in 2006, there was no discussion at all of progress because the methodology used to measure literacy had completely changed. In the first two survey waves, respondents were asked to declare whether they were literate or not, while in 2006 they were administered a literacy test requiring them to read at least part of a sentence, making the new rates incomparable with the old. Not surprisingly, literacy rates were much lower when based on a reading test than when based on self-evaluations.

Even seemingly clear-cut measures such as infant mortality, which counts the number of children who are born and survive until the age of one or five, are subject to discretion. Globally, 11 million children die each year before their fifth birthday. But how many are born? If a child is born but does not survive the first day, does the baby count in the denominator or not?[12]

Yet another weakness stems from the uneven temporal coverage and frequency of measurement of many key public service indicators. Censuses typically occur only once per decade. Meanwhile, ambitious survey efforts, including the World Bank's Living Standards Measurement Study (LSMS) and the Demographic and Health Surveys (DHS) conducted by the United States Agency for International Development (USAID), are often able to revisit countries only once every few years, not least because these efforts are inordinately expensive. Without consistent and frequently updated data, it is difficult to parse the effects of political institutions from other secular trends such as medical advances, technological innovation, and globalization.

These measurement problems are compounded because most data underlying international datasets are derived from self-reported government data, and different agencies use varying definitions and data collection methods. Moreover, government agencies may face pressures that can affect the accuracy

---

[12] There is a vibrant debate on the relationship between democracy and infant mortality (Przeworski et al. 2000; Zweifel and Navia 2000; Franco, Álvarez-Dardet, and Ruiz 2004; Besley and Kudamatsu 2006; Ross 2006; Kudamatsu 2012; Ramos 2014).

of their reports, including efforts to satisfy donors, international observers, or domestic watchdogs (Jerven 2013; Kerner, Jerven, and Beatty 2014). Without reliable and consistent data, it is hard to know whether our conclusions are driven by true variations in the signal or confounding movements in the noise.

Implications

The argument presented in this chapter emphasizes the political value of public goods schemes in electoral settings. Commitments to deliver public goods are especially valuable in democratic contexts given the efficiency by which they can help secure broad bases of support. But they are also appealing to politicians because in their implementation, public goods schemes provide myriad opportunities for politicians to influence the timing, siting, and management of projects – choices that carry important electoral costs and benefits. These campaign tactics are particularly powerful in the periphery because such goods are highly valued by the rural poor, who are electorally numerous and whose votes may be more easily swayed by delivery of these scarcities. When voters believe that their best chance of accessing these goods depends on how they vote, politicians can exploit that belief to their advantage.

A potentially discouraging interpretation of this argument may be that it affirms the suspicion that many democracies underinvest in true nontargetable public goods at the expense of more targetable spending programs. However, as the discussion has shown, there is no straightforward way to classify a good as targetable or not based only on its inherent characteristics and properties. Rather, public policies shape the way any scheme actually benefits their intended constituents, and these policies are formed in political space by actors with political interests.

The account offered here may also help explain a troubling paradox of democracy and the provision of public goods. If the incentives for public goods provision are so high in democracy, why is there so little evidence that democracy helps improve the day-to-day welfare of the poor? Indeed, many scholars have questioned whether democracies actually provide higher quality public goods, or whether they simply spend more and are getting less return on their investments. If the argument proposed here is correct, then the choices of democratic leaders are shaped by electoral concerns, inducing an emphasis on maximizing short-term gains and away from the kind of long-term investments that require fiscal sacrifices in the present. Thus the visible electrification of a village, the installation of street lights, and the creation of new household connections are appealing outcomes for which politicians can claim credit. By contrast, the expensive costs of ensuring quality into the future remain largely hidden from public view. It is far less compelling for a politician to campaign to maintain aging equipment or replace deteriorating transformers. Even the construction of desperately needed power plants to ensure adequate power supply is difficult in democracy, given that the benefits accrue long into the future while voters focus on short-run costs and immediate environmental impacts.[13]

The argument presented here also does not imply that democracy is a necessary prerequisite for rural development. The rural poor can benefit from public goods even in the absence of electoral competition. In China, civic organizations can induce pressure on local officials to provide public services (Tsai 2007). In many African countries, voluntary "home town" associations, often formed along ethnic lines, are organized to provide mutual benefits for their members and ancestral regions. According to Barkan, McNulty, and Ayeni (1991), such associations in Côte d'Ivoire have provided an array of basic services to residents of local communities – secondary schools, health clinics, utility poles for electricity and telephone lines, roads, public meeting halls, and postal services (462).

Autocratic governments may also actively target the rural poor with public goods. Dictators may prioritize rural interests when the threat of rural rebellion is high (Lichbach 1994; Fox 1996; Azam 2001; Smith 2008), or when they recognize interests in suppressing urban migration and placating citizens in their villages. Ideological commitments to rural development have certainly played a role in the delivery of rural public goods under autocratic regimes in the Soviet Union, China, and Cuba (Oi 1985). Yet, although political threats and ideological commitments can waver within autocracies, the institution of competitive elections under democracy is persistent in how it privileges certain political strategies to attend to the masses, regardless of the specific ideological preferences of those in power.

Taken together, my theory results in three empirical implications that are tested in the remainder of the book. First, I expect electricity to be more broadly provided by democratic governments. Second, democracies will provide more electricity to their rural poor than nondemocracies. Third, efforts to deliver electricity to voters will be heightened during election periods when access to public services is most politically salient.

Conclusion

Scholars tend to neatly classify goods as "public" or "private" in theoretical and empirical research. Yet this tendency is problematic. Many things called "public goods," such as electricity, roads, clean water, and schools, have broad, universal benefits befitting the designation. However, in their rollout and delivery, such goods also deliver discrete benefits that can be targeted to communities, groups, or individuals in intricate ways. The mixed characteristics that describe many goods and services provided by the state make them particularly

---

[13] See, e.g., the controversy over the Medupi power plant in South Africa and the Narmada Valley hydroelectric dam project in India.

valuable to political leaders, who can exploit different dimensions of these goods according to political context and circumstance (Diaz-Cayeros 2008).

Trying to decide whether to classify electricity as a public good or not is a misguided exercise. Electricity provision has aspects that are both broad and nonexcludable, but also benefits that are discrete and targetable. In the aggregate, the presence of an electrical power grid may be a public good in the Samuelsonian sense.[14] Yet in its provision, the practical need to locate power lines and streetlights along specific streets and in specific buildings provides discretion in shaping who benefits and who is excluded.

Consider the challenge of classifying street lighting as a public good or not. Once the lighting is installed, everyone on the street benefits from its consumption and there is no way to restrict its value or exclude anyone from its benefits. As the sun sets and darkness descends, streetlights allow people to travel more comfortably. With people staying outdoors longer, shops stay open later. Cars and bicycles can navigate more safely. People can wander farther to sell their goods or purchase daily necessities. The hum and buzz of street life extends later into the day. Befitting the classic economic definition of a pure public good, street lighting is wonderful because it benefits everyone without exclusion or restriction. It costs no more to provide its benefits to many people than to just one, and so the marginal cost of delivering its benefits to more people approaches zero.

Yet by unpacking the way outdoor public lighting is delivered and managed, we can observe the intricate ways in which political opportunities arise to shape its provision. Why does one town get streetlights but not another? Why are some streets lit while others are dark? What influences whether electricity is actually flowing to power the bulbs on any given night? Who replaces the bulb when it burns out? Who pays the lighting bills? As this book shows, these everyday decisions are not only technical questions but political questions as well. Given public responsibility for electricity provision, political actors are centrally involved in shaping the answers to each of these questions, influenced not only by cost–benefit calculations about economic viability, but also by political motivations shaped by the abiding priority to stay in office.

---

[14] Many scholars have identified aspects of electricity provision as a public good including the efficiency of the electricity network (Alesina, Baqir, and Easterly 1999), the presence of electricity in villages (Chhibber and Nooruddin 2004; Besley et al. 2004; Banerjee, Somanathan, and Iyer 2005; Banerjee and Somanathan 2007), village expenditures on electricity (Zhang et al. 2004), and the ability of electricity to augment existing markets (Besley and Ghatak 2006). Emphasizing the stability of the power supply as a public good, Abbott (2001) describes: "Any expansion in capacity designed to meet growth in demand not only reduces the risk of blackouts for those being supplied from the new plant but also reduces everyone else's risk at no extra cost. This means that security [of electricity supply] is nonrival in public good terms. Security of supply also appears to be nonexclusive in that it is difficult to exclude people from benefiting from that reduced risk..." (32).

3

Power and the State

Introduction

Electricity undergirds the modern economy. In 2010, the world used 18.7 trillion kilowatt-hours of electricity – a third more than all the energy used to fuel every car and truck on the planet.[1] Since 1990, global electricity consumption has nearly doubled, exceeding population growth, which increased by 30 percent, and even outpacing the growth of average incomes, which improved by 48 percent in real terms.[2]

The world's thirst for electricity is not abating. Total electricity generation soared from 6,115 terawatt-hours (TWh) in 1973 to 22,126 TWh in 2011, an increase of 360 percent. By contrast, global oil production increased only 45 percent over the same period, from 21 to 29 billion barrels per year (International Energy Agency 2012). By 2012, there were some 62,500 power plants around the world.[3] Despite this frenzied expansion, many countries have been unable to keep pace with demand, which continues to be spurred on by economic development and population growth. The specter this poses for climate change is alarming, a concern to which I return in the book's conclusion.

Satisfying the great demand for electricity remains among the most important and difficult challenges facing governments across the world, as it has ever

---

[1] In 2010, 8.09 billion barrels of oil were used for motor gasoline, equivalent to 4.94 × 10^{19} joules. By contrast, electricity consumption was 6.7 × 10^{19} joules. Source: US Energy Information Administration, International Energy Statistics online database, http://www.eia.gov/ies.

[2] The world population grew from 5.3 billion in 1990 to 6.9 billion in 2010 according to estimates from the US Census Bureau. Meanwhile, average per capita income in the world went from $8,691 in 1990 to $12,888 in 2010, as reported by the World Bank in constant 2011 international dollars using purchasing power parity rates.

[3] Power plant data from Platts UDI Database, June 2012, as reported by *The Washington Post* Wonkblog, December 8, 2012.

since power grids were introduced.[4] By 2013, more than 1.3 billion people, a fifth of the world's population, still had no access to electricity. The electrification challenge is most formidable in rural areas, where customer densities are low and poverty can be pervasive. Because of the expense and complexity of this challenge, four in five of those in the world without electricity can be found in rural areas (International Energy Agency 2013).

No country has ever completed rural electrification without the intensive financial support of its government (Barnes and Floor 1996).[5] Especially in the developing world, governments have played central roles in the financing, construction, management, and regulation of the power sector. As Brown and Mobarak (2009, 196) note, "It is difficult to overstate the role of politics in the supply of electricity." According to their research, governments fully owned the power sector in 103 countries in 2000. In another 50 countries, some part of the power sector had been opened to private investment, and only in 11 was it primarily in the hands of private investors. Given the economies of scale and benefits of uniform standards in electricity provision, governments often retain full ownership and management of utilities. Even when they relinquish power distribution to private companies (a path pursued in very few developing states), governments preserve oversight and regulatory authority, continuing to influence distribution by subsidizing energy prices or imposing taxes, enabling investments in generation and transmission projects, and steering grid extension efforts. The importance of the state when it comes to electricity provision is especially acute in states where electricity grids are still being built and service delivery issues can have immediate and critical impacts on economic welfare and political stability.

At the founding of the Soviet Union in the 1920s, Vladimir Lenin famously placed electricity at the center of his vision of the future: "Communism is Soviet power plus the electrification of the whole country." His State Commission for Electrification of Russia (GOELRO) sought to extend the power grid to the entire country and formed the basis of the first Soviet plan for national economic recovery. The plan reflected Lenin's belief in a reorganized industry based "on electrification which will put an end to the division between

---

[4] It is estimated that $1 trillion in investments will be needed globally by 2030 to cover the basic energy needs of those with no household electricity or clean cooking facilities (International Energy Agency 2011).

[5] One common question is whether electricity in rural areas must always come from the state, given that electricity can also be privately generated. Indeed, many large industrial operations in the developing world generate their own electrical power, including cement factories, mines, and oil refineries. In India, airports, hotels, shopping malls, and a growing number of private residences are equipped with diesel power generators to supply power when the grid is not working. But in rural areas, especially among the poor, access to generators is limited simply because generators are expensive to buy, as is the fuel to power them. Other renewable off-grid solutions, such as solar panels and wind turbines, are also expensive. In rural areas, access to electricity almost always depends on whether villages are connected to the national power grid.

town and country and ... overcome, even in the most remote corners of land, backwardness, ignorance, poverty, disease, and barbarism." Implementation of GOELRO led to a near doubling of the country's total national power output by 1931 (Kromm 1970) and full electrification of the entire Soviet Union in the years that followed. Meanwhile, in Germany, Holland, and Scandinavia, the electrification of every home was seen as a desirable political goal and 90 percent of homes were electrified by 1930 (Nye 1992, 140).

Not all governments have been as enthusiastic about the public provision of electricity. Most famously, private firms dominated the US power sector well into the twentieth century, spurred by the lobbying of powerful individuals such as Thomas Edison and George Westinghouse. The result was a balkanization of electricity distribution across numerous private distributors, most of whom focused their business in the wealthy urban centers. Extending the power grid from cities to rural areas required high fixed cost investments in infrastructure including new power plants, long haul transmission lines, substations, and shorter distribution lines to the end user. Rural areas with low customer densities were unattractive markets to profit-minded firms. By the time of the Great Depression, only one in ten rural Americans had access to electricity compared to 90 percent of city dwellers. With the collapse of the economy, even private power utilities in the most lucrative urban markets were struggling to stay solvent. Farmers seemed destined to stay in the dark had it not been for Franklin Roosevelt's celebrated establishment of the Tennessee Valley Authority (TVA) in 1933 and Rural Electrification Administration (REA) in 1935. At the end of 1934, only 12.1 percent of all US farms had electricity, with only 3 percent in Tennessee and fewer than 1 percent in Mississippi having been electrified. By 1943, the TVA and REA had brought electricity to four out of ten American farms (see Figure 3.1). Within one more decade, nine out of ten were connected (US Census Bureau 1975, 827). Former US Secretary of Agriculture Bob Bergland recalled, "The day the lights finally came on at our farm, I remember my mother cried." Another farmer reminisced, "I remember singing with robust glee in celebration as our little strip of houses along a dirt road was connected to electricity. We sang out with joy and no small amount of amazement: Oh the lights, the lights, Lottie Mae got light and we got lights! Oh the lights, the lights" (Campbell 2000).

The historical experiences of the Soviet Union and the Western industrial economies would play an influential role in guiding future government efforts to build power grids in the developing world. In China, purposeful government policies led to electrification for 700 million people over two decades – an achievement of unprecedented scale and scope. In one program promulgated in State Council Document No. 190 in 1983, local development of rural hydropower facilities was mandated in 100 mostly remote rural counties and funded through subsidies and low-interest loans. By 2000, an additional 553 counties had also been electrified through this program, bringing the total number of beneficiaries of rural hydropower to nearly 140 million people. Overall, total

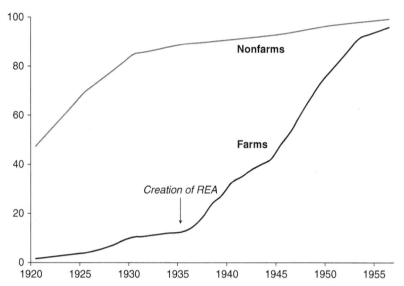

FIGURE 3.1. Electrifying America: Percentage of US dwelling units with electricity, 1920–1956.
Source: US Census Bureau, *Historical Statistics of the United States, 1975*, S 108–119.

electricity consumption in rural China increased tenfold between 1978 and 2000. The number of villages without electricity decreased from 55,000 in 1993 to 9,300 in 2002. According to official estimates, more than 98 percent of Chinese homes have an electrical connection (Pan et al. 2006).[6]

Just west of China, in the world's most populous democracy, electricity provision was a foundational concern in postcolonial India. At independence, fewer than 4,000, or less than 1 percent, of villages and towns in India had electricity. Lamenting this critical state of affairs, India's leaders emphasized in its first five-year plan, "Cheap electric power is essential for the development of a country ... Extensive use of electricity can bring about the much needed change in rural life in India."[7] Jawaharlal Nehru famously declared that dams were the temples of modern India and in numerous speeches promoted massive investments in hydroelectric power to speed the development of rural parts of the country. According to Dubash and Rajan (2002), "For much of the history of post-independence India, the electricity sector has been an entrenched symbol of the nation's state-led economic development approach. Publicly owned, and operated and managed by state employees, the sector was conceived of and run as an instrument of development policy" (51). Nevertheless, rural

---

[6] Interestingly, the satellite-derived estimates I describe in Chapters 4 and 5 observe a much lower proportion of the Chinese population benefiting from electricity.
[7] Source: Planning Commission of India, First Five-Year Plan (1954, 345).

electrification progressed slowly: by 1971, still only 18 percent of India's villages were electrified.

Today, India's power grid is among the most intricate in the world. In 2008, its power grid served nearly a billion people, sending out 723 billion kilowatt-hours (kWh) of electricity from hundreds of power plants into 4 million transformers along some 4.5 million miles of transmission and distribution lines – enough wire to get to the moon and back nine times. Nevertheless, India continues to trail on a variety of other metrics. In 1950, India's electricity consumption per capita was 14 kilowatt-hours (kWh), as compared to 1,100 kWh in the United Kingdom and 2,200 in the United States. By 2009, power consumption in India had risen to 571 kWh per person, but in relative terms it had fallen even further behind, with the United States at about 13,000 kWh per person. Meanwhile, China now consumes more than 2,600 kWh per person.[8] Moreover, even by conservative estimates, 10 percent of demand for electricity goes unmet because of a severe shortage of supply. Most of the time, the system maintains itself in something of a low-level equilibrium (Strand 2012), where users receive inadequate power service and pay even less adequately for the privilege. One third of all electrical power sent out in India is not paid for, collectibles presumably lost due to transmission losses, billing irregularities, excess use by flat-rate consumers, and theft (Min and Golden 2014).

The Politics of Electricity

Governments are the intermediaries linking citizens to electricity. They play a central role in managing power generation, controlling prices, shaping regulations, and overseeing electricity distribution. Jeffrey Sachs (2006) notes, "Governments are critical to investing in public goods and services like primary health care, roads, power grids, ports, and the like" (59). But even when governments pursue universal provision of public goods such as electricity, choices must be made in implementation that carry important distributive effects and political spillovers. After the fall of apartheid, the new South African government launched the massive National Electrification Programme (NEP) to provide universal access to electricity. In 1993, fewer than one in three South Africans had electricity and 80 percent relied on wood for fuel and heat. By 2001, two million more households were connected to the grid, almost a quarter of all households in the country. Yet where these new connections were made was guided as much by the African National Congress's (ANC) political priorities as by other factors. Dinkelman (2011) notes, "Almost by definition, networked infrastructure of any kind requires that consumers be connected in some order. And, in the context of the NEP, local political pressures and connections costs each played an important role in prioritizing communities for electrification." Supporting this claim, Kroth, Larcinese, and Wehner (2013)

---

[8] Source: World Bank Data Indicators.

found that new electricity connections increased faster in areas with many newly enfranchised, and presumably ANC-leaning, voters.

In India, numerous government schemes have aimed at expanding access to electricity in its villages. Here too, politics have played a role, if not the central role, in shaping the implementation of these efforts. In the late 1990s in Uttar Pradesh, Chief Minister Mayawati Kumari initiated the Ambedkar Village Programme (Ambedkar Gram Vikas Yojana) to provide over 11,000 of the poorest villages with electrification, roads, and irrigation. Despite its populist pretense, the program was widely regarded as a targeted effort to win Scheduled Caste votes and was closely associated with Mayawati and her Bahujan Samaj Party (BSP).[9] Critics argued that the blatant targeting of low caste villages was meant to reinforce caste divisions and reflected Mayawati's "obsession with the Dalit agenda."[10] Program audits revealed that from 1997 to 2001, elected politicians used their influence to get numerous villages electrified, sidestepping the formal process. In the Barabanki district just east of Lucknow, six villages were electrified that had not been authorized to receive electrification funds. Several other villages were found to have been selected for electrification by intervention of the energy minister, contrary to program guidelines (Wilkinson 2006).

Similar patterns of politically motivated public goods provision have been described in Mexico. A massive poverty alleviation program, Programa Nacional de Solidaridad (PRONASOL), began in 1989 to provide or improve access to water, electricity, nutrition, and education in poor communities. Municipalities dominated by the ruling Partido Revolucionario Institucional (PRI) received significantly higher per capita transfers than those voting for another party (Diaz-Cayeros, Magaloni, and Estévez forthcoming).

In Zaire, Mobutu Sese Seko famously ensured that Zaire's copper mines had to rely on the hydroelectric power stations he built at the Inga Falls more than a thousand miles away. Bueno de Mesquita and Smith (2011) explain, "This empowered him to cut off electricity at the touch of a button, guaranteeing that he, and not some local entrepreneur, controlled the flow of copper wealth" (119). In Iraq, Saddam Hussein diverted electricity from the provinces to keep power flowing to Baghdad and favored areas like his hometown of Tikrit. After he was deposed, subsequent governments have adopted new priorities in the distribution of electricity, amidst persistent accusations of favoritism.[11] The small farming village of Haenam in South Korea's Cholla province was electrified in the 1960s, enabling the use of streetlights, indoor lights, and a public

---

[9] The BSP was founded in 1984 to consolidate caste and religious minority interests in India. As a staunch advocate of Scheduled Caste issues, it has been most successful in Uttar Pradesh, where it won nearly 60 percent of the Scheduled Caste vote in 1998 (Chandra 2004). The Ambedkar program gets its name from B. R. Ambedkar, an untouchable who rose to prominence as a jurist and architect of the Indian constitution in the post-independence period.

[10] Tripathi, Purnima S., "Mayawati in Deep Trouble," *Frontline* 19(19): September 14–27, 2002.

[11] Zavis, Alexandra, "It's a power struggle every day." *Los Angeles Times*. March 24, 2008. See also Agnew, Gillespie, Gonzalez, and Min (2008).

announcement system. Yet Haenam residents grumbled at how long they had waited for electricity, long after their member of parliament's hometown was electrified, and even longer still after many villages in the president's home province of Kyongsang. In Zambia, a rural respondent noted how political allegiances affect who receives services from the state:

> One time I was watching a program on TV which showed Chiluba's village. It was being electrified. [It had a] good road network. They are doing so because that is where he comes from. It shows that you have to elect someone from your place because development will be there. (Posner 2005, 96)

Because electricity is so highly valued by citizens, it often receives prominent attention in electoral campaigns. In Liberia, Ellen Johnson Sirleaf won the presidency in 2006 on an uplifting campaign to restore stability and bring back electricity to the war–ravaged country. In a prominent ceremony soon after she took office, Sirleaf flipped a switch turning on streetlights in Monrovia that had been dark since 1990 when rebels had knocked the city off the power grid. As one newspaper account described: "Ms. Johnson Sirleaf decided to emphasize electricity because even beyond its economic importance, it has deep symbolic value. 'Even though we have a long way to go, at least we have reinforced hope,' Ms. Johnson Sirleaf said. 'We have brought back what we call the light at the end of the tunnel. Finally light has taken over from darkness … Small light today, big light tomorrow.'"[12] Yet by 2012, it remained clear that despite these broad promises, the actual benefits of electricity were available only to a favored few. According to one account, "There are street lights in parts of the city. Government buildings, NGOs, hospitals, some schools and the UN all have electricity. However, the average Liberian is still in the dark. Just 0.6% of Monrovians have access to electricity."[13]

The need for standardization also renders an important responsibility for governments. Users benefit when electricity is delivered in a reliable, consistent, and standard way. However, supply voltages, power frequencies, receptacle configurations, and rates can all vary. At the turn of the twentieth century, London lagged far behind many other leading cities in the quality of its electrical service, largely because its sixty-five separate utility companies could not agree on a common standard. Instead, electricity in London was characterized by variation: 70 generating stations, 49 different supply systems, 10 different frequencies, 32 voltage levels for transmission, 24 levels for distribution, and 70 pricing methods (Hughes 1983, 227). Following the trauma of the Great War, London's inability to agree on a consistent power architecture became a severe hindrance to growth: from 1920 to 1925, the economies of France and Germany grew twice as fast as that of the United Kingdom. A government committee report showed that per capita consumption of electricity in the United

---

[12] "One new light in Liberia, an inch back from abyss." *The New York Times*, July 27, 2006.
[13] "Liberia's battle to put the lights back on." *The Guardian*. February 6, 2012.

Kingdom was lower than in California, Chicago, Canada, and even Tasmania and Shanghai. Finally in 1926, Prime Minister Stanley Baldwin secured passage of the Electricity Supply Act, a landmark bill that would establish a national power grid and ensure a more uniform system of supply, all to be regulated by a Central Electricity Board. As the historian Thomas Hughes notes, "This achievement, in a country whose electric supply had long been parochial, was more political than technological and economic" (1983, 350).

Governments also have the ability to affect electricity prices by setting rates and providing subsidies. Manipulating prices represent a powerful lever by which leaders can seek to bolster public support, though lower rates to some usually imply higher rates to other sectors. As Brown and Mobarak (2009) argue, governments regularly use their authority to cross-subsidize prices: "Even in the most liberalized and privatized electricity markets, governments still can manipulate unit prices" (195). These policies often result in sectoral prices that reflect political priorities, because, as Berry (1979) notes, "The setting of rate structures is inherently redistributive" (263). In India, industry pays the highest rates for electricity, which subsidizes tariffs for the politically important agricultural and residential sectors. According to Dubash and Rajan (2002), "from 1977 onward, electricity increasingly became an instrument of populist politics. By offering electricity at flat rates – based on pump capacity rather than metered consumption – or even completely free, several state governments cultivated farmers as a vote bloc" (53). According to a recent International Monetary Fund (IMF) study, electricity subsidies amounted to almost 1 percent of gross domestic product in Latin America and the Caribbean. Often, subsidies are motivated by political concerns: in Buenos Aires, rates are set based on generation and transmissions costs but "remain subject to political discretion," while in the Dominican Republic, tariffs are set "by [the] regulator subject to political involvement" (Di Bella 2015, 17). In Venezuela, Hugo Chavez repeatedly lowered residential electricity prices to rates as low as 3 cents per kilowatt-hour, compared to rates of 15 cents or more in Brazil.

In these myriad ways, from shaping the priorities of electrification initiatives to the setting of prices, states and their agents exert weighty influence over the power sector. Accordingly, even ostensibly technical and economic matters can be deeply politicized, as a country's leaders respond to the competing demands for electricity and its benefits. Political incentives are thus critical factors in shaping who gets electricity and why, whether they be electoral considerations in democracies or the need to satisfy elites or powerful factions in nondemocratic settings.

Blackouts

For many in the developing world, electrification is a slow and drawn-out process, characterized by uneven access and low-quality service. Even for those fortunate to have an electrical connection, the reliability of the power supply can be unpredictable. Power outages are a common occurrence in much of the world, though few could imagine the discomfort and frustration they would cause when power grids were first being built. As the historian of technology David Nye observes, "Blackouts presuppose an electrical grid that did not yet exist" (Nye 2010, 13). As grids expanded, society became ever more vulnerable to the impact of failures in its provision. As Graham and Thrift (2007) note, breakdowns of complex systems "are not aberrant but are a part of the thing itself. To invent the train is to invent the train crash, to invent the plane is to invent the plane crash" (4).

As electrical grids expanded and grew, so too did the probability and impact of power failures. Regionally interconnected grids sharply reduced the price of electricity to consumers, allowing local utilities to sell excess power or import it when their supply was insufficient. Yet they also increased the likelihood of catastrophic interconnected failures. As electricity becomes woven into the daily life of citizens and the everyday reality of the interconnected power grid establishes itself, so does its converse, the blackout. As one villager in Senegal put it, "Now when the power goes out, it feels even darker than it did before we had electricity." Another factory manager lamented India's notoriously unreliable electricity service: "It's very frustrating. Power is a basic need. Everything is dependent on power."[14] As they live in uncertainty, many find themselves relying on a bricolage of methods to meet their energy needs, switching between electric light bulbs and candles and kerosene lamps when the power is not working.[15]

Massive outages are both inconvenient and costly. In addition to the great blackout of India in 2012, 15 million lost power in Europe in 2006, and 60 million more in Brazil and Paraguay in 2009. In August 2003, 55 million people lost power in the northeastern United States and Canada at an estimated cost of $US 6.4 billion. As *The New York Times* reported, "Many saw the blackout as emblematic of a wider problem, one brought about by a lack of government oversight for years of the electric industry."[16] It is estimated that power outages negatively impacted the US economy to the tune of $79 billion in 2004.

Blackouts can occur for a variety of reasons. Electricity is sent from power-generating plants to a country's users through an intricate network of wires interconnected by transformers and substations. A fault or failure at any point can mean a loss of power for all downstream users. Sometimes the faults are due to downed wires or short circuits. More commonly in the developing world, utilities intentionally shut power to parts of the grid to protect sensitive

---

[14] "India struggles to deliver enough power." *The New York Times*. April 19, 2012.
[15] Karekezi and Majoro (2002) found that in Zambia, household electrification resulted in a decline in the use of kerosene but a sevenfold increase in the ownership of candles. For those who can afford it, an extravagant accessory is the combination of car batteries and inverters to store power for use during blackouts.
[16] "The blackout that exposed the flaws in the grid." *The New York Times*, November 11, 2013.

infrastructure. Not only do wires heat up when placed under excess loads, but so too do transformers which can explode spectacularly.

Transformers are critical nodes in the power grid, stepping up power to the high voltages necessary for efficient transmission across large distances, and stepping down the voltage at service drops to the 220 or 110 volts useful for household use. A blown transformer is expensive and laborious to replace. More than 200 villages were plunged into darkness in western Uttar Pradesh when a large 132-kilovolt transformer caught fire on a scorchingly hot day in June 2012. Power utility officials explained, "the demand for power has been touching an all time high in the recent times. It was possibly the high load on the transmission transformer that resulted in the crisis."[17] Only the power company and its staff can repair such costly equipment. As a result, when a transformer fails, it can mean days or even weeks without electricity for its users. Because of the high costs of equipment failure, power companies will preemptively disable the supply of electricity entirely to sections of the grid during periods of excess demand. These rolling blackouts, also referred to as load shedding, protect the infrastructure but cut off service, often when people need power the most.

If all consumers would reduce their power consumption slightly, total demand could be reduced enough to obviate the need for load shedding. However, as in a classic tragedy of the commons, no user has an incentive to reduce demand if he or she believes his or her neighbors are unlikely to curb their use as well. Imagine a bustling marketplace on a hot summer day. Significant energy savings could be achieved and load shedding could be averted if shopkeepers would turn off their air conditioners and lights.[18] Certainly, owners should all feel invested in preventing a power cut that would hurt sales as shoppers stay away from darkened stores. Nonetheless, it is unlikely that owners will coordinate to lower their power consumption when the payoffs for defection are more attractive. As a result, power companies resort to imposing forced and regular blackouts in many parts of the world. The World Bank reports that the average Nigerian firm suffers 25 power outages in a typical month. The number is 34 in Albania, 39 in Kosovo, 41 in Iraq, 51 in Nepal, and 52 in Yemen. In Bangladesh, firms reported more than *100* power outages a month in 2007.[19]

Load shedding requires power companies to engage in a difficult and perilous balancing act. All consumers want power. Residents depend on electric lighting in their homes and the use of fans on sweltering days and nights.

---

[17] "Power crisis in 200 villages as transformer catches fire." *Times of India*, June 17, 2012.

[18] As incomes rise, air conditioning can quickly become the single largest variable load on a power grid. Following a spike in power cuts in 2012, Egypt's electricity minister blamed the use of air conditioners, which account for up to 20 percent of total electricity use. In 2012, Egyptians owned 6 million air conditioning units, up from 3 million in 2009 and 196,000 in 1999. "Egypt's electricity ministry ducks blame for power cuts." *Al-Ahram*, English edition, July 26, 2012.

[19] World Bank Enterprise Surveys, most recent year data reported. http://data.worldbank.org/indicator/IC.ELC.OUTG

Commercial businesses need electricity to illuminate storefronts and run equipment. Industry requires power to operate machinery. Farmers require electricity to pump water and irrigate their fields. The decision about whose power gets cut and whose power is preserved is loaded with economic, social, and political consequences. According to one newspaper account, "India's basic power problem is that the country's rapid development has led demand to far outstrip supply. That means power officials must manage the grid by shutting down power to small sections of the country on a rotating basis. But doing so requires quick action from government officials who are often loath to shut off power to important constituencies."[20]

In some countries, utilities have attempted to formalize their load shedding policies to appear fair and transparent. In Nepal, a popular Android app from the country's electricity authority transmits the load shedding schedule to users' smartphones (assuming they are charged!).[21] Yet because utilities control how rolling blackouts are imposed under the watchful gaze of the state and its leaders, the timing and geographic incidence of blackouts can be subject to political control, in ways both risible and shrewd. On the evening of a championship cricket match between Pakistan and India, the president of Pakistan ordered that load shedding be suspended during the match so that televisions would work across the country.[22] In September 2008, the ruling government of Uttar Pradesh, India, increased the number of hours of electricity to a set of majority-Muslim localities by imposing blackouts on several industrial zones, a move that many viewed as an effort to pander to the Muslim vote.

Blackouts are technical failures but also political opportunities. Because their frequency and incidence are subject to discretion, those in control of the power grid have the ability to manipulate the grid for political purposes. This feature is significant for numerous reasons. First, it reflects an important reality in the developing world: access to *infrastructure* does not necessarily imply access to the *services* they are designed to deliver. School buildings provide no benefit when teachers do not show up.[23] Roads are of little value when rain storms wash them away or leave potholes that make them impassable. Electrical wires are of no use when there is no power flowing through them.

Second, the governance of blackouts reveals an important way in which politicians can manage the delivery of supposed "public goods" for political gain. Scholars have postulated that risk-averse politicians may be disinclined to deliver permanent public goods because there is no way to ensure that voters will continue to support them once these goods have been provided. But

---

[20] "As power is restored in India, the 'blame game' over blackouts heats up." *The New York Times*, August 2, 2012.

[21] Nepal Electricity Authority Load Shedding Schedule, http://nea.org.np/loadshedding.html.

[22] "No load shedding during Pakistan-India match Zardari orders PM." *The News Tribe*, September 30, 2012.

[23] Chaudhury et al. (2006) used unannounced visits to schools and clinics to find that 9 percent of teachers and 35 percent of health workers were absent in the developing world.

public service delivery requires two interlocking components: the physical stock of capital infrastructure and the ongoing flow of service. Politicians can seek political advantage in two stages: first by negotiating where infrastructure projects are built and second by managing the ongoing flow of services. Why the power only works sometimes for some and not for others is thus an intrinsically political question.

Do Voters Care about Electricity?

As temperatures plummeted below 20°F in the winter of early 2008, residents of Bishkek, Kyrgyzstan, were shocked as their heaters shut off and lights flickered off across the city. Low water levels at Kyrgyzstan's hydroelectric reservoirs had crippled its already overstretched power grid, and officials at the state-run utility had been forced to cut power to whole swaths of the country during the coldest winter in decades. In a state where half the population lives in poverty, citizens were outraged when President Kurmanbek Bakiyev's primary response to the energy crisis was to raise electricity tariffs. Yet power outages would become increasingly frequent and severe in the months ahead. By 2009, outages lasting five hours per day were costing firms in Kyrgyzstan up to 10 percent in lost sales and had become the number one problem facing businesses, more troublesome than taxes, corruption, or political instability. Following yet another steep rise in energy tariffs in early 2010, frustrations against the government reached a tipping point. In April 2010, bloody riots in Bishkek ousted President Bakiyev in a coup and sparked ethnic violence that displaced 400,000 and left hundreds dead (Nichol 2009).

In early 2013, thousands of Bulgarians marched in protests against surging electricity prices.[24] Violent demonstrations were marked by four self-immolations and dozens of injuries in cities across Bulgaria. The protests, sparked by a sudden rise in electricity prices, escalated into an expression of broader discontent against the ruling government. By late February, a day after violent clashes in Sofia, the center-right government led by Prime Minister Boiko Borisov collapsed.

When power outages swept across South Africa in late 2007, citizens directed their outrage toward their political leaders. South Africa had long been a haven from power outages that plague the rest of Africa. To many South Africans, the power crisis was an embarrassment, a devastating result of poor planning and government oversight. In an extraordinary admission of failure, President Thabo Mbeki acknowledged "that this government got its timing wrong."[25] The crisis overshadowed the efforts made by the African National Congress, which had more than doubled the percentage of the population connected to

---

[24] "Bulgaria government to resign, PM Boiko Borisov says." *BBC News*, February 20, 2013.
[25] "Power failures outrage South Africa." *The New York Times*, January 31, 2008, quoting Alec Erwin, South Africa's Minister of Energy and Public Enterprises.

the grid since 1994 to more than 70 percent. Mere months later, amidst a crisis of legitimacy, Mbeki resigned.

Even still, South Africa has continued to be rocked by hundreds of so-called "service delivery protests" in recent years, as disenchanted protesters have taken to the streets in frustration over the government's failures to provide sanitation and electricity. Police were called out to nearly 600 protests over a three-month span in Gauteng province alone.[26] According to one protester, "The ANC makes all these promises but they can't deliver. No water, no electricity, they can't fix the roads."

The upheavals in Kyrgyzstan, Bulgaria, and South Africa are not isolated occurrences. In 2011, newspaper sources reported protests over electricity shortages and quality issues in some 50 countries around the world. In at least two dozen of these, the protests were violent, resulting in personal and property damage. These protests reflect the intersection of powerful currents linking development, poverty, citizen pressure, and public responsibility. Failures to provide consistent and reliable electrical power are among the daily reminders of a weak and unresponsive state. Governments are legitimized by their provision of public goods. But when governments fail to deliver basic public services such as electricity, they show that leaders are unable to fulfill their mandates. Protests are an extraordinary expression of frustration by citizens against their governments, and the fact that so many protests in recent years have been sparked by energy concerns reflects the critical relationship between energy access and overall social welfare.

In a 2007 preelection survey in Uttar Pradesh, nearly four in ten voters noted that development issues including electricity, road, and water concerns were their most important consideration in deciding for whom to vote.[27] Indeed, it is often said that Indian politics centers around *bijli, sadak, paani* (electricity, roads, water). Voters in one village confronted their elected state legislator about the lack of power during a campaign visit, crying, "no electricity, no vote."[28] In the World Bank Enterprise Survey of Indian businesses in 2006, more firms cited access to reliable electricity as the number one obstacle facing their business (35 percent) than any other concern, including taxes (25 percent) and corruption (11 percent). Indian firms estimated losing 6.6 percent of sales as a result of power outages.

In a nationally representative survey of 8,388 respondents in 2001–2002, Indian voters were asked about various problems relating to public services facing their lives. Three-quarters of Indians ranked electricity as an important problem. Many fewer reported concerns about sanitation, crime, and pollution. Indians believe overwhelmingly that responsibility for electricity issues rests in the hands of government and not private business or individuals.

---

[26] "Informal settlements ablaze with disenchantment." *Mail & Guardian*, February 8, 2014.
[27] Lokniti, *Uttar Pradesh Pre-Election Poll 2007*.
[28] "Mayawati MLA accused of beating up voters over electricity," NDTV.com, January 5, 2012.

Among respondents, 93 percent said they perceived the government as having primary responsibility for electricity problems, a higher proportion than for any other category of public service including roads, health, education, or water (Chhibber et al. 2004).

Even when governments attempt to hand over the power sector to private interests, citizens still hold them accountable for failures. In 2000, the disastrous deregulation of California's electric industry led to rolling blackouts across the state. Analysts observed that the newly empowered private providers, including Enron, were intentionally reducing the power supplied to the grid during periods of high demand, raising spot prices and firm profits. The eventual fallout was certainly severe for Enron, but also for California's political leadership, which many citizens believed were ultimately responsible. Governor Gray Davis declared a state of emergency in January 2001 that lasted more than two years and attempted to deflect blame, saying "I inherited the energy deregulation scheme which put us all at the mercy of the big energy producers. We got no help from the Federal government. In fact, when I was fighting Enron and the other energy companies, these same companies were sitting down with Vice President Cheney to draft a national energy strategy."[29] Voters were not assuaged, and Davis was removed from executive office in the recall election of October 2003.

All these cases show that electricity is politicized because it is of such high value to citizens. Especially in democratic contexts where citizens demand public services from their leaders, and where politicians recognize the influence and responsibility they have over the power sector, electricity can become a critical electoral issue.

What Electricity Can Tell Us about Political Systems

Beyond its intrinsic value in providing energy, electricity provides a clear window into how political institutions work. Electricity is a critical input that can enable economic growth *as well as* social welfare. How do governments balance this choice? When electricity is plentiful, it can serve both goals simultaneously, fueling growth while also supplying the basic needs of the poor. But in much of the world, electricity is scarce relative to demand and governments must make difficult choices about how to prioritize where it goes and who gets to use it.

Electricity enables job creation and industrial production. Without electricity, modern economic growth is not possible. For industry and commerce, electricity is a sine qua non – it is a basic necessity for production. Firms without electricity cannot compete against those that use it to power factories and run machinery (Asher and Novosad 2013; Allcott, Collard-Wexler, and O'Connell 2014).

---

[29] "Davis Blasts GOP Tactics," *San Jose Mercury News*, August 20, 2003.

But electricity is also valuable because it increases social welfare. In their homes, people benefit from electric lighting, fans, and refrigeration. It also improves information access through phones, radios, and televisions. In town squares and along streets, outdoor lights illuminate roadways and enhance safety. When the United Nations agreed on its ambitious Millennium Development goals, electricity was not explicitly on the list. Yet as Thomas Friedman (2008) has noted, "Every problem of the developing world is also an energy problem" (197). Access to energy is a basic prerequisite for eradicating poverty, improving access to education, lowering infant mortality, and improving access to health services. Without electricity, the poor are deprived of economic opportunities to improve their welfare and well-being. Every day, the poor burn precious calories to forage for wood and fuel, to pump drinking water, and to keep themselves warm.[30] And every day, they fall farther behind those who can produce goods more efficiently, study longer into the night, and live healthier lives because of their access to electricity and the conveniences it enables.

The economic and social welfare benefits of electricity are at odds when the domestic sector and industrial sector must compete over the same scarce supply of power. In the zero-sum game that constrains electricity supply in much of the world, every watt of electricity going to one sector means one less going to another. The juxtaposition of these competing needs and demands presents a thorny challenge to governments. How does a government allocate resources, prioritize access, and focus its policies when it seeks both to enable economic growth but must also be concerned about maintaining political support among the masses?

The chapters ahead will show that the answer depends on how governments stay in power and that the need to win elections induces democratic leaders to allocate a greater share of electricity towards voters and away from industry and other sectoral interests. Importantly, democracies provide broader provision of electricity to the rural poor, a constituency that is far easier to overlook in regimes that do not depend on their votes. These patterns are not driven by a greater normative commitment to poverty alleviation or an attachment to the peasantry, although such commitments may well exist. Rather, it is because the logic of winning votes induces elected leaders to target those most likely to be swayed by new promises and commitments. These dynamics are particularly salient among the rural poor who have access to few alternatives other than state-provided public goods, and may be more willing to switch their votes based on their provision.

---

[30] In rural Africa, many women living without electricity must carry 20 kg of fuelwood an average of 5 km every day (International Energy Agency 2002, 367).

4

Measuring Electricity from Space

Introduction

On September 4, 1882, Thomas Edison flipped a switch at his Pearl Street Station and electric lights flickered on across lower Manhattan. So began the era of electric power transmission, setting off the proliferation of power plants distributing electrical power across the world. Yet today, 1.3 billion people continue to lack electricity, relying instead on kerosene, wood, and agricultural residues to meet their energy needs (International Energy Agency 2013). Where do these 1.3 billion people reside? And what do they reveal about how their governments choose to electrify some before others, and some not at all?

Despite its significance, there are little reliable data on how electricity is distributed in much of the developing world. High levels of uncertainty pervade official estimates of electrification rates, a vital and basic public service that is typically provided by governments in most of the rural world. Surveys from the World Bank, the Demographic and Health Surveys (DHS), and household survey programs provide invaluable data on household electrification rates and use. But these exist only for a subset of countries and rarely enable estimation of electrification rates at lower sub-national levels. Moreover, such surveys are expensive and difficult to conduct in areas that are remote, dangerous, or without the cooperation of local officials.

This book proposes a new method to estimate the provision of electrification using satellite imagery of the earth at night to identify lit and unlit areas across the globe. Stable concentrations of outdoor lighting are a uniquely good indicator of electricity access, because electricity is the most reliable energy source for outdoor illumination of streets and buildings and the only source that can do so at the levels required for satellite detection. Compared with traditional data on energy production and consumption, the satellite images explicitly reveal the geographic distribution of electrical power, providing a clearer picture of who benefits from electricity across every corner of the globe.

Satellite Imagery of Nighttime Lights

Since the early 1970s, the Defense Meteorological Satellite Program's Operational Linescan System (DMSP-OLS) has been flying in polar orbit capturing high-resolution images of the entire earth each night, typically between 7PM and 10PM local time. Captured at an altitude of 830 km above the earth, these images reveal concentrations of outdoor lights, fires, and gas flares at a fine resolution of 0.56 km. On-board averaging of 5 by 5 blocks of fine data produces "smoothed" data with a nominal spatial resolution of 2.7 km. Most data are made available in the smooth spatial resolution mode. Although the original purpose of the DMSP-OLS was to detect clouds using moonlight, it is also able to detect outdoor illumination from towns and cities and the ephemeral light from forest fires, gas flares, and heavily lit fishing boats.

Early images from the DMSP-OLS were recorded on film strips, limiting their usefulness to most scholars. Beginning in 1992, digitized data began to be archived at the NOAA National Geophysical Data Center, facilitating their analysis and use by the scientific community. The nighttime low-light sensing capabilities of the OLS permit the detection of radiances down to 10^{-9} W/cm^2/sr/μm. This is not sensitive enough to detect individual point sources of light, but it can detect large concentrations of electric lighting. For example, large boats used for squid fishing are regularly visible in nighttime images captured off the Japanese and Korean coasts. These boats, weighing between 60 and 100 tons, can be equipped with as many as 50 incandescent lamps with an average power of 3,500 watts per lamp to attract squid to the sea surface (Nakayama and Elvidge 1999). Analysis shows that the light from just one of these fishing boats can be clearly distinguished by the DMSP-OLS sensors (Elvidge et al. 2001).

Although raw satellite imagery is recorded every night, the primary data products used by most scientists are a series of annual composite images. These are created by overlaying all nightly images captured during a calendar year, dropping images where lights are shrouded by cloud cover or overpowered by the aurora or solar glare (near the poles), and removing ephemeral lights such as fires and other visual noise.[1] The result is a series of images of time stable night lights covering the globe for each year since 1992 (Elvidge et al. 1997a, 2001; Imhoff et al. 1997). As the DMSP program may have more than one satellite in orbit at a time, some years have two annual images created from composites from each satellite. Images are scaled onto a georeferenced 30-arcsecond grid (approximately 1 km^2 at the equator), creating a global image with a resolution of 43,200 by 21,600 pixels.

Each pixel is encoded with a measure of its annual average brightness on a 6-bit scale from 0 to 63, providing an unusually rich perspective of how dark

---

[1] The geographic range of usable DMSP data is −65 to +65 latitude. This results in missing data for portions of the world within the Arctic and Antarctic circles, home to an exceedingly small share of the global population.

and bright different corners of the earth appear at night. Because of differences in the sensitivity and calibration of sensors across years, the brightness values of a pixel in one annual composite cannot be easily compared to the brightness values from those of other years. However, statistical calibration techniques, such as the use of fixed effects in regression models, can help account for systematic differences across annual composites. For social science research, a great virtue of the nighttime image data is that they are automatically collected using a consistent recording protocol across time and space with complete geographic coverage. As a result, the data are resistant to human reporting biases and sampling concerns that are potentially worrisome in data collected using traditional survey methods.

Figure 4.1 shows an annual composite image of the earth at night in 2009. The image reveals large variation in light intensity around the world, with especially broad and brightly lit areas across the eastern United States, Western Europe, India, and East Asia. Meanwhile, inhospitable environments in the frozen Arctic deserts of Canada, Alaska, and Siberia and the deserts of Africa, China, and Australia are cloaked in darkness. At first glance, the distribution of lights might appear to be a reflection of population distributions. But closer examination reveals that there are important anomalies in the relationship between population concentration and light output. For example, much of Africa is dark, even though it is home to 15 percent of the world's population. Although more than one in three people in the world live in India and China, the light output of these two countries accounts for only a tenth of the global total. The distribution of global population, shown in Figure 4.2, shows an inconsistent correlation between population and light output.[2]

A better predictor of why some countries are brighter than others is a country's level of industrialization. South Africa has a similar population density but larger economy than neighboring Zimbabwe and a correspondingly higher light output. The difference across the 38th parallel on the Korean peninsula is especially striking, revealing the impact of political institutions and economic development in a region with identical cultures and similar geography. Indeed, numerous studies have shown that nighttime light output from the DMSP-OLS imagery is highly correlated with gross domestic product at the national level (Elvidge et al. 1997b; Doll 2000; Chen and Nordhaus 2011; Henderson, Storeygard, and Weil 2012).

Scientists are also using these data to model urbanization (Lo 2001; Small et al. 2005) the environmental consequences of natural disasters (Kohiyama et al. 2004; Gillespie et al. 2014), and the destructive impacts of violent conflict (Agnew et al. 2008; Li and Li 2014). For social science research, a great virtue of the nighttime image data is that they are unbiased by human factors,

[2] The population data come from the LandScan project (Dobson et al. 2000) and are discussed in more detail in Chapter 5.

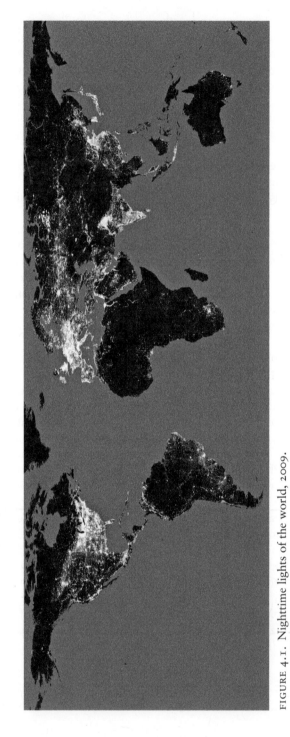

FIGURE 4.1. Nighttime lights of the world, 2009.
Source: DMSP-OLS F182009. Image and data processing by NOAA's National Geophysical Data Center. DMSP data collected by US Air Force Weather Agency.

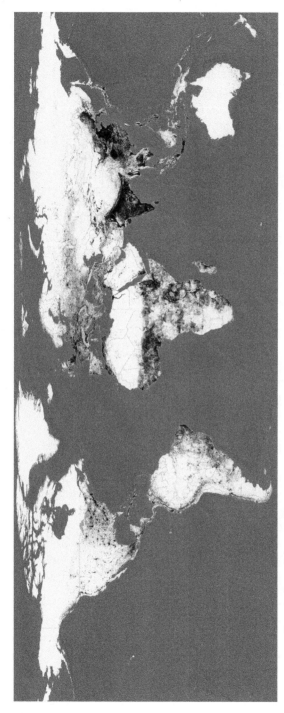

FIGURE 4.2. Population of the world.
Source: Oak Ridge National Laboratory, LandScan 2008.

consistently measured across time and space, and complete in their geographic coverage.

Some research has identified important technical limitations of the nighttime lights sensors and data, including saturation and blooming. However, these are concerns that apply mostly to urban environments and other very brightly lit regions. They are much lower concerns in the rural, dimly lit contexts I focus on in this book. *Saturation* occurs because of the limited dynamic range of the satellite sensor. To detect dimly lit areas, light entering the satellite sensors are amplified using high gain settings on the photomultiplier tube. While higher gain increases detection of dimly lit areas, it also results in the loss of detail in very bright areas, similar to overexposure of bright areas in a conventional photograph. The result is censored data in the most brightly lit areas of the world, notably in the center of large cities that are uniformly coded with the maximum brightness value in the data stream. *Blooming* occurs when lights from an area appear to spill into neighboring areas, resulting in an overglow of light that extends beyond the immediate ground-based sources of lighting. For example, many of the largest coastal cities have light profiles that spill over the coast. This means that nighttime light images tend to overestimate the extent of light coverage, especially around large cities. However, the effects of blooming are unlikely to be correlated at the country level with the presence of elections, which are the primary focus of my analysis. The *limited sensitivity* of the DMSP sensors means that not all dimly lit regions are detectable in satellite images. Field checks have revealed that lights from US towns with as few as 150 residents are detectable (Doll, Muller, and Elvidge 2000). In another field test, light produced by a single 1000-watt high-pressure sodium lamp was detected by the satellite (Tuttle et al. 2014). However, even sparse cloud cover and minor atmospheric disturbances can cloak ground-based light output, and thus the image processing algorithms used to create the annual composite images may filter out many dimly lit or irregularly lit areas. The result is that the annual composite DMSP images will underestimate access to electrification in the most dimly lit settlements. This is a significant limitation, although this concern would affect the analysis only if this under-estimation is systematically correlated with key independent variables like level of democracy, which I assume to be unlikely.

Although access to electricity is clearly related to a country's level of development, the relationship is not absolute. The International Energy Agency (IEA) produces the most cited source of data on electrification levels around the world in its annual World Energy Outlook publications. As the IEA data in Figure 4.3 show, many countries with comparable poverty levels have very different levels of electrification. Income levels in Indonesia and the Philippines are comparable but nearly half of Indonesians lack electricity compared to only one in eight in the Philippines. Benin is among the poorest countries in the world but has the same proportion of unelectrified citizens as Botswana, where average income is six times higher. These variations suggest that although the

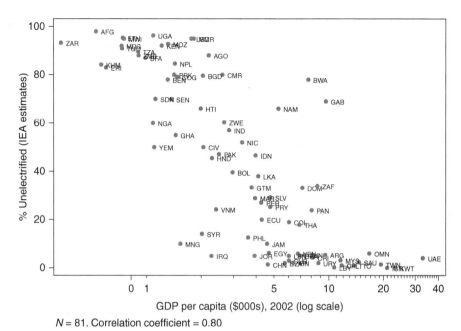

FIGURE 4.3. Official estimates of electricity access and poverty, 2000.
Source: International Energy Agency (2002).

level of development is important, it cannot by itself explain why some states provide electrification to more of their citizens than others.

The IEA data also illustrates some of the potential weaknesses that are typical in cross-national datasets. Given the impracticality of single-handedly collecting data on electrification using a single team of researchers following a consistent and unified process across the world, IEA's data are instead derived from disparate sources, including self-reported government data, nongovernmental organization (NGO) estimates, World Bank studies, and regional organization reports. Moreover, because there is no universal definition of what it takes for a home or village to be considered electrified, the comparability of country-specific estimates is difficult to gauge. Official definitions of electrification can differ even within the same country. For decades in India, a village was considered electrified in official records if it had even a single electrical connection anywhere within the village being used for any purpose. Thus a village with one electrified water pump but not a single working light bulb was nevertheless classified as electrified. But in 2004, the official definition changed, requiring a broader level of service provision including basic electrical infrastructure, electrification of public buildings, and a minimum 10 percent household electrification rate. As a result, official government reports show a *decline* in India's village electrification rates over that decade, an improbable trend that is simply an artifact of the definitional change. In addition to differences in methodology and definitions, the bureaucratic capacity to collect dependable statistics varies widely by country. The precision and reliability of electrification estimates is probably lower in poorer countries, places overwhelmed by civil war, and closed regimes inaccessible to outsiders. Yet properly accounting for presumed variations in the quality of data measures across cases is difficult. Finally, the IEA lists data for only 86 countries, resulting in a pattern of missing data that is unlikely to be random and can lead to sample biases in statistical analysis.

Nighttime satellite imagery provides an opportunity to sidestep these concerns. Yet for this strategy to be effective, we need confidence that the presence of outdoor illumination actually reflects the availability and use of electricity on the ground. In the following sections, I present a range of evidence drawn from statistical analysis and "ground truthing" efforts at multiple geographic scales and across diverse settings that confirm the strong relationship between outdoor illumination and electricity use. Overall, the consistent and compelling pattern that emerges across these comparisons provides confidence that satellite imagery can be used to study how states allocate and deliver electricity, even across the poorest parts of their countries where we know least about how public goods and services are distributed.

Validating Night Lights as a Measure of Electrification

Lights and Electrical Infrastructure Across Countries
The World Bank, drawing on data from Canning (1998), reports the total electricity production capacity in millions of kilowatts for all countries of the world. In Figure 4.4, I compare this total against each country's 2003 nighttime light output, summed across all pixels within a country's borders. Overall, the correlation is high, at 0.83 for 146 countries. Countries with lower electricity production capacities generate less light while the larger and wealthier countries at the top right are the brightest countries visible from space. These data indicate that nighttime lights are a reliable measure of a country's electrical production capacity. In a related comparison, Elvidge et al. (1997b) report an R^2 of .96 in a regression of 21 countries' lit area and electric power consumption.

Electrical Infrastructure in Italian Provinces
Golden and Picci (2005) collected data on public investments and capital stocks for numerous infrastructure categories in up to 103 provinces in Italy. The data include a measure of 1997 energy infrastructure stocks normalized by geographic area and indexed as a ratio to the national average. I compare this measure against nighttime light output. To create a comparable "per unit area" measure, I divide the total 1997 light output for each province by its size to

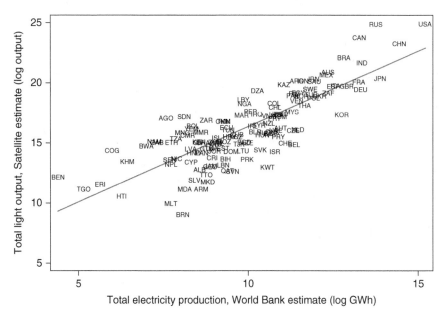

N = 130. Correlation coefficient = 0.81

FIGURE 4.4. Comparison of nighttime light output from satellite against World Bank estimates of electricity production.

Sources: DMSP-OLS F152003, 2007 update to Canning (1998).

create a measure of light per square kilometer.[3] Figure 4.5 shows Italy at night and Figure 4.6 plots these two variables against each other, showing a correlation of 0.52 for 91 provinces.

In the OLS regression shown in Table 4.1 and Figure 4.6, I find that energy infrastructure stock is a powerful predictor of light output, even after controlling for population density and economic activity. This suggests that nighttime light output reflects public investments into electrical infrastructure and is not simply a proxy for private economic activity or industrial output.

Lights and Public Spending in US Cities

Especially in the United States, it seems plausible that nighttime light output might be a better indicator of private economic activity and not a reflection of public investments into infrastructure and public services. To examine this question, I follow Alesina, Baqir, and Easterly (1999), who analyze local public spending data for all US cities in 1990. The expenditure data come from the 1994 *County and City Data Book*, which provides 1992 spending totals for various categories, including local highway spending. I recorded data for a

---

[3] Italian provincial boundaries were taken from ArcGIS Europe basemap province level 2.

FIGURE 4.5. Italy at night, 1997. Reverse color image (darker pixels have higher light output).
Source: DMSP-OLS F141997.

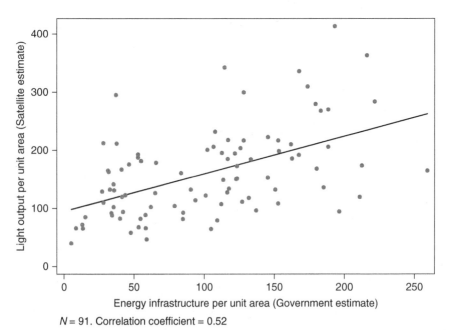

N = 91. Correlation coefficient = 0.52

FIGURE 4.6. Nighttime light output and energy infrastructure in Italian provinces.
Source: DMSP-OLS F141997 and Golden and Picci (2005).

TABLE 4.1. *Light output in Italian provinces*

	The Dependent Variable is Light Output per km^2
Population density	0.0454**
	(0.016)
Economic intensity per area (VAT)	0.0002
	(0.0005)
Infrastructure stocks per unit area	
Energy	0.3622**
	(0.112)
Transportation	−0.2875
	(0.158)
Communication	−0.3813**
	(0.136)
Water	0.2032
	(0.143)
Sanitation	−0.2075
	(0.164)
Constant	103.08**
	(27.11)
Observations	91
R^2	0.787

Huber–White robust standard errors in parentheses.
**p-value ≤ 0.01; *p-value ≤ 0.05.

sample of 172 metropolitan statistical areas (MSAs) going alphabetically from Abilene, TX to Reading, PA – roughly three-quarters of all metropolitan areas.[4]

In the highly industrialized US context, shown in Figure 4.7, I assume that city lights visible from space come from public streetlights on residential streets, thoroughfares, and freeways; leakage from indoor lights from homes and office buildings; illumination of billboards and signs; outdoor lighting of buildings; traffic and other signal lights; outdoor lighting of private parking lots and other outdoor venues; and automobile headlights. Among these various sources of illumination, it seems plausible that the most significant light producers would be streetlights and the headlights of automobiles on busy highways. Should this be true, lights should be highly correlated with streets and highways, which are publicly funded. Figure 4.8 plots nighttime light output against local highway spending for 172 MSAs, with a strong correlation of 0.80.

Because light can also be generated by other sources unrelated to public activities, I conduct regression analysis to control for other potential factors. My dependent variable is light output per capita, measured as the total radiance

---

[4] Shapefiles for all MSAs and PMSAs as of 1990 were originally obtained from the US Census Bureau. These can now be accessed at the National Historical Geographic Information System of the University of Minnesota.

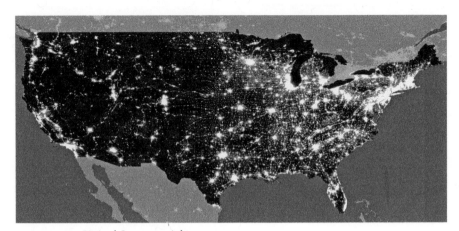

FIGURE 4.7. United States at night, 1992.
Source: DMSP-OLS F101992.

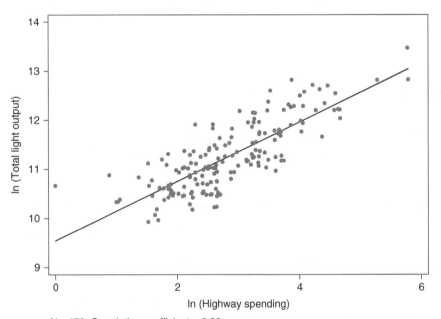

N = 172. Correlation coefficient = 0.80

FIGURE 4.8. Nighttime light output and local highway spending in US metro areas.
Source: DMSP-OLS F101992 and *County and City Data Book, 1994*.

TABLE 4.2. *Light output in US metro areas*

The Dependent Variable is Light Output per Capita	(1)	(2)
Population, log	−0.0955**	−0.1101**
	(0.007)	(0.008)
Area, log	0.0850**	0.0951**
	(0.010)	(0.010)
Local per capita income	0.0048	0.0074*
	(0.003)	(0.003)
Private businesses, per capita	0.0010	0.0014*
	(0.0005)	(0.001)
Local government spending per capita		
Highways	0.4638**	
	(0.175)	
Education	0.0759*	
	(0.031)	
Health	0.0264	
	(0.033)	
Police	−0.4640	
	(0.310)	
Welfare	−0.0275	
	(0.087)	
Constant	1.4569**	1.6629**
	(0.101)	(0.099)
Observations	172	172
R^2	0.641	0.593

Huber–White robust standard errors in parentheses.
**p-value ≤ 0.01; *p-value ≤ 0.05.

of a metropolitan statistical area divided by its population. My independent variables include population; size of the metro area; local per capita income; number of private business establishments per capita; and per capita spending by local governments on highways, education, health, police, and welfare. The results are presented in Table 4.2.

Model 1 reveals that light output from US cities is strongly predicted by local government spending, especially spending on highways. Meanwhile, economic variables including local per capita income and the number of businesses are not significant predictors of light output. These economic measures become highly significant once the public spending categories are removed in model 2. These results suggest that even in US cities, nighttime light output reflects government investments in public services and not simply private economic activity.

Streetlights in Elmira, New York

Elmira is a small city in upstate New York with a population of 30,940 as of the 2000 census in a 20 square kilometer area. To evaluate more closely

FIGURE 4.9. Comparing streetlight location and night lights imagery in Elmira, New York. Rectangular cells represent 30-arcsecond pixels. Lighter cells indicate higher light output.
Sources: NOAA-NGDC DMSP-OLS F152003 and City of Elmira.

whether nighttime light output is correlated with outdoor public lighting, I requested data from the city on the location of each of the city's 4,076 streetlights, as plotted in Figure 4.9. The image also shows nighttime light output in 2003 and an outline of Elmira's city limits. At this local level of geography, the rectangular shape of each 30-arcsecond pixel of the DMSP imagery is clearly visible. Each pixel encompasses an area roughly five to ten city blocks per side, a size similar to common notions of a neighborhood. With the city's area divided into some two dozen pixels, variations in light output can be distinguished across Elmira's neighborhoods. Typical of the level of development characteristic of most industrialized countries, light output is generally very high, ranging from a low of 49 at the city's southeast corner to a high of 60 downtown at the city center. On the other hand, the pixel size is not small enough to distinguish individual lights, nor is it possible to identify whether the light is coming from streetlights, outdoor building illumination, leakage from indoor lighting, or automobile headlights.

However, as expected, the correlation between streetlight density and light output is high, with more light generally shining from neighborhoods with more streetlights.

The figure also shows the precision of the georeferencing process by which satellite imagery and other locational data such as street locations and city boundaries can be matched. Once image layers are placed in the same geographic coordinate system, the spatial matching of different kinds of geographic information is automatic and precise. This geographic accuracy makes it possible to measure light emissions down to the neighborhood level for any location in the world. I apply this process in Chapter 7, where I measure and analyze changes in nighttime light output for all 98,000 villages in Uttar Pradesh, India.

Electricity and Night Lights in Senegal and Mali

How reliable are satellite images as an indicator of actual levels of electricity consumption on the ground? Previous studies have found high correlations between nighttime light output and electricity use at the national level (Elvidge et al. 1997b) but the relationship at smaller subnational units has not been robustly evaluated, especially in low income settings. In 2011 in collaboration with Kwawu Mensan Gaba at the World Bank, I directed a survey of more than 200 villages across Senegal and Mali to collect ground-based data on electricity availability and use for comparison against night lights imagery (Min et al. 2013). To our knowledge, this was the first systematic "ground truthing" effort to validate the use of DMSP-OLS night lights imagery to detect rural electrification in the developing world. The sampled villages were chosen to be representative of the range of conditions that characterize electrified villages in the respective countries. These are settings with low levels of electricity access and use: in Senegal electricity consumption was 187 kWh per capita and only around 35 kWh per capita in Mali at income levels of $2,140 and $1,590 respectively. Senegal's household electrification rate in 2008 was 42 percent, with 75 percent connected in urban areas and 18 percent in rural areas. In Mali, the rural electrification rate was estimated to be 13 percent in 2009, up from 1 percent in 2006.

Because the primary goal was to collect data on the range of electricity use in villages and not necessarily to identify national patterns, we did not pursue the goal of drawing a nationally representative sample of villages. Instead, we used a two-stage selection design. The first step divided the country into geographic regions. Then within each region, villages were selected largely via convenience sampling. Given time and process constraints, villages were selected so as to be relatively accessible by automobile or motorcycle.

The surveys collected information about the use of electricity in each village. Questions asked when the village was electrified, how many homes have access to electricity, how many streetlights are in the village, how many hours of power are available, the frequency of power outages, and opinions about the quality of electricity service. In addition, background information about population size and local economic conditions was also collected. In each village, the geographic coordinates of the village center and the brightest outdoor evening location were recorded using handheld GPS devices.

The analysis revealed that electrified villages are consistently brighter than unelectrified villages across annual composites, monthly composites, and a time series of nightly imagery. The number of streetlights in a village was the single most important and robust predictor of brightness. Overall, we observed a 1-point increase in average nighttime light output for every additional 20 to 60 public outdoor streetlights present in a village, depending on which compilation of nightly imagery is used. Although the presence of streetlights does vary around the world, they are installed consistently in electrified villages in Senegal. Government officials confirmed that streetlights were part of all village electrification plans and that they were highly valued by villagers. By contrast, the correlation with household electricity use and access was low, probably because residential electricity consumption is so low in these settings.

Figure 4.10 illustrates the ability of satellite imagery to detect rural electrification from space. The top image shows the electrification plan for Rao, a village of 2,000 people located 20 km from Saint Louis in Senegal. The locations of 71 outdoor streetlights are highlighted by large red markers. The lower image shows annual average nighttime light output from Rao, observed by satellite in 2009. Overall, light output corresponds well with the roughly southwest to northeast axis of the village. By contrast, the same region observed by satellite in 1997 shows no nighttime light output from Rao.

Electricity Consumption in Vietnam

In a second study with the World Bank focusing on Vietnam, we evaluated the relationship between electricity consumption and light output at the province level from 2000 to 2012 (Min and Gaba 2014). Official data on electricity consumption were provided by the state's main power utility, Vietnam Electricity (EVN). For each year, we also computed the total brightness of each province from the corresponding annual composite imagery of time-stable night lights. This was done by summing the brightness levels of each 30-arcsecond pixel located within the boundaries of each province, using boundary shapefiles from the Food and Agriculture Organization of the United Nations (FAO's) Global Administrative Unit Layers (GAUL) project.

Vietnam has experienced a dramatic increase in electrification in recent decades. The share of households with electricity access has grown from 2.5 percent in 1975 to 96 percent by 2009, an increase benefiting more than 80 million people over 33 years. According to the World Bank Development Indicators, average electricity consumption in Vietnam in 2011 was 1,073 kWh per person, at an average per capita income of $4,510 (in 2014 international purchasing power parity dollars). The level of electricity consumption in Vietnam is similar to that of more developed countries such as Ecuador

A. Electrification Plan for Village of Rao, Senegal

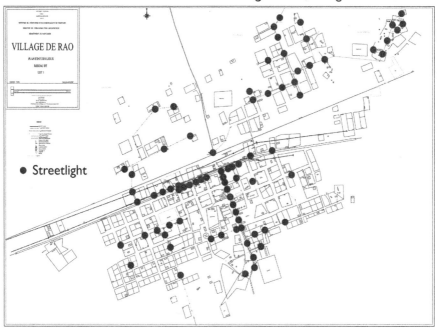

B. Satellite Imagery of Night Lights over Rao

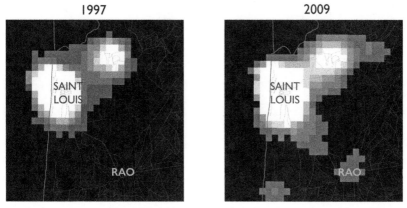

FIGURE 4.10. Comparing streetlight location and night lights imagery in Rao, Senegal. *Source*: Min et al. 2013.

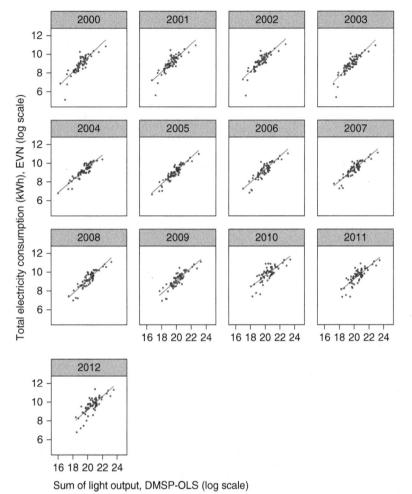

FIGURE 4.11. Nighttime brightness and electricity consumption in sixty-eight Vietnam provinces, 2000–2012.
Source: Min and Gaba 2014.

(1,192 kWh/capita; $9,420 income/capita) and Peru (1,248 kWh/capita; $9,950 income/capita) in Latin America. Meanwhile, electricity consumption in Vietnam is higher per person than in India (683 kWh/capita; $4,840 income/capita) and Pakistan (449 kWh/capita; $4,450 income/capita).

Figure 4.11 plots the relationship between electricity consumption reported by the power company against total brightness measured by satellite for each of Vietnam's 68 province-level units in each year. Each of the correlations is statistically significant and positive with a Pearson's correlation coefficient ranging from 0.77 to 0.92, indicating that satellite imagery provides a reliable measure of the intensity of electricity use in Vietnam. Across all 680 observations over the time series, the two measures correlate at a level of 0.85 with a *p*-value of less than 0.001, evidence of a clear positive relationship between electricity use and total brightness observed from space. Overall, these results indicate that satellite data provide a reliable and valid indicator of electricity consumption at the subnational level.

To study the relationship between electricity use and nighttime light output in Vietnam further at an even more disaggregated level, our project team administered surveys in 200 village-level units across Vietnam in August and September 2013. The villages were drawn from seven provinces representing a range of geographic and economic conditions. As in our earlier work in West Africa, the surveys collected information on the use of electricity in each village, including the number of public outdoor lights, the number of electrified public facilities, the frequency of power outages, and complaints regarding electricity issues. To compare these data against satellite imagery, we acquired nightly DMSP-OLS imagery captured between 19:00 and 22:00 local time over a three-month period overlapping the survey dates. In addition, we acquired monthly composite images for the period produced by NOAA-NGDC that depict average brightness across each month. Finally, we compared our survey data against light output in the 2012 annual composite of time-stable night lights over Vietnam, the most recent annual image available at the time of our study.

Our analysis reveals that villages with more streetlights appear consistently brighter in all compilations of the night lights imagery, as summarized in Figure 4.12. On average, villages with no streetlights had a brightness of 10.1 in the 90-night time series and 9.3 across the three monthly composites spanning August to October 2013, and 8 in the 2012 annual composite. In contrast, the 12 villages with more than 500 streetlights were two to almost five times as bright: 21.3 in the nightly series, 35.5 in the monthly composites, and 37 in the annual composite image.

Further statistical analysis reported in Min and Gaba (2014) predict a 1-point increase in brightness for every 60 public streetlights and an additional 1-point increase for every 240,270 electrified homes. Although these are findings specific to the Vietnam setting, they provide detailed and credible support for the claim that night light output is closely related to the availability and use of electricity, even for rural villages in a developing context.

Electricity Consumption in Uttar Pradesh, India

In India, the Uttar Pradesh Power Corporation (UPPCL) provided me with monthly reports of electricity consumption for each of its 150 electricity supply divisions which I then aggregated up to the district level to enable spatial comparisons against satellite imagery. Figure 4.13 plots UPPCL's district-level electricity consumption against the pixel-by-pixel sum of all light output within each district in 2002. The high correlation between these two sources indicates a log-linear relationship between electricity provision from the power station and nighttime light emissions detected from space.

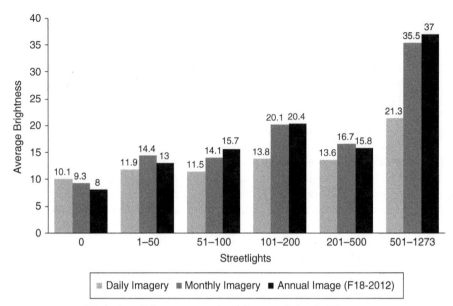

FIGURE 4.12. Nighttime light output and public streetlights in Vietnam.
Source: Min and Gaba 2014.

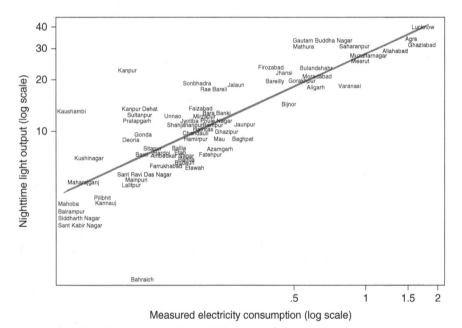

N = 66 a districts. Correlation coefficient = 0.82

FIGURE 4.13. Comparing satellite-derived and official electricity data, Uttar Pradesh
Districts, 2002.
Sources: Author's calculations from DMSP-OLS data; Uttar Pradesh Power Corp.

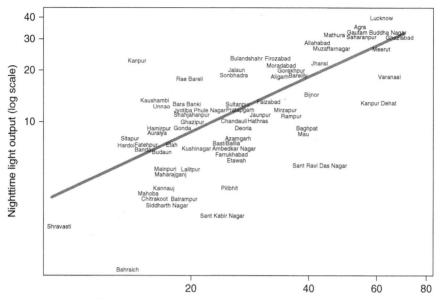

Percentage households using electricity for lighting (log scale)
N = 69 districts. Correlation coefficient = 0.70

FIGURE 4.14. Comparing satellite data and household electrification rates, Uttar Pradesh Districts, 2001.
Sources: Author's calculations from DMSP-OLS data; *2006 Uttar Pradesh Human Development Report*.

How do nighttime lights compare against household electrification rates? Based on 2001 India Census tables, the *Uttar Pradesh Human Development Report* provides estimates at the district level of the percentage of households using electricity as the primary source of lighting. These household electrification data are plotted against the total light output within each district in Figure 4.14. There is again a clear log-linear relationship, though the pattern is noisier than the comparison with energy consumption data.

An alternative government indicator of electrification comes from the Village Amenities database of the Indian Census. Collected decennially, the census reports dichotomous indicators of local public goods availability in villages, including the availability of "power supply" for all 98,000 villages in Uttar Pradesh. According to the definition of electrification used in the 2001 census, *any* use of electricity, including a single household connection or one electrified pumpset for irrigation, qualified a village as being electrified.[5]

---

[5] India's official definition of village electrification was changed in 2005, requiring at least 10 percent of households to be connected and the provision of electricity to public places like schools and the village Panchayat office.

TABLE 4.3. *Village electrification by census and by satellite*

	Unlit in Satellite Imagery (%)	Lit in Satellite Imagery (%)	Total (%)
"Power Supply Unavailable" in Census	52.1	47.9	100
"Power Supply Available" in Census	21.3	78.7	100
Total	30.0	70.0	100
			97,926 villages

Note: Indian Census data reflects the reference date of March 31, 1999.

Table 4.3 presents a contingency table comparing the Census "power supply available" measure against an indicator of visible nighttime lights derived from satellite imagery. Specifically, the village is coded as "lit by satellite" if a positive light value is detected in any annual composite image from 1992 to 1999. This approach helps avoid excessive false negatives by recognizing that many villages on the power grid appear lit in some years but dark in others, reflecting the large variations in electrical supply and reliability described later in Chapter 7.

By this comparison, 79 percent of villages are jointly identified as electrified by the Census and satellite imagery. There are a few possible explanations for why some villages classified as electrified nevertheless appear dark at night. First, because of the expansiveness of the Census's electrification definition, some barely electrified villages might not have the infrastructure or connections to even support a single light. Second, lights from very small or dispersed villages may not be detected given the limited sensitivity of the satellite sensor.

The classification of villages without power supply availability is much more mixed. Only half of these villages are consistently classified, suggesting that the detection of nighttime lights alone may not reliably indicate that a village is connected to the power grid. Analysis of these villages shows that many unelectrified villages that appear lit are close to large towns or urban centers, in which the blooming of city lights spills over the village. Looking only at rural villages located more than 10 km from the nearest town, 62 percent of these unconnected villages now appear dark. Another possibility is that there may be errors in the Census classifications that contribute to the appearance of type I and type II errors. Several media reports have described village residents protesting such incorrect classifications.

Conclusion

This chapter has presented multiple comparisons of satellite-based data against traditional indicators of electricity use and access. I compared nighttime imagery of light output against cross-national data on electrical infrastructure; energy infrastructure stocks in Italian provinces; public spending on highways in the United States; streetlight density in settings as diverse as the town of Elmira, New York, Western Africa, and Vietnam; and finally district-level electricity consumption in Uttar Pradesh, India. Although the correlations are not perfect, the comparisons suggest that satellite-derived indicators of nighttime lights are a highly reliable indicator of electricity provision, and a good but varying predictor of other electricity measures including the presence of electrical infrastructure, energy consumption rates, outdoor public lighting, and household electrification rates. Despite some shortcomings, the data provide the most detailed perspective on the distribution of electricity across and within countries, with more complete and reliable coverage than any other data source. By carefully studying the patterns of light output in these images, the data enable a more robust analysis of how politics affects the provision of electricity than has ever before been possible.

5

Democracy and Light

Introduction

For decades, political scientists have debated whether democracies are more likely than other regime types to provide valuable public goods to their citizens. Basic public goods such as clean water, sanitation, and electricity are critical because they are foundations for poverty alleviation and economic growth. Such public goods are often undersupplied by private markets, especially in the developing world, and governments must decide whether and how to address these market failures. Liberal theorists argue that free and open elections are the key to effective and responsive states. Elections create powerful incentives for politicians to pursue the preferences of the citizenry, despite the constraints that may otherwise exist within a country. Because voters have the ability to reward and punish the performance of their leaders, democratic politicians are more likely to channel a state's resources toward welfare-enhancing outcomes. Without elections, voters lack the ability to control and direct their politicians.

Yet, if democracies are supposed to be responsive to their citizens, why do so many more people in democratic India lack electricity compared to autocratic China? In an opinion piece in *The New York Times*, Amartya Sen laments, "The far greater gap between India and China is in the provision of essential public services... China has done far more than India to raise life expectancy, expand general education and secure health care for its people."[1] Across the world, more than half of the 1.3 billion people who lack electricity reside in democratic states. And within many developing democracies, glaring inequalities in public service provision challenge the norm of universalism, equality, and fairness many presume to be key features of democracy.[2]

[1] Sen, Amartya. "Why India Trails China." *New York Times.* 20 June 2013.
[2] See, for example, discussions of the norm of universalism observed within democratic legislatures such as the US Congress (Weingast, Shepsle, and Johnsen 1981; Collie 1988; Groseclose and Snyder 1996).

Using satellite imagery of the earth at night to develop new estimates of electricity access across every corner of the world, this chapter presents compelling evidence that democracies provide significantly broader levels of electricity to their citizens than do nondemocratic governments. This is not only because democratic leaders respond to citizens' preferences for public goods: democracies have an added incentive to provide public goods because of the political externalities created by their creation and distribution. Although access to electricity is proclaimed to the masses as a pure public good with universal benefits, democratic politicians can capture additional electoral payoffs because of the discretion they exert over the delivery and implementation of electrification projects.

Importantly, the higher levels of electricity access in democracies persist across all levels of income, including in the world's poorest regions. The results strongly affirm the power of competitive elections to induce more extensive public service delivery, even in contexts where state capacity may be low. Moreover, I demonstrate that the positive effect of democracy cannot be replicated using "official" statistics on electrification. This suggests that official data collected from state agencies can be unreliable, perhaps helping to explain the wide variation in reported results about the performance of democracies across the developing world.

The chapter proceeds as follows. In the next section, I argue that political externalities explain why democracies provide broader access to public goods than do nondemocracies. I then describe my method of estimating electrification rates by tracking populations in lit and unlit areas for all countries of the world. Using regression analysis, I next present cross-national evidence showing that democracy is associated with a significant and substantial increase in electrification rates.

Democracy and Light

At least three types of mechanisms have been proposed to explain why democracies will provide more public goods than nondemocracies: preference matching, performance accountability, and cost efficiency. The first mechanism is laid out most influentially by Meltzer and Richard (1981), who argue that under democracy, public policies are more likely to match the preferences of the median voter. Because the median voter is typically poor, policy outcomes should better reflect the preferences of poorer citizens, including preferences for more public goods and services that the poor value highly.

A second argument suggests that democracy induces more public goods provision because leaders are held accountable for their performance (Manin, Przeworski, and Stokes 1999; Przeworski et al. 2000). Because voters value economic development and welfare, politicians will focus on efforts that visibly improve economic outcomes, such as investments in public goods and services (Mani and Mukand 2007). A closely related claim is made by Harding and Stasavage (2014), who show that democratic politicians will concentrate more on policies with verifiable outcomes, because voters are more likely to judge their leaders for things they can control, such as abolishing school fees, and less for outcomes that are indirectly affected by politicians, such as local school quality.

The third argument expects democracies to systematically favor the provision of public goods because they are the most cost-effective way to secure the support of multitudes of voters. This argument, from Bueno de Mesquita et al. (2003), suggests that in systems in which the number of beneficiaries required to sustain political support is large, public goods are more efficient at securing broad support than private goods, which are effective only when the needed winning coalition is small.

Although these arguments have been highly influential, scholars have struggled to validate their theoretical predictions against the uneven record of public goods provision by democracies in the real world. Many cross-national studies find that even if democracies do spend more on public-facing services and social expenditures, these funds rarely reach the poorest or most vulnerable segments of society (Ross 2006). Keefer and Khemani (2005, 2) observe that "policymakers in poor democracies regularly divert spending away from areas that most benefit the poor or fail to implement policies that improve the services that are known to disproportionately benefit poor people." One reason is that graft and political manipulation of funds might actually be more likely to occur with programs designed to aid the poor. Schady (2000) notes that "the kind of targeted poverty-alleviation programs which have become increasingly widespread in Latin America and elsewhere may be particularly vulnerable to political interference" (291).

Such failures seemingly contradict the expectations of the median voter theorem, and the theory has become increasingly maligned by critics. For one, the median voter theorem assumes that candidates and voters are aligned only along a single policy dimension, a modeling conjecture that does not hold in most situations. Moreover, the standard median voter result emerges only in a setting with two candidates. By contrast, elections typically feature multiple candidates, especially in the developing world, where weak party systems can lead to a proliferation of choices for voters (Gallagher and Mitchell 2005; Golder 2005). In such multiparty settings, the policy space can become fragmented as parties seek to capture groups of supporters, resulting in a preference for goods that can be strategically targeted rather than those providing broad-based benefits (Chhibber and Nooruddin 2004).[3]

Another explanation for why democracies fail to meet the needs of the poor is that the repeated nature of elections makes governments vulnerable to

---

[3] Relatedly, Milesi-Ferretti, Perotti, and Rostagno (2002) show that in proportional representation systems, politicians prefer spending that can be targeted towards groups of voters while majoritarian systems will induce a preference for spending that can be targeted geographically.

"political failures," in which leaders fail to enact economically desirable policies that may reduce their likelihood of reelection, for example, by empowering the poor and thereby changing the income distribution (Besley and Coate 1998; Acemoglu and Robinson 2006a). Besley and Burgess (2002, 1415) also suggest that "the poor and vulnerable may not obtain the full attention of politicians even in a democracy where they have numerical strength," especially if they lack access to information on government performance and are unable to distinguish between high- and low-quality candidates.

Existing theories provide an incomplete account of how political institutions affect public goods delivery. I argue that democracies lean toward public goods provision for deeper reasons than just their cost effectiveness at winning support and because so many citizens value them. Under democracy, electorally minded politicians are motivated to provide public goods because of their strategic usefulness. In the hands of skilled politicians, the same public goods projects are on the one hand trumpeted as universal resources to benefit the nation, while on the other, they are used to entice supporters with promises of improved personal welfare, jobs, and other localized benefits. It is not only that public goods are an economical way to secure large numbers of votes; it is that such goods are also malleable, offering politicians fluid means of using the public purse to seek out and maximize electoral payoffs.

Unlike the reproach and censure that can result from explicit pandering to groups or outright vote buying, broad-based promises to electrify the masses, improve education, or enhance public safety reflect a veneer of universalism that masks the tartan patchwork of benefits that politicians can shape and target. Electorally minded politicians enjoy myriad opportunities to influence the timing, siting, and mode by which public goods are delivered to their constituents. When it comes to electricity, its plausibility as a pure public good despite its private good properties, and its high salience and value to voters, create an electoral payoff in its provision. This political externality provides added incentives for democratic politicians to expand access to electricity in ways that do not exist in nondemocratic settings. This implies that electricity policy is driven not merely by technical and feasibility constraints, but also by a logic of political exigency.

If this argument is correct, we should find that more citizens enjoy the benefits of electrification in democratic regimes with competitive elections, and that the positive benefits of democracy should compound over time as elected leaders continually seek out votes through the provision of public goods such as electricity. Indeed, this is the pattern I find and that I describe in the rest of the chapter.

Data and Methods

This chapter introduces a new method of estimating how many people in a country have access to electricity. Specifically, I calculate the proportion of a country's population living in areas that are consistently and brightly lit at night, indicating both the presence of electrical infrastructure and the ongoing provision of stable electricity supply. This approach relies on a systematic comparison of high-resolution data of nighttime light output and population distribution across all countries of the world.

To identify populated regions, I draw on the 2006 LandScan population count map produced by the Oak Ridge National Laboratory (see Figure 4.2). Drawing on subnational census data, the map is produced by apportioning populations onto a 30-arcsecond grid (roughly 1 square kilometre at the Equator) using country-specific likelihood coefficients based on proximity to roads, slope, land cover, and other information (Dobson et al. 2000). The LandScan population maps have been thoroughly vetted and are widely used by the United Nations, World Health Organization, and Food and Agricultural Organization. LandScan uses satellite-based inputs to create the map, including high-resolution daytime imagery and land cover databases. It does not use night lights images, resulting in a data source that is independent of the Defense Meteorological Satellite Program's Operational Linescan System (DMSP-OLS) night lights data.

A direct comparison of the raw LandScan and 2003 DMSP-OLS data reveals a very large number of populated cells with no light output. While this may reflect the lack of electricity, it could also be because electrified areas with very low population counts may not generate a sufficient concentration of outdoor light to be seen from space. Thus a direct comparison of these data sources will not yield an accurate count of people living in electrified areas. To better estimate the electrification rate, we need to focus on areas where we can reliably infer that lighting would be detectable *if it were present*. I do so by identifying what the typical population counts look like in the most dimly lit parts of each country. For example, it may be that in a given country, the only villages detectable in nighttime satellite imagery have at least 100 people. Since this affirms that electricity use for villages with at least 100 people are visible from space, I then assume that villages that meet this threshold but look dark at night can be reliably classified as lacking electricity. Because lighting technology, norms of streetlight density, and cultural preferences for outdoor illumination vary across the world, I conduct this procedure separately for each country. Practically speaking, I identify the median population count in the most dimly lit cells within each country individually. I then sum the population in all unlit cells of a country whose population exceeds the country-specific threshold. This provides a relatively conservative estimate of how many people live in unlit areas that presumably would appear lit if electricity were available. I then calculate the electrification rate accordingly.

To illustrate, here is how the method works in the case of India. India is home to 1.1 billion people as of 2003 and is the second most populous country and largest democracy in the world. The DMSP satellite image of India for 2003 is composed of 4 million pixels at 30-arcsecond resolution with a mean light output of 2.2 (4.9 excluding unlit cells) on the 0–63 scale. The median

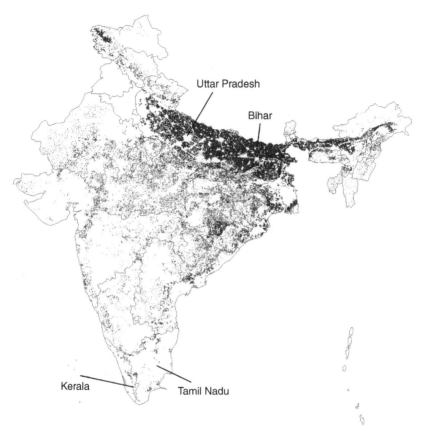

FIGURE 5.1. Estimated unlit populations in India, 2003. Darker areas have more people living in unlit areas. Each dot represents a populated 30-arcsecond cell with no detectable light output. Estimated using DMSP F152003 and LandScan 2006 data.

population count of the most dimly lit cells is 58, providing observational evidence that in India, outdoor lighting technology is detectable for cells with at least 58 people. Of the more than 2 million unlit cells in which no stable light is detected in the annual composite, about 690,000 have a population of at least 58. Summing the population counts across these unlit cells with at least 58 people yields a total estimate of about 275 million Indians living in unlit areas. Given that India has a population of 1.1 billion, using this procedure reveals that 75 percent of the country has access to electricity.[4]

The distribution of populations living in unlit areas in India is plotted in Figure 5.1, with each dot indicating an unlit settlement and darker dots

---

[4] By comparison, IEA (2002) estimates 440 million unelectrified homes in India, but many of these are in electrified cities and towns. The population living in unelectrified villages, which my measure most closely resembles, is not reported.

TABLE 5.1. *Estimated electrification rate using nighttime satellite images, 2003*

Region	Total Population (millions)	Unlit Population (millions)	Access to Electricity Rate (%)
Western democracies and Japan	778	7	99.1
North Africa and Middle East	414	34	91.9
Eastern Europe	405	35	91.5
Latin and Central America	546	71	87.1
Asia	3,450	895	74.1
Sub-Saharan Africa	746	349	53.2
Other	88	2	97.9
WORLD	6,427	1,391	78.4

indicating higher population counts. The highest concentrations of populations in dark areas lie across India's northern region, spanning two of India's
poorest states, Uttar Pradesh and Bihar. Note that even in these impoverished
regions, urban cores are white, including the state capitals Lucknow and Patna,
indicating the prevalence of electrical infrastructure in urban areas. In comparison, Kerala and Tamil Nadu, on the southern tip of the Indian peninsula,
have only a scattering of unelectrified communities. Indeed, India's Ministry
of Power estimates that 42 percent of villages in Uttar Pradesh and 51 percent
in Bihar lacked electricity in 2005. Meanwhile, the estimated rates for Kerala
and Tamil Nadu were 3 percent and 0 percent, respectively. Meanwhile, the
satellite-based method estimates that 37 percent of the people in Uttar Pradesh
and 64 percent of those in Bihar lived in unlit areas, compared to 3 percent in
Kerala and 1 percent in Tamil Nadu.

Applying the method described above, I estimate that 1.4 billion people,
or 22 percent of the global population, lived in unlit areas of the world in
2003. Regional breakdowns are presented in Table 5.1 and country totals are
listed in the book's appendix. This global estimate compares reasonably well
with the International Energy Agency (IEA) projection of 1.6 billion people living without electricity in 2002, a number that includes the urban unelectrified
(International Energy Agency 2002). Figure 5.2 plots the satellite estimates of
the proportion unlit against the IEA's estimates of the proportion unelectrified, derived from official government and UN statistics. Among the 86 countries for which IEA data exist, there are some notable outliers, including China
which looks far darker by satellite than official data would suggest. Overall,
the satellite method yields lower estimates of electrification access than the IEA
data. This is not surprising since the indicators measure different things. My
satellite method identifies populations that live in electrified areas that appear
lit at night, focusing on whether the public goods nature of electrification is

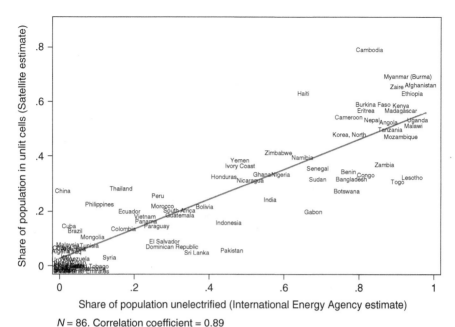

FIGURE 5.2. Comparison of satellite and official estimates of electrification.
Sources: DMSP-OLS F152003, LandScan 2006, World Energy Outlook 2002.

available in a community. By contrast, IEA data focus on variations in household electrification, which can depend on a household's private income as much as on whether the government has chosen to provide electricity to a community. Still, the overall correlation between the satellite and IEA estimates is high, with a correlation coefficient of 0.89.[5]

Unlike the self-reported government data that are used in most widely used datasets, the accuracy of satellite-derived data is not affected by political motivations to embellish performance, economic circumstances that make proper record-keeping difficult, or definitional variations that make estimates incomparable across cases. The satellite estimates provide instead unbiased and objective estimates of lit and unlit populations, whose measurement errors are unlikely to be correlated with political variables. Furthermore, the satellite images provide spatially disaggregated information at the subnational and local levels, offering opportunities for more detailed analysis that are not possible using official country data alone (see Chapters 6 and 7).

---

[5] I show elsewhere that variations between the satellite estimates and the government-reported IEA estimates are not random and are systematically predicted by levels of development and bureaucratic capacity. If the IEA-reported totals include systematic measurement error, regressions using the reported data are likely to be biased and inconsistent.

Some plausible objections exist that outdoor lights might not be an accurate indicator of publicly funded electrification. If electrified areas do not have substantial outdoor lighting, they will be incorrectly classified as unelectrified by my procedure. Although this certainly is a concern, reports and anecdotal evidence suggest that outdoor lighting is among the most highly desired benefits of electricity, especially at night. Many rural electrification agencies incorporate public outdoor lighting as part of every village electrification plan.[6] Attaching an outdoor lamp to a preexisting electric utility pole is of low marginal cost but delivers large public benefits. For politicians seeking to win the favor of a community, ensuring that there is outdoor lighting is a very public and visible way to demonstrate the success of an electrification project.

A different concern is that the presence of outdoor lighting will not be a reliable indicator of government public goods provision if electricity is provided privately. In many parts of the developing world, privately owned diesel and kerosene power generators can provide electricity absent the state. However, it is unlikely that private generators are widely used to provide the kind of outdoor lighting detected by the satellite sensor. The cost of electricity produced by a generator can be several times the cost of grid electricity, depending on the price of fuel. As a result, business owners are unlikely to shine light into public spaces at their own expense because they have no way of charging the public for these benefits. It is more likely that generators are used primarily to power indoor lighting and other devices unlikely to be visible from space.

Nevertheless, the effect of these concerns will not bias inferences about the effects of democracy, unless they are correlated with political regime type. Nonsystematic measurement error on the dependent variable does not bias the slope coefficient but leads to larger standard errors, which would make it more difficult to find a statistically significant effect of democracy. On the other hand, systematic errors on the dependent variable will bias coefficient estimates toward zero when the errors are correlated with the predictor variables, which should make it more difficult to identify a democracy effect if the concerns raised earlier are valid.

Electrification and Regime Type

If voters hold their politicians accountable for the provision of electrification, then democratic leaders should face a more compelling incentive to deliver electricity to their citizens than leaders in autocracies. To assess the influence of democratic elections on electrification rates, I construct a measure of *Democratic history* that calculates the number of years between 1946 and 2002 that a country has had democratic and competitive elections. I use the

---

[6] For example, in Senegal, the Agence Sénégalaise d'Electrification Rurale (ASER) provides public outdoor lighting as part of every new village electrification effort. Engineers report that such outdoor lighting is among the most highly prioritized benefits of electricity in villages (Min et al. 2013).

dichotomous coding of democracy, originally attributable to Przeworski et al. (2000) and updated by Cheibub and Gandhi (2004) and Cheibub, Gandhi, and Vreeland (2010). Their definition of democracy is clear cut: executives must be elected, there must be competition between more than one party, and there must be alternation of power between different parties. The definition is particularly appropriate because it places primacy on the competitiveness of elections, which is the mechanism that leads to the political externalities that are central to this book's argument. Certainly, other features of democracy are valuable and important in their own right, from the presence of checks and balances on executive power, to freedom of expression, or to a normative preference for liberty and equality. Yet my analysis shows that the presence of competitive elections alone is sufficient to motivate a broader distribution of public goods.[7]

It is important to account for history because electrical infrastructure observed in 2003 is a *stock* measurement, reflecting the current extent of the grid built up through the *flow* of investments over years and decades. Looking only at the current level of democratization might yield incorrect inferences because the extent of the power grid in 2003 depends on investments made in the past, perhaps under a different regime type. That said, almost half of the countries in the dataset have not changed regime type at any point during the postwar period: 52 countries have always been autocratic while 31 have stayed democratic.

Figure 5.3a shows satellite-based electrification rates for 183 countries at all levels of democratic history (the sample size is limited only by the availability of regime-type data). Among sustained democracies, the provision of electrification is impressively uniform. In these 21 countries, only about 2 out of every 100 people live in unlit areas, with India appearing as a notable outlier. Among authoritarian regimes, the variance in electrification rates is much wider. In Rwanda and Burundi, more than three-quarters of the population live in the dark compared to less than 1 percent in Egypt and Jordan. Some of these differences are likely to be linked to oil wealth, but variation persists even among dictatorships without oil.[8]

In the middle region of the figure lie almost half of the world's countries that have experienced some mix of democratic and autocratic rule since 1946. The pattern here remains consistent with theoretical expectations: countries

---

[7] To evaluate robustness, I also compare my results using other widely used democracy measures constructed from Polity and Freedom House data (see later). Although these measures are highly correlated with the dichotomous scores of Cheibub, Gandhi, and Vreeland (2010), I focus less on those measures as they incorporate other dimensions of democracy that are outside the scope of my theory.

[8] Nighttime lights in oil producing countries may lead to an overestimate of the distribution of electrification: gas flares on oil wells and rigs generate high levels of outdoor light visible in the satellite images. Gas flaring is known to be particularly pronounced in Nigeria, Russia, Iran, Algeria, Mexico, Venezuela, and Indonesia (Elvidge et al. 2009).

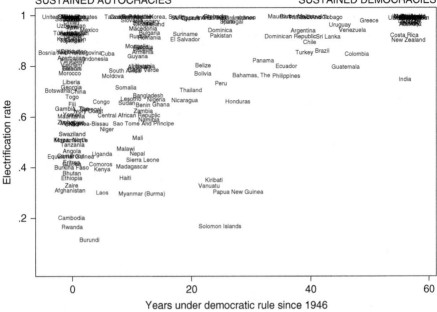

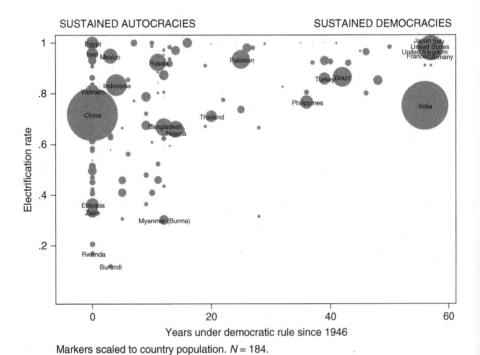

Markers scaled to country population. N = 184.

FIGURE 5.3. Satellite estimates of electrification rates by history of democratic rule. *Sources*: Author calculations based on data from DMSP-OLS F152003, LandScan 2006; Cheibub and Gandhi (2004).

with a longer history of democratic rule have higher rates of electrification. In addition, variation in electrification rates appears to decrease with longer experience under democracy.

Figure 5.3b shows the same scatterplot but uses markers weighted by the population size of each country. Dominating the plot are the large markers associated with China and India. In stark contrast to the official electrification estimates reported by the IEA that claim nearly complete electrification in China but dismally low access in India, the shares of populations living in lit areas are surprisingly similar for China and India using the satellite-based methodology. In fact, a full quarter of China's population live in areas that emit no stable light output at night, with most concentrated in the poorer central provinces of Sichuan, Yunnan, and Guizhou. Meanwhile, the IEA reports a 98% electrification rate in China, an incredible rate that may reflect widely recognized reliability limitations with China's official energy statistics (Sinton 2001).[9]

Partially obscured in both figures is the large number of countries that are effectively fully electrified: 43 countries have less than 1 percent of their population in unlit cells and 64 countries have less than 5 percent in dark areas. Many of these countries are wealthy (e.g., Norway, Saudi Arabia), have small territories (e.g., Jamaica, Lebanon), or both (e.g. Kuwait, Israel). The majority are democracies though about a quarter are autocracies.

To what extent does this pattern simply reflect differences in development between the (mostly) wealthy democratic West and the (mostly) autocratic developing world? Even comparing countries at similar levels of development reveals that differences in democratic history matter. Among the poorest half of the world's countries with incomes below $4,589 per capita in 2002, those with no history of democratic rule had 63 percent of their populations in electrified areas. Among democracies below that income level with at least 10 years of democratic history, the electrification rate was 68 percent, a small but nevertheless important difference.

Many scholars have asserted that the choice of government may not be relevant in the very poorest states. As Przeworski et al. (2000, 163) write, "Poor countries cannot afford a strong state, and when the state is weak, the kind of regime matters little for everyday life." But satellite images of the earth at night show otherwise. Even among states with income levels in the bottom quartile – below $1,534 per capita – 59 percent of citizens in democracies with at least 10 years of democratic history live in electrified areas, compared to 48 percent

---

[9] Barry Naughton, in his influential textbook, *The Chinese Economy*, reports: "There have been serious problems with Chinese energy data in recent years. According to official Chinese data, after decades of sustained growth total energy production began a sharp decline in 1996, and by 2000 it was 19.3 percent below the 1996 peak; the entire decline was accounted for by coal production, which supposedly declined 29%, while GDP officially grew 36%. These figures are preposterous. Of all the data problems mentioned in this text, this is the most flagrant and egregious case" (2007, 335).

in countries that have always been autocracies. For the average country in this group, this translates into 2.3 million more people living with access to electricity in democracy versus autocracy. The difference is significant at the $p = 0.04$ level. These results suggest that even at low levels of development, more citizens benefit from electrification in democracies than in nondemocracies. Still, these highly suggestive results might be caused by other factors unrelated to but correlated with democratic rule, such as differences in geography or demography. I explore these concerns using regression analysis.

Cross-National Analysis of Unlit Populations

To evaluate the effects of democracy on the provision of electrification, I conduct cross-national regressions on the electrification rate as measured by satellite. The dependent variable is the electrification rate, calculated from the proportion of a country's population living in lit and unlit areas as of 2003. My key independent variable is a count of the number of years between 1946 and 2002 during which a country was a democracy in which elections were competitive.

Because my dependent variable is a proportion bounded at 0 and 1, ordinary least squares (OLS) regression is problematic because it will generate predicted values outside of this range. Instead, I use a fractional logit model following Papke and Wooldridge (1996) and Wooldridge (2002, 661). In the fractional logit model, the dependent variable, y is assumed to be a proportion generated by the logistic function:

$$E(y|x) = \exp(x\beta)/[1 + \exp(x\beta)]$$ (5.1)

The β's are easily estimated by specifying a generalized linear model with a binomial distribution and logit link function. The partial effects of a change in an independent variable in a fractional logit model are roughly comparable to changes estimated based on the coefficients of an OLS model.[10]

Among nonpolitical variables, other important determinants of electrification are a country's level of industrialization and the distribution of its population. The level of industrialization indicates a country's ability to afford the provision of electrification. Moreover, the more advanced an economy, the higher the demand for electrical power. I estimate the level of industrialization using the log of a country's *GDP per capita* in 2002. These data come from the Penn World Table 6.2 and are denominated in thousands of 2000 US dollars. A country's *Population density* will also affect the feasibility of electrification because sparsely populated countries must absorb higher per capita costs to electrify remote areas.

---

[10] An alternative would be to use the log-odds transformation, $\log[y/(1 - y)]$, as the dependent variable, since $\log[y/(1-y)]$ ranges over all real values while y is strictly bounded between 0 and 1. However, the log-odds transformation fails when y takes on the boundary values of 0 and 1 where the transformation is undefined.

I use the log of the population density, which is counted in people per square kilometer and is computed from LandScan 2006 population numbers and World Development Indicators data on surface area. To account for differences in urbanization across countries, I also control for a country's *Rural population*, calculated as the percent of the population living in rural areas in 2002 as defined by national governments and recorded in the World Development Indicators.

I include several other control variables. Violent civil wars and conflicts can quickly destroy infrastructure that might have taken years to build. As a result, countries that have suffered from a higher *Number of civil armed conflicts* might have lower levels of electrification. This variable, derived from the Peace Research Institute Oslo's (PRIO) Armed Conflicts Dataset 3.0, counts the total number of internal conflicts with at least 25 battle-related deaths from 1946 to 2002. Many scholars have found a relationship between ethnic diversity and public goods provision. I include a measure of *Ethno-linguistic fractionalization* that comes from Fearon and Laitin (2003). The physical geography of a country might make it more difficult for a government to provide rural electrification. For example, the presence of rough and *Mountainous terrain* increases construction and maintenance costs for electrical infrastructure. This measure also comes from Fearon and Laitin (2003). Geography may also affect the underlying demand for electricity. Places at a higher *Absolute latitude* have more variation in sunlight and colder temperatures. I use the latitude of a country's capital city as coded by Gleditsch (2003).

Access to natural resources such as oil might affect the incentives of governments to electrify their rural populations, both by diverting state resources toward resource extraction activities and by diminishing the accountability of governments toward their populations. I include a measure of *Oil production per capita* in barrels as recorded for 2002, derived from Humphreys (2005) and BP's *Statistical Review of World Energy 2007*.

Table 5.2 presents fractional logit regression results to test the effects of democratic rule on the electrification rate. I run all models using the Huber–White sandwich estimator to correct for heteroscedasticity. Model 1 shows the bivariate relationship between years of democratic rule and electrification. As the dependent variable is the share of the population living in lit areas, the democratic coefficient should have a positive sign, as seen here. Going from fully sustained autocratic rule to fully sustained democratic rule is linked with a 25 percent increase in the lit population. Although this is a large effect, it might be generated by other confounding factors not included in the model but correlated with democracy. Moreover, we know from Figure 5.3 that because there is so much variance among autocracies, regime type alone is a relatively poor predictor of electrification levels absent other information. What we would like to know is whether autocracies and democracies with similar levels of income and population densities provide different levels of electrification. I account for these and other potential factors in the next model. Model 2 shows that

TABLE 5.2. *Fractional logit analysis of electrification rate*

	All Countries		Excluding OECD	Less Developed Countries Only[a]
	(1)	(2)	(3)	(4)
Democratic history[b]	0.0355**	0.0170**	0.0176**	0.0149*
	(0.0053)	(0.0053)	(0.0062)	(0.0071)
log (GDP/capita)[c]		0.3206**	0.2595*	0.3290
		(0.1230)	(0.1203)	(0.1696)
log (Population density)[c]		0.1017	0.0902	0.0515
		(0.0619)	(0.0615)	(0.0684)
Rural population (%)[c]		−0.0215**	−0.0210**	−0.0219**
		(0.0053)	(0.0053)	(0.0067)
Absolute latitude of capital		0.0278**	0.0274**	0.0323**
		(0.0066)	(0.0070)	(0.0077)
Civil armed conflicts[b]		−0.0195	−0.0179	−0.0184
		(0.0457)	(0.0456)	(0.0456)
Ethno-linguistic fractionalization		0.1203	0.1457	0.2320
		(0.3283)	(0.3244)	(0.3632)
log (Mountainous terrain)		−0.0753	−0.0617	−0.1107*
		(0.0467)	(0.0489)	(0.0506)
Oil production per capita[c]		0.0891*	0.1214*	0.0786
		(0.0416)	(0.0476)	(0.1008)
Constant	−0.8255**	−1.5993	−1.1714	−1.3531
	(0.1175)	(1.1597)	(1.1395)	(1.6002)
Observations	184	147	119	88

The dependent variable is the share of country population in lit areas, 2003. Huber–White robust standard errors in parentheses.
**p-value ≤ 0.01; *p-value ≤ 0.05.
[a] GDP per capita < $6,500.
[b] From 1946 to 2002.
[c] As of 2002.

the effect of democratic rule is substantial even after controlling for a wide range of country-level differences. When comparing two countries with similar mean levels of all variables except that one has been democratic over the entire post–World War II period and the other has stayed autocratic, the results show that the democratic state provides electrification to 10 percent more of its citizens than the dictatorship. This is a sizeable difference, given that 29 percent of the population lived in the dark in the average autocracy. Put another way,

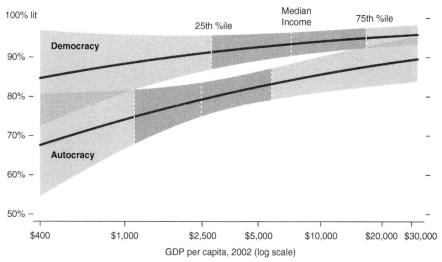

FIGURE 5.4. Predicted electrification rates by regime type and income level.
Note: Predicted values based on Table 5.2, Model 2 with bootstrapped 95% confidence intervals. Autocracy is a country with no history of democratic rule, while Democracy is a country with sustained democratic rule from 1946 to 2002 (i.e., 57 years). All other variables are held at their mean or modal values. Darker regions show interquartile range of observed per capita income values in 2002 among autocracies and democracies.

in a typical autocracy with 35 million citizens, an alternate history of sustained democratic rule would have provided electrification for an additional 3.5 million residents.

The population and income variables are highly significant, as expected. Wealthier countries provide more electricity: an increase of $1,000 in per capita income from the observed mean is associated with a 1.1 percent gain in the electrification rate. The population density result has a positive sign as expected, suggesting that more densely populated countries are likely to have greater access to electricity. With these factors taken into account, a country's war history and ethnic diversity do not predict electricity provision. Countries with more rugged terrain have fewer people in electrified areas, though the coefficient misses standard levels of significance. Finally, higher levels of oil production are linked with more widespread electrification, perhaps because some oil-rich states use diesel to generate electricity.

The effects of regime type and income are plotted in Figure 5.4, based on the equation in model 2. At every level of development, democracies are predicted to have a higher proportion of their population living in lit areas than autocracies. The difference is statistically significant, except at very low levels of income (where there are few democracies) and high levels of income (where there are few autocracies).

To what extent is the positive effect of democratic rule driven by the wealthy Western democracies? To evaluate this possibility, model 3 excludes the highly developed Organisation for Economic Co-operation and Development (OECD) nations; it yields nearly identical results. Model 4 focuses the analysis on the developing world, excluding countries with per capita income greater than $6,500.[11] The results are again nearly identical, suggesting that even poor and middle-income democracies provide electrification to more citizens than their autocratic counterparts. Drawing on codings from the Polity IV and Freedom House projects allows us to see that the results are also robust to alternative measures of democratic history. The coefficients on these measures of democratic history, presented in Tables 5.3 and 5.4, are consistent in size and significance to the main results.[12]

Table 5.5 evaluates the robustness of the main results to different model specifications. Model 1 includes only the sample of sustained democracies and autocracies to obviate the concern that existing electrification rates might have been the result of previous regimes. The size and sign of the democratic history coefficient remain similar to the results for the full country sample. Model 2 runs a population weighted regression to see whether the cross-sectional results might be driven by a handful of small countries. The largest country in my sample (China) has a population three orders of magnitude larger than the smallest (Trinidad and Tobago). The size and significance of the democratic history variable is reduced, though the sign remains positive as before. Model 3 shows that the inclusion of region fixed effects has no effect on the democratic history coefficient. Model 4 explores several potential interaction effects. For example, it might be that democracies are just more efficient at translating economic wealth into public goods provision. To ease the interpretation of interactions between two continuous variables, I center the democratic history, per capita income, and population density variables. Although the interaction effects between democratic history and income, democratic history and population density, and income and population density are all significant, the independent effect of democratic rule remains as strong as before. These results

---

[11] The $6,500 cutoff is arbitrary, though results are robust to a wide range of cutoff levels. Interestingly, Przeworski et al. (2000, 98) note that no democracy has fallen since World War II in a country with a per capita income higher than that of Argentina in 1975, $6,055.

[12] The different democratic history measures are:
- Years Polity>0: number of years from 1946 to 2002 in which Polity score is positive.
- Years Polity≥6: number of years in which Polity score surpasses Polity's recommended threshold for "democracy."
- Years with competitive elections: number of years in which the chief executive is chosen through competitive elections (i.e., Executive Recruitment Concept 8 in the Polity data).
- Σ Polity: the sum of the annual Polity scores (from −10 to + 10), scaled to a 0–100 score.
- Years Free: number of years since 1972 (the earliest year available) a country has been coded as "Free" by Freedom House.

TABLE 5.3. *Robustness checks: Fractional logit analysis of electrification rate using alternative democracy measures (all countries)*

All Countries	(1) Years Polity >0	(2) Years Polity ≥6	(3) Years with Competitive Elections	(4) Σ Polity
Democratic history,	0.0142*	0.0162**	0.0150**	0.0193**
1946–2002	(0.0056)	(0.0059)	(0.0057)	(0.0068)
log (GDP/capita), 2002	0.3214*	0.3407**	0.3289**	0.3020*
	(0.1292)	(0.1282)	(0.1272)	(0.1282)
log (Population density),	0.1057	0.1217	0.1051	0.1114
2002	(0.0643)	(0.0646)	(0.0646)	(0.0647)
Rural population (%),	−0.0220**	−0.0230**	−0.0223**	−0.0221**
2002	(0.0052)	(0.0053)	(0.0053)	(0.0053)
Absolute latitude of	0.0273**	0.0252**	0.0266**	0.0272**
capital city	(0.0065)	(0.0064)	(0.0062)	(0.0064)
Civil armed conflicts,	−0.0210	−0.0284	−0.0224	−0.0214
1946–2002	(0.0439)	(0.0456)	(0.0449)	(0.0448)
Ethno-linguistic	0.0461	0.1336	0.0635	0.0779
fractionalization	(0.3327)	(0.3273)	(0.3290)	(0.3325)
log (Mountainous	−0.0630	−0.0570	−0.0589	−0.0618
terrain)	(0.0475)	(0.0471)	(0.0469)	(0.0472)
Oil production per	0.0894*	0.0794*	0.0829*	0.0898*
capita, 2002	(0.0424)	(0.0393)	(0.0400)	(0.0413)
Constant	−1.5935	−1.7133	−1.5888	−1.4860
	(1.1844)	(1.1889)	(1.1783)	(1.1769)
Observations	147	147	147	147

The dependent variable is the share of country population in lit areas, 2003. Huber–White robust standard errors in parentheses.
**p-value ≤ 0.01; *p-value ≤ 0.05.

are nearly identical for the reduced sample that excludes the OECD countries (Table 5.6).

Finally, I evaluate whether we could have reached the same conclusions by relying on existing measures of electrification rates. It is by now well known that missing data, inconsistent definitions, and variable data collection practices across states impair many traditional cross-national data sources. In fact, the best available data on electrification rates suffer from many of these limitations. The IEA's World Energy Outlook volume reports electrification rates for 86 countries compiled from various sources including government self-reports, private research notes, and OECD and World Bank estimates.

TABLE 5.4. *Robustness checks: Fractional logit analysis of electrification rate using alternative democracy measures (excluding OECD)*

Excluding OECD	(5) Years Polity >0	(6) Years Polity >6	(7) Years with Competitive Elections	(8) Σ Polity
Democratic history, 1946–2002	0.0153* (0.0062)	0.0169* (0.0073)	0.0150* (0.0065)	0.0210* (0.0082)
log (GDP/capita), 2002	0.2434 (0.1254)	0.2782* (0.1250)	0.2672* (0.1240)	0.2323 (0.1245)
log (Population density), 2002	0.0944 (0.0636)	0.1119 (0.0644)	0.0940 (0.0642)	0.0999 (0.0645)
Rural population (%), 2002	−0.0215** (0.0052)	−0.0228** (0.0052)	−0.0218** (0.0052)	−0.0217** (0.0052)
Absolute latitude of capital city	0.0269** (0.0067)	0.0247** (0.0067)	0.0259** (0.0065)	0.0271** (0.0068)
Civil armed conflicts, 1946–2002	−0.0199 (0.0440)	−0.0276 (0.0462)	−0.0202 (0.0449)	−0.0207 (0.0452)
Ethno-linguistic fractionalization	0.0675 (0.3271)	0.1651 (0.3248)	0.0864 (0.3243)	0.1037 (0.3284)
log (Mountainous terrain)	−0.0454 (0.0491)	−0.0400 (0.0488)	−0.0433 (0.0484)	−0.0453 (0.0488)
Oil production per capita, 2002	0.1247** (0.0483)	0.1101* (0.0456)	0.1144* (0.0466)	0.1232** (0.0463)
Constant	−1.0475 (1.1533)	−1.2719 (1.1627)	−1.1442 (1.1487)	−0.9991 (1.1468)
Observations	119	119	119	119

The dependent variable is the share of country population in lit areas, 2003. Huber–White robust standard errors in parentheses.
**p-value ≤ 0.01; *p-value ≤ 0.05.

Affirming the difficulty of compiling reliable data from such diverse sources, IEA researchers made adjustments to country estimates in at least a dozen cases: "Where country data appeared contradictory, outdated or unreliable, the IEA Secretariat made estimates based on cross-country comparisons, earlier surveys, information from other international organizations, annual statistical bulletins, publications and journals." In addition, there are a large number of missing observations in the IEA data, which will exacerbate bias if the pattern of unavailable data is not random (King et al. 2002; Groves 2006).

As reported earlier, the IEA data on electrification rates correlate at 0.89 with my satellite-derived estimates of population proportions that are lit. Yet

TABLE 5.5. *Robustness checks: Fractional logit analysis of electrification rate using alternative model specifications (all countries)*

	All Countries			
	Sustained Autocracies & Democracies Only	Population Weighted	Region Fixed Effects	Interactions
	(1)	(2)	(3)	(4)
Democratic history, 1946–2002	0.0164 (0.0092)	0.0096 (0.0057)	0.0189** (0.0069)	0.0128* (0.0050)
log (GDP/capita), 2002	0.2999 (0.2442)	0.6523** (0.1732)	0.3060** (0.1044)	0.3380* (0.1381)
log (Population density), 2002	0.0927 (0.0902)	0.1477 (0.0814)	0.0690 (0.0665)	0.2166** (0.0720)
Rural population (%), 2002	−0.0234* (0.0115)	−0.0149* (0.0069)	−0.0175** (0.0055)	−0.0209** (0.0050)
Absolute latitude of capital	0.0356** (0.0120)	0.0160 (0.0083)	0.0135 (0.0098)	0.0268** (0.0061)
Civil conflicts, 1946–2002	0.0146 (0.0782)	−0.0826 (0.0440)	−0.0081 (0.0450)	−0.0389 (0.0379)
Ethno-linguistic fractionalization	0.1945 (0.5267)	0.7783* (0.3841)	0.2243 (0.3536)	0.1783 (0.2873)
log (Mountainous terrain)	−0.0447 (0.0939)	−0.0818 (0.0722)	−0.0983 (0.0513)	−0.0510 (0.0444)
Oil production per capita, 2002	0.0696 (0.0388)	0.2319* (0.0968)	0.0466 (0.0334)	0.1253** (0.0429)
Latin America and Caribbean			−0.9803* (0.4376)	
Eastern Europe and former Soviet Union			−0.4041 (0.4479)	
Asia			−1.1571* (0.4729)	
Sub-Saharan Africa			−1.1662* (0.5252)	
North Africa and Middle East			0.1133 (0.5438)	
Democratic history × log (GDP/capita)				0.0103* (0.0044)
Democratic history × log (Population density)				0.0028 (0.0038)
log (GDP/capita) × log (Population density)				0.2494** (0.0490)
Constant	−1.5400 (2.5572)	−4.7575** (1.4080)	−0.3228 (1.2991)	1.7336** (0.3530)
Observations	67	147	147	147

The dependent variable is the share of country population in lit areas, 2003. Huber–White robust standard errors in parentheses.

**p-value ≤ 0.01; *p-value ≤ 0.05.

TABLE 5.6. *Robustness checks: Fractional logit analysis of electrification rate using alternative model specifications (excluding OECD)*

	Excluding OECD		
	Population Weighted	Region Fixed Effects	Interactions
	(5)	(6)	(7)
Democratic history, 1946–2002	0.0072	0.0234**	0.0111*
	(0.0064)	(0.0075)	(0.0055)
log (GDP/capita), 2002	0.5593**	0.2507*	0.3148*
	(0.1642)	(0.1016)	(0.1392)
log (Population density), 2002	0.1416	0.0476	0.1980*
	(0.0776)	(0.0685)	(0.0773)
Rural population (%), 2002	−0.0139*	−0.0161**	−0.0219**
	(0.0066)	(0.0055)	(0.0050)
Absolute latitude of capital	0.0157	0.0142	0.0258**
	(0.0087)	(0.0102)	(0.0064)
Civil conflicts, 1946–2002	−0.0605	−0.0090	−0.0485
	(0.0516)	(0.0467)	(0.0403)
Ethno-linguistic	0.6977	0.2747	0.1359
fractionalization	(0.3714)	(0.3508)	(0.2909)
log (Mountainous terrain)	−0.0774	−0.0900	−0.0292
	(0.0760)	(0.0511)	(0.0477)
Oil production per capita, 2002	0.2526**	0.0669	0.1430**
	(0.0919)	(0.0353)	(0.0415)
Latin America and		−1.2942**	
Caribbean		(0.4456)	
Eastern Europe and		−0.6912	
former Soviet Union		(0.3799)	
Asia		−1.4571**	
Sub-Saharan Africa		(0.3994)	
North Africa and		−1.4545**	
Middle East		(0.4116)	
Democratic history ×			0.0062
log (GDP/capita)			(0.0060)
Democratic history ×			0.0068
log (Population density)			(0.0046)
log (GDP/capita) ×			0.2708**
log (Population density)			(0.0536)
Constant	−4.0866**	0.3201	1.7605**
	(1.2777)	(1.1397)	(0.3836)
Observations	119	119	119

The dependent variable is the share of country population in lit areas, 2003. Huber–White robust standard errors in parentheses.

**p-value ≤ 0.01; *p-value ≤ 0.05.

TABLE 5.7. *Comparing results using satellite and official data*

	Satellite Data (1)	IEA Data (2)
Democratic history, 1946–2002	0.0168**	0.0103
	(0.0062)	(0.0078)
log (GDP/capita), 2002	0.5028**	0.6872**
	(0.1401)	(0.2165)
log (Population density), 2002	0.1840*	0.2261
	(0.0847)	(0.1375)
Rural population (%), 2002	−0.0152*	−0.0255**
	(0.0063)	(0.0091)
Absolute latitude of capital city	0.0295**	0.0302*
	(0.0089)	(0.0135)
Civil armed conflicts, 1946–2002	−0.0565	−0.0334
	(0.0450)	(0.0736)
Ethno-linguistic fractionalization	0.2452	−0.1274
	(0.3287)	(0.4495)
log (Mountainous terrain)	−0.0946	0.0085
	(0.0487)	(0.0879)
Oil production per capita, 2002	0.1160*	0.0373
	(0.0464)	(0.0442)
Constant	−3.9120**	−5.7301**
	(1.2622)	(1.7972)
Observations	80	80

The dependent variable is the share of country population in unlit areas, 2003. Huber–White robust standard errors in parentheses.
**p-value $\leq$ 0.01; *p-value $\leq$ 0.05.

running the same exact statistical test on the same sample of countries produces different results (Table 5.7). Although democratic history continues to have a statistically significant effect on the rate of electrification observed by satellite (model 1), democracy is insignificant if one uses the IEA data (model 2). In other words, we would have mistakenly concluded that democracy has no effect on electrification if we used official IEA data.

This inconsistency demonstrates the potential perils of measurement problems in cross-national analysis (Treier and Jackman 2008). When the dependent variable is measured with random error, then coefficient estimates on the independent variables will be biased toward zero. But regression estimates can be biased if the measurement error in the dependent variable is systematically related to one or more explanatory variables. Moreover, if there are systematic errors in the recording of any independent variable, then regression results will be attenuated on that variable while other coefficients will be biased and inconsistent in unknown direction and magnitude (Wooldridge 2002, 70–76).

Taken together, these findings support the claim that electoral incentives induce higher public goods provision in democracies. Across a range of samples and model specifications, democratic leaders provide substantially broader levels of electrification than do autocrats, even after controlling for differences in wealth, population density, and other factors. Nevertheless, the results should be interpreted with some caution. Recent work has challenged the use of standard cross-sectional research methods in comparing democracies and dictatorships (Przeworski et al. 2000; Keefer and Khemani 2005; Ross 2006). Because the causal factors that lead countries to democratize might also be correlated with the outcomes we seek to evaluate, inferences about the effects of democracy might be weakened by selection bias. Some of this concern is mitigated by my measure of democratic history, which takes period under democratic rule and not just the current level of democracy into account. However, it is still possible that observed electrification levels are not causally linked to democracy. For example, a country that transitions to democracy might already have had high levels of electrification, and inferring that it was democracy that led to the provision of lighting would be incorrect. One way of mitigating this concern is to compare only the subsample of states that have not experienced a regime transition during the postwar period. Within this group, the average electrification rate was 26 percent lower in the 51 fully sustained autocracies compared to the 17 sustained democracies.

Competitive Elections or State Capacity?

The findings in the preceding text argue that there is broader public goods provision in democracies than in nondemocracies. But is it the presence of free and open elections that induces this effect? Or could the effect be due to higher state capacity, in which the occurrence of elections is simply a confounding factor that tends to exist in many states with high capacity?

Theories stressing the importance of state capacity extend at least as far back as Weber, who argued that states were defined by their ability to maintain a monopoly on violence and manage a bureaucracy capable of effectively implementing policy. According to Weber's many followers, a state's capacity determines the effectiveness with which it can enact and enforce policies and laws, whereas its absence is reflected in mismanagement, corruption, and disorder (Huntington 1968; Geddes 1996; Bates 2008). Without a strong and functional state apparatus, rules about how to select leaders to fill national offices are largely inconsequential. Indeed, states vary widely in their ability to meet the needs of their citizens:

Efficacious states simply have more power at their disposal than less efficacious ones... Some states are simply more purposive and better organized than others. Some states also choose to work closely with their dominant classes, whereas others, facing a variety of pressures, maintain some distance. (Kohli 2004, 20–21)

Geddes (1996) defines the most important feature of the state as its capacity to translate preferences into actions:

Preferences matter very little if officials cannot carry out the policies they choose. The capacity to implement state-initiated policies depends on the ability to tax, coerce, shape the incentives facing private actors, and make effective bureaucratic decisions during the course of implementation. (14)

According to this view, a state's institutional capacity is more important for many outcomes than the electoral rules that decide how its leaders are chosen. For Huntington (1968), highly institutionalized states are more adaptable, complex, impervious to outside interference, and unified. Strong states, he says, have the ability to "command the loyalties of their citizens and thus have the capacity to tax resources, to conscript manpower, and to innovate and to execute policy" (1). Without such capacity, elections matter very little to a country's people. Consistent with this view, Lipset (1959) argued, "Only in a wealthy society in which relatively few citizens live at the level of real poverty could there be a situation in which the mass of the population intelligently participate in politics and develop the self-restraint necessary to avoid succumbing to the appeals of irresponsible demagogues" (75). Democracy may thus be of limited benefit then when states are too poor to implement policies. More recently, Barro (1996) stated that democracy is "a sort of luxury good. Rich places consume more democracy because this good is desirable for its own sake" (24).

Are states characterized by high capacity – competent bureaucracies, civil order, and the fiscal and organizational ability to implement policy – better at providing basic public services to their citizens? Or do democratic states, led by political leaders who must win elections, perform better? A stylized dichotomy places the competing expectations of these two perspectives in stark relief. Functionalists expect higher levels of state capacity to improve outcomes regardless of regime type. Institutionalists expect that at any level of state capacity, democracy will improve outcomes. The juxtaposition of these claims results in sharply divergent expectations regarding the distribution of public goods by governments around the world. On the one hand, democracy is expected to improve outcomes regardless of a state's capacity. On the other hand, state capacity is argued to lead to better outcomes irrespective of regime type. Yet empirical research has yielded little consensus on how state capacity and regime type influence the welfare of the world's citizens.

Although the analysis that follows will not provide a definitive answer, it is a first step in comparing the effects of elections against the role of efficacious state institutions in enabling the provision of electricity. I use several measures to account for state capacity. The most widely used indicator may be tax revenues, without which governments cannot finance their activities (Tilly 1990; Lieberman 2002; Brownlee 2004; Brautigam, Fjeldstad, and Moore 2008; Besley and Persson 2009; Hendrix 2010). As Herbst (2000, 113) writes, "There is no better measure of a state's reach than its ability to collect taxes."

TABLE 5.8. *Democracy or state capacity? Fractional logit analysis of electrification rate*

	(1)	(2)	(3)	(4)	(5)	(6)
Democratic History[a]	0.0118*	0.0167**	0.0150**	0.0135*	0.0147**	0.0168**
	(0.006)	(0.005)	(0.005)	(0.006)	(0.005)	(0.006)
log (GDP/capita)[b]	0.3813*	0.3610**	0.2159	0.2357	0.2003	0.3159*
	(0.151)	(0.119)	(0.135)	(0.124)	(0.123)	(0.123)
log (Population density)[b]	0.2664**	0.0973*	0.1021	0.1017	0.1425*	0.1021
	(0.080)	(0.050)	(0.061)	(0.063)	(0.060)	(0.062)
Rural population (%)[b]	-0.0260**	-0.0199**	-0.0229**	-0.0232**	-0.0237**	-0.0215**
	(0.007)	(0.005)	(0.005)	(0.005)	(0.005)	(0.005)
Absolute latitude of capital	0.0181**	0.0285**	0.0272**	0.0257**	0.0306**	0.0276**
	(0.007)	(0.007)	(0.007)	(0.007)	(0.007)	(0.007)
Civil conflicts[a]	-0.0822	-0.0195	-0.0126	-0.0012	-0.0461	-0.0181
	(0.045)	(0.042)	(0.044)	(0.045)	(0.046)	(0.047)
Ethno-linguistic fractionalization	0.0137	0.1942	0.0881	0.0819	-0.0991	0.1191
	(0.349)	(0.298)	(0.329)	(0.335)	(0.342)	(0.327)
log (Mountainous terrain)	0.0186	-0.0531	-0.0603	-0.0517	-0.0379	-0.0740
	(0.056)	(0.048)	(0.048)	(0.047)	(0.057)	(0.049)
Oil production per capita[b]	0.1118	0.0940*	0.1010*	0.0962*	0.0920	0.0895*
	(0.080)	(0.046)	(0.049)	(0.049)	(0.047)	(0.042)
Tax revenues (% of GDP)[c]	0.0032					
	(0.011)					
Central government Expenditures (% of GDP)[c]		-0.0040				
		(0.008)				

Government effectiveness			0.2074			
			(0.158)			
Rule of law				0.2513		
				(0.136)		
ln (Homicides/100,000)[d]					−0.0150	
					(0.075)	
State fragility index[e]						−0.0008
						(0.006)
Constant	−2.6788*	−1.9797	−0.5916	−0.6686	−0.6327	−1.5021
	(1.326)	(1.069)	(1.294)	(1.205)	(1.211)	(1.291)
Observations	103	138	147	147	128	147

The dependent variable is the share of country population in lit areas, 2003. Huber–White robust standard errors in parentheses.

**p-value ≤ 0.01; *p-value ≤ 0.05.

[a] From 1946 to 2002.
[b] Measured in 2002.
[c] Average, 2001–2005.
[d] Measured in 1998.
[e] Average, 2005–2008.

Tax revenue is measured as tax revenue of the state as a percent of GDP, averaged from 2001–2005. A related indicator is *Central government expenditure*, recorded as a percent of GDP, averaged from 1998 to 2005. Both measures are from the World Bank.

State capacity may also be reflected in the quality of a state's governance. From the Worldwide Governance Indicators project (Kaufmann, Kraay, and Mastruzzi 2005), I use the two measures that most clearly reflect the capacity of a state's bureaucratic and governing institutions to carry out policy: *Government effectiveness*, which measures the competence of the bureaucracy and the quality of public service delivery; and *Rule of law*, which measures the quality of contract enforcement, the police, and the courts, as well as the likelihood of crime and violence.

Measures of internal security and violence may also reflect the strength of a state. As indicators of a state's domestic capacity to control violence and security, I use data on the *Homicide rate*, measured as the log number of homicides per 100,000 people in 1995 (Neumayer 2003) and a composite measure of *State fragility*, averaged over the first years of data collection, 2005–2008 (Fund for Peace 2008).

The results are presented in Table 5.8. In every single case, the effect of competitive elections is far more important than the capacity of a state's institutions in predicting access to electricity. Thus although the ability to collect taxes, govern effectively, and maintain peace and domestic security are important characteristics of a strong state, they do not override the importance of democratic and competitive elections in motivating politicians to ensure broad access to critical public goods.

Conclusion

This chapter demonstrates that democracies provide electrification to many more of their citizens than autocracies. Drawing on new estimates of electrification whose reliability and validity are not sensitive to endogeneity with the political institutions we want to evaluate, I show a positive link between democratic rule and electrification that is robust to differences in development, demographics, and geography.

These results affirm the central theoretical claim of this book: that public goods provision is especially attractive to democratic leaders because of the political benefits they can capture during elections. In countries with longer histories of democratic rule, the ongoing pursuit of votes results in broader access to electricity. The results hold across all levels of income, affirming the power of democratic elections in inducing higher public service delivery, even in contexts where state capacity appears to be low.

6

Lighting the Poor

Introduction

In the previous chapter, I demonstrated that democracies across the world provide electricity to a larger share of their populations than do autocracies. This
is an especially important result for the developing world, where many wonder
whether democracy is effective in contexts of high poverty and low state capacity. Although the results from the last chapter show that democracy leads to
greater electricity provision in *poor countries*, does democracy actually benefit
poor people? This chapter evaluates this question by comparing electricity provision in the poorest areas of countries across the developing world.

Poverty has long been a central concern of states. Charles Booth, who
coined the idea of a poverty line in his groundbreaking 1889 study of poverty in London, defined the poor as those "living under a struggle to obtain
the necessaries of life and make both ends meet, while the 'very poor' live in a
state of chronic want." For Booth, the persistence of abject poverty demanded
public action by the state, and he was among the first proponents of a publicly
funded social safety net. More than a century later, poverty alleviation efforts
continue to accentuate the role of the state in providing public goods that communities and markets fail to deliver. Besley and Burgess (2002) argue that in
poor countries where markets are weak, "vulnerable populations rely in large
measure on state action for their survival" (1415). This means that the poor
depend heavily on the state for basic public goods such as electricity, education,
and health services.

Despite the high demand for public goods among the poor, it is far from
obvious that the state will supply such goods to them. Clearly, poor areas have
the highest need and greatest demand for public goods. However, the poor lack
economic clout, contribute little to state revenues, and participate less actively
in the political process. In many advanced democracies, they are less likely
to vote than better off groups (Powell 1986; Schlozman and Brady 1995).

Moreover, the votes of the poor are thought to be easily captured, whether by vague promises made by co-ethnics (Chandra 2004; Dunning and Nilekani 2013) or the fear of retribution (Stokes 2005; Stokes et al. 2013). Yet the poor also represent a powerful resource for democratic politicians. They are numerous and constitute the majority of voters. Moreover, many among them are nonaligned voters, with shorter histories of electoral participation and thus potentially weaker partisan attachments. It is precisely in this context of numerically large groups of marginal voters where political entrepreneurs may have the greatest opportunity to reshape the coalitions that define the political landscape. Given the high demand for basic public goods and services among the poor, strategic efforts to market and distribute such goods can offer lucrative opportunities for democratic politicians as they seek to win large numbers of votes. Such electoral incentives do not exist in autocracies.

Drawing on a new subnational dataset constructed at the 1-degree latitude by 1-degree longitude level across the developing world, I compare rates of electrification in the poorest areas of a country, and show that democracies provide consistently higher rates of access in these economically disadvantaged regions than do non-democracies.

Although this pattern is consistent with the theoretical expectations of Meltzer and Richard (1981), Bueno de Mesquita et al. (2003), and Lake and Baum (2001), my results go further than these models. Prevailing theories emphasize that democracies provide more public goods because they satisfy the preferences of the median voter, they are a cost-effective means of securing mass support, or because leaders are held accountable if they withhold them in favor of rents. Although these accounts predict that democracies will provide higher levels of public goods, my theory helps explain *how* such public goods will be distributed and targeted. I argue that the institutional preference for public goods under democracy emerges from their extraordinary political usefulness. Because demand for public goods is high, and because political leaders enjoy influence over their supply, their provision results in political externalities that, in the context of elections, result in valuable electoral payoffs. Consequently, democratic leaders can be expected not only to provide more public goods, but also to exploit them and distribute their benefits in ways that yield political advantages.

Affirming this expectation and exploiting the disaggregated nature of my data, I show that the distribution of electricity within poor areas reflects an electoral logic: especially where poor voters are more concentrated, democracies provide more public services. By contrast, in autocracies, the spatial distribution of citizens has no systematic effect on the provision of electricity. Taken together, the patterns revealed in this chapter bolster the evidence that democracies favor public goods because of their electoral value.

My research strategy seeks to overcome several barriers obstructing previous research. First, I exploit the advantages of nighttime satellite imagery to construct measures of electricity provision in the world's poorest regions where traditional data are sparse and unreliable. The use of a common data source for the subnational estimates in this chapter and the national estimates in the previous one ensures decomposability and alleviates concerns about aggregation bias and ecological inference problems. Second, I draw on subnational data to construct a new dataset of cells at the 1-degree latitude by 1-degree longitude level. For all developing countries (i.e., non–Organisation for Economic Co-operation and Development [OECD]), I identify the cells in which the poorest quartile of citizens reside. Given the difficulties associated with assessing poverty, I construct separate measures to discern where the poor reside within each country, the first using subnational infant mortality rates, the second using disaggregated economic output data, and the third a combined measure that identifies areas with both the highest infant mortality rates and the lowest income levels.

Identifying the Poor

Identifying where the poor reside in the developing world is no easy task. My strategy draws inspiration from the use of poverty mapping and small-area estimations of poverty. In this approach, scholars use household surveys to estimate the relationship between poverty and household characteristics and then apply this relationship to similar households across a country using census data, generating maps that show the spatial distribution of poverty as opposed to simple national headcounts of the poor (Henninger and Snel 2002; Hentschel et al. 2000; Minot 2007). However, because comprehensive household surveys and census data are not available for all developing countries, I adopt a more feasible approach, combining spatial data on average infant mortality rates as well as disaggregated estimates of economic output with population maps to identify a country's poorest areas.[1] I focus only on non-OECD states and organize all of my data into cells at a resolution of 1-degree latitude by 1-degree longitude (roughly 100 km × 100 km at the equator), which is the smallest common unit across my subnational data sources.

Infant mortality is considered by many to be a highly reliable measure of social welfare in poor settings (Ross 2006; McGuire 2010; Diaz-Cayeros, Magaloni, and Estévez forthcoming). Death rates are usually similarly defined and well recorded, even in the developing world. Moreover, high rates of childhood death are likely to indicate conditions of impoverishment. The data come from the Global Subnational Infant Mortality Rates (GSIMR) project, which estimates the number of children who die before their first birthday for every

---

[1] Given the lack of household or other lower-level data for most developing countries, I do not have the data, for example, to estimate the proportion of people who are poor in each cell.

10,000 live births in the year 2000. Data are available for more than 10,000 national and subnational units.[2]

To complement the infant mortality–based poverty measure, I also create estimates following a more traditional approach that relies on economic output data. The most comprehensive source for spatially disaggregated economic data is the G-Econ project, which estimates total economic output for sub-national cells at the 1-degree latitude by 1-degree longitude level (Nordhaus et al. 2006). This provides an unparalleled perspective on subnational variation in economic activity. However, the data may underestimate poverty since the total economic output of a cell may be dominated by point source industrial output or resource extraction which reflect little about the welfare of typical households. Still, cells with the lowest economic output within a country should reflect areas that are relatively poorer.

I organize all the subnational data in cells at the same 1-degree latitude by 1-degree longitude level as the G-Econ data. When a cell lies across a national border, it is divided into smaller country-specific cells. Because cells are not uniform in size, I control for *area* in the regressions. There are a total of about 27,000 terrestrial cells in the subnational dataset; 21,000 once you exclude Antarctica. Russia, the world's largest territory, is composed of 3,448 cells; China has 1,092 cells; India comprises 363 cells.

The G-Econ dataset also provides additional geographic variables that describe variations in climate and terrain (Hood 2005). I include measures of the average *Precipitation, Temperature, Elevation,* and *Roughness* of each cell. These data are derived from the Climate Research Unit Average Climatology 10-arcminute datasets (New et al. 2002). Precipitation and temperature are long-term monthly averages from 1961 to 1990.

For my dependent variable I compute the *Population in lit areas* as a proportion of each cell's population. The proportion lit for each cell is computed based on the underlying 30-arcsecond pixel data using the same 2003 night lights imagery and LandScan population map as in Chapter 5. Using the same data sources to construct both the earlier national and these new subnational estimates of lit populations ensures decomposability, a desirable feature not common to most measures of public service provision. The global distribution of electricity access by cell is presented in Figure 6.1. The map reveals variations at the national level, and for the first time, large variations at the subnational level. An analysis of variance (ANOVA) reveals that almost half of the variation in the proportion lit variable is between countries and half within countries. This highlights the potential magnitude of variation that goes unexplained in traditional cross-national studies that rely only on national-level averages.

---

[2] The level of subnational detail varies substantially by country and includes as few as one data point for the entire country, as in Chad, and more than 2,000 county-level observations for China. See http://sedac.ciesin.columbia.edu/povmap/.

Proportion in Lit Areas

- 0.0–0.25
- 0.25–0.50
- 0.50–0.75
- 0.75–0.9
- 0.90–0.95
- 0.95–0.98
- 0.98–1.0

FIGURE 6.1. Electrification rates by 1-degree × 1-degree cell, 2003. Lighter cells have a higher proportion of the population living in lit areas. OECD countries excluded.

(a)   (b)

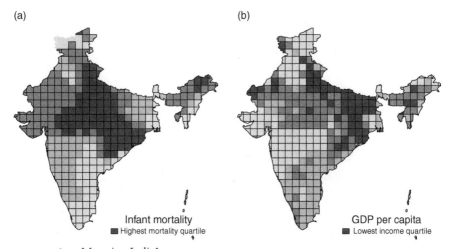

FIGURE 6.2. Mapping India's poor.
Sources: Global Subnational Infant Mortality Rates Project, G-Econ Project.

To identify population counts in poor areas, I rely on the Gridded Population of the World (GPW) dataset from Columbia's Earth Institute, because this is the data source used by both the GSIMR and G-Econ projects. For the measures of both infant mortality and per capita income, I overlay their distributions against the GPW population map to identify the cells that make up the poorest population quartiles using both measures. For example, for the infant mortality data, I locate the cells in which the quarter of the population with the highest infant mortality rates reside.

After identifying the cells that are home to the poorest quartiles, I then look at nighttime satellite imagery and compare rates of electricity provision within these poorest areas. Consider India and China, the world's largest democracy and autocracy, respectively. In India, stark inequalities exist in wealth and social welfare across its population of 1.2 billion. From the bustling information technology hubs of Bangalore and Hyderabad to the impoverished farmlands across Bihar and Uttar Pradesh, levels of development vary widely across regions, with some evidence of divergence in welfare across states during the 1990s (Deaton and Drèze 2002). Applying the mapping methods described previously, Figure 6.2 shows two perspectives on where India's poorest quartile lives, identified by the darkest cells. Infant mortality rates are highest in India's north, including the states of Uttar Pradesh, Madhya Pradesh, Chhattisgarh, and Orissa. The quartile of India's population with the highest infant mortality is spread across 84 cells. Per capita income is also lower in the north, with the poorest quartile living in 71 cells across Bihar, Orissa, and some parts of Uttar Pradesh.

Electricity provision across India is plotted in Figure 6.3, showing much higher rates of unlit populations in the northeast than in the south and around

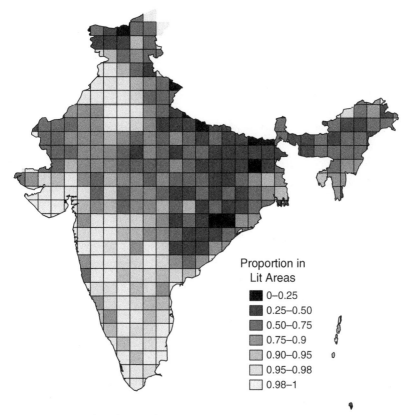

Proportion in
Lit Areas
■ 0–0.25
■ 0.25–0.50
■ 0.50–0.75
■ 0.75–0.9
□ 0.90–0.95
□ 0.95–0.98
□ 0.98–1

FIGURE 6.3. India's lit population.
Sources: DMSP F152003, LandScan 2005.

the New Delhi capital region. Visually comparing the maps, one observes that the proportion lit is low in many of the cells where Indians with the highest rates of infant mortality and lowest incomes live. Notably, rates of electrification are exceedingly low in cells identified as poor across both poverty measures, such as in Orissa.

Inequality is also high in neighboring China. Figure 6.4 shows China's 1,092 cells, home to 1.3 billion people. Although infant mortality rates in some eastern areas (80 deaths per 10,000) are as low as in some industrialized nations, rates are 8.5 times higher in the 525 cells that are home to the highest infant mortality quartile. These include the western province of Xizang (Tibet) and the central provinces of Sichuan, Yunnan, and Guizhou. Meanwhile, income levels are lowest in the central region, with the bottom quartile located in 169 cells, including Sichuan province. Interestingly, many western provinces that look underdeveloped when observing infant mortality rates nevertheless appear to have impressive rates of economic output. One driver for this has been the

(a)

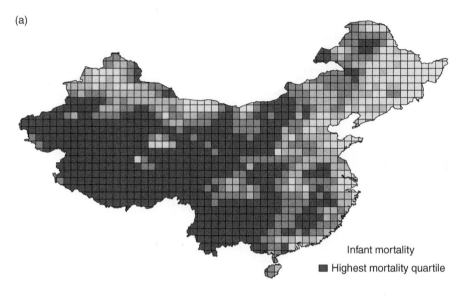

Infant mortality
■ Highest mortality quartile

(b)

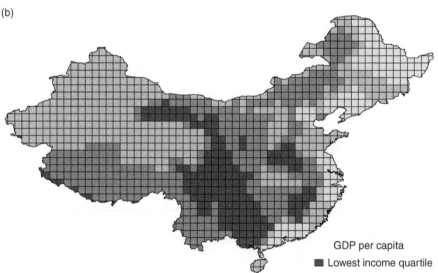

GDP per capita
■ Lowest income quartile

FIGURE 6.4. Mapping China's poor.
Sources: Global Subnational Infant Mortality Rates Project, G-Econ Project.

implementation of China's "Western Development" policy since 1999, which has resulted in billions of dollars of investment in infrastructure and industrial development to secure growth and sustain political stability. However, to date, these sizable expenditures appear to have only had limited impacts on

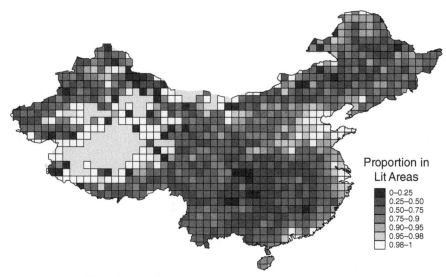

FIGURE 6.5. China's lit population.
Sources: DMSP F152003, LandScan 2005.

improving social welfare, at least partly due to corruption and misappropriation of funds (Lai 2002; Démurger et al. 2002).

Figure 6.5 shows the proportion of people living in electrified areas in China. Many cells in the Tibetan Plateau show no data, as I do not compute lit populations in areas with very low population counts (see discussion in Chapter 5). As with India, the maps show that in many of China's cells with the highest rates of poverty, electricity provision is low.

How do India and China differ in the rates of electricity provision to their poorest citizens? To compare, Figure 6.6 shows kernel density plots of the distribution of proportion lit per cell in the poorest quartiles. Higher densities toward the right of the plot mean more poor cells are highly electrified and have fewer people living in the dark. Higher densities toward the left suggest instead that most living in these poor cells lack electricity.

These distributional plots show a somewhat mixed picture. Electricity provision to the disadvantaged is higher in democratic India when the poor are identified by infant mortality rates (Figure 6.6a). However, when looking at poor areas identified by relatively lower per capita incomes, electricity provision appears slightly higher in autocratic China (Figure 6.6b). That these patterns are similar at all is in itself surprising, given the widespread belief that China has outpaced India in the delivery of electricity. In fact, the results here suggest that India has done as well, and maybe even better, than China, at providing electricity to its poorest citizens. Although India and China represent

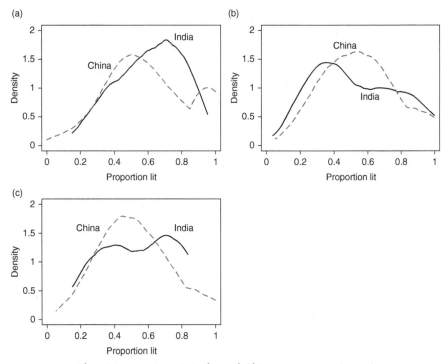

FIGURE 6.6. Electricity provision in India and China's poorest regions.
Note: Kernel density plots using the Epanechnikov kernel.

an important paired comparison, what systematic patterns hold across the broader developing world? I turn to this global comparison next.

Global Patterns of Electricity Provision to the Poor

Do regimes differ systematically in whether they provide electricity to their poorest citizens? In autocracies, the poor have little oversight or authority over their governments. By contrast, the impoverished in democracies can wield their ballots to demand that elected leaders be responsive to their basic needs.

Figure 6.7 provides a global perspective of where the poorest quartile reside as identified by the highest infant mortality rates. Similarly, Figure 6.8 shows areas with the lowest per capita incomes from the G-Econ data in all countries of the developing world. By comparing electrification rates within these poorest quartile cells (see Figure 6.1), I find that for those living in a country's poorest areas, the likelihood of being electrified is substantially higher in a democracy than in an autocracy.

Figure 6.9 presents kernel density plots showing the distribution of electrification in the poorest regions of developing democracies and autocracies.

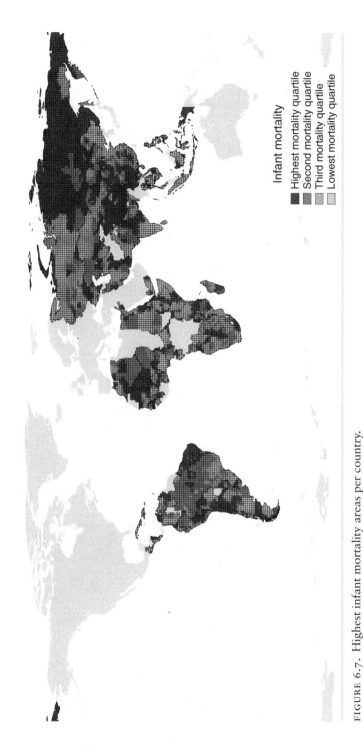

Infant mortality

- ■ Highest mortality quartile
- ▨ Second mortality quartile
- ▨ Third mortality quartile
- ☐ Lowest mortality quartile

FIGURE 6.7. Highest infant mortality areas per country.

Sources: Global Subnational Infant Mortality Rates (GSIMR) and LandScan projects. OECD countries excluded.

GDP per capita

■ Lowest income quartile
■ Second income quartile
□ Third income quartile
□ Highest income quartile

FIGURE 6.8. Lowest income areas per country.
Sources: G-Econ and LandScan projects. OECD countries excluded.

The top graph, identifying the poorest quartile using infant mortality rates, contrasts electricity provision in 23 developing democracies over 1,561 cells versus 33 developing autocracies over 1,042 cells.[3] The next graph uses lowest per capita income to identify the poorest quartile. Here, the density plot traces electricity provision across 1,122 cells in 38 developing democracies and 1,274 cells in 56 developing autocracies.[4] Both of these perspectives on poverty provide the same finding: poor areas are more likely to be electrified in democracies than in autocracies.

Among the highest infant mortality quartile areas, 84 percent of the population was lit in countries that were democratic and had at least 10 years of democratic rule in their recent history. By contrast, 70 percent of the population was lit in autocratic states. When using income to identify the poor, the difference is 79 percent lit in democracies versus 72 percent in autocracies.

Although these results are suggestive, they show only bivariate comparisons among large pooled samples of diverse countries and cells. One concern about these patterns is that poor areas in democracies like India might differ in important respects from poor areas in autocracies like China. For example, there might be higher geographic barriers such as more mountainous terrain and higher elevations in poor parts of China than in India. If such factors can influence the ability of governments to provide electricity, *and* these factors are correlated with regime type, then it is important to account for such differences.

To account for such effects, I run fractional logit regressions controlling for several potential confounders. I include country-level controls for GDP per capita and population density. I also include cell-level measures of infant mortality, income per capita, and population density. I also add cell-level

---

[3] The developing democracies in the high infant mortality sample are Argentina, Armenia, Bangladesh, Benin, Bolivia, Brazil, Chile, Colombia, Costa Rica, Dominican Republic, El Salvador, Guatemala, India, Mali, Mongolia, Namibia, Nicaragua, Philippines, Russia, Thailand, Uruguay, Venezuela, and Zambia. The developing autocracies are Algeria, Angola, Botswana, Burkina Faso, Cambodia, Cameroon, China, Cuba, Egypt, Eritrea, Ethiopia, Gabon, Gambia, Guinea, Iran, Jordan, Kazakhstan, Lebanon, Mauritania, Morocco, Mozambique, Paraguay, Rwanda, Somalia, Sudan, Tanzania, Togo, Turkmenistan, Uganda, Uzbekistan, Vietnam, Yemen, and Zimbabwe.

[4] The developing democracies in the low-income sample are Albania, Argentina, Armenia, Bangladesh, Benin, Bolivia, Brazil, Bulgaria, Chile, Colombia, Costa Rica, Croatia, Dominican Republic, Estonia, Guatemala, Honduras, India, Israel, Jamaica, Latvia, Lithuania, Macedonia, Mali, Mongolia, Namibia, Nicaragua, Panama, Papua New Guinea, Philippines, Romania, Russia, Slovenia, Sri Lanka, Thailand, Ukraine, Uruguay, Venezuela, and Zambia. The developing autocracies are Afghanistan, Algeria, Angola, Azerbaijan, Belarus, Bosnia and Herzegovina, Botswana, Burkina Faso, Cambodia, Cameroon, Chad, China, Democratic Republic of Congo, Cuba, Egypt, Eritrea, Ethiopia, Gabon, Gambia, Georgia, Guinea, Iran, Iraq, Jordan, Kazakhstan, North Korea, Kyrgyzstan, Laos, Lebanon, Liberia, Libya, Malaysia, Mauritania, Morocco, Mozambique, Myanmar, Oman, Paraguay, Rwanda, Saudi Arabia, Serbia and Montenegro, Somalia, Sudan, Swaziland, Syria, Tajikistan, Tanzania, Togo, Tunisia, Turkmenistan, Uganda, United Arab Emirates, Uzbekistan, Vietnam, Yemen, and Zimbabwe.

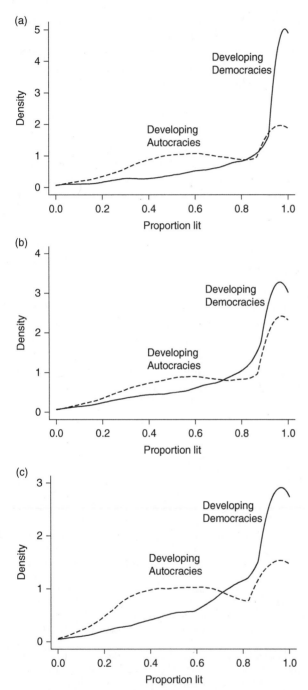

FIGURE 6.9. Electricity provision in the poorest regions of developing states.
Note: Kernel density plots using the Epanechnikov kernel.

controls to account for differences in geography, including average roughness, elevation, precipitation, temperature, latitude, and area. The results are presented in Table 6.1. I run three models using different samples: (1) highest infant mortality quartile cells, (2) lowest per capita income quartile cells, and (3) cells that are both in the highest mortality and lowest income cells. In models 1 and 2, democracy is associated with higher lit populations, though the coefficients just miss standard levels of statistical significance ($p = 0.087$ and $p = 0.064$). For the cells identified as most poor in model 3, democracy is significant ($p = 0.038$).

In the next section, I use matching to identify cells that are essentially identical along a wide range of cell-level variables but that differ in whether they are governed by a democracy or an autocracy.

Matching

To address concerns of selection bias and reduce the dependence of results on model specification and parametric assumptions, I use matching in an effort to achieve the highest level of balance across all observed covariates between democratic and nondemocratic cases. Matching seeks to make the treatment group look as similar as possible to the control group, allowing analysis that is less sensitive to choices of functional form and model selection. By achieving balance, matching reduces model dependence and reduces bias and variance (Ho et al. 2007).

The goal is to identify cells that are as similar as possible across all potentially relevant aspects except for their regime type. One way to think of this is to consider areas that lie along opposing sides of national borders that share similar geography, access to natural resources, and settlement patterns, but that differ in their political institutions (Posner 2004; Miguel 2004). China and India, for example, share a common border extending over 2,000 miles. Today, the Tibetan population is divided by this border in Xizang province in China and the Indian state of Himachal Pradesh. There are numerous cultural and geographic similarities across these areas, yet a clear difference in political institutions. The impact of political differences can be stark. One newspaper account described how in another area straddling the India–China border to the southeast, Indians living in unelectrified villages in Arunachal Pradesh would gaze in frustration at the twinkling lights of lit villages across the Chinese border.[5] The 38th parallel dividing the Korean peninsula provides another well-known example. While South Korea is bathed in light, North Korea is almost completely dark except for lights in the capital city and in a few isolated pockets, including the area around the Yongbyon nuclear facility.

---

[5] Rao, Raghvendra. "Shining China in Sight, Villages to Finally Get Power." *The Indian Express*, December 25, 2007.

TABLE 6.1. *Regime type and electricity provision in the poorest quartiles*

	Highest Infant Mortality Quartile	Lowest Per Capita Income Quartile	Most Poor (Highest Mortality and Lowest Income)
	(1)	(2)	(3)
Democracy	0.3336	0.3493	0.4316*
	(0.195)	(0.189)	(0.208)
GDP per capita (country)	0.0194	0.0091	−0.0047
	(0.049)	(0.039)	(0.069)
Population density (country)	−0.0030**	−0.0042**	−0.0056**
	(0.001)	(0.001)	(0.001)
Infant mortality rate (cell)[a]	−0.0130	−0.0716**	−0.0496*
	(0.020)	(0.025)	(0.024)
Gross cell product per capita (cell)[a,b]	0.1456**	0.1618*	0.2006*
	(0.049)	(0.073)	(0.080)
Population density (cell)[a]	−0.0000	0.0006*	0.0004
	(0.001)	(0.000)	(0.001)
Cell-level controls			
Roughness	−0.6008	0.2530	0.3215
	(0.424)	(0.305)	(0.300)
Elevation, average	0.0003	0.0001	0.0003**
	(0.000)	(0.000)	(0.000)
Precipitation, average	−0.0019	−0.0059**	−0.0038**
	(0.001)	(0.001)	(0.001)
Temperature, average	0.0611**	0.0459*	0.0871**
	(0.021)	(0.023)	(0.019)
Latitude, absolute	0.0302*	0.0055	0.0303*
	(0.012)	(0.011)	(0.015)
Area (10^3 km^2)	−0.0136	−0.0270	−0.0299
	(0.019)	(0.017)	(0.022)
Constant	−0.9244	0.8572	−0.8992
	(0.826)	(0.812)	(0.746)
Cell observations	2,557	1,971	689

Huber–White robust standard errors, clustered on country, in parentheses.
** p-value ≤ 0.01; * p-value ≤ 0.05.
[a] Estimate for 2000.
[b] In 1995 purchasing power parity (PPP) US dollars.

Borders are not the only places where similar cases can be found. Using the language of counterfactual analysis, Haber and Menaldo (2011) match cases of countries that discovered oil against similar neighbors that did not to estimate the effect of resource wealth on political development. They note, "If one wanted, for example, to specify the counterfactual path that would have been followed by oil- and gas-rich Kazakhstan had it not discovered those resources, the best approximation would be the other Central Asian Republics that have not emerged as major resource producers (e.g., Uzbekistan) – but that share Kazakhstan's history of repeated invasions and occupations, as well as broad geographic and cultural characteristics" (3).

A similar logic underpins the Przeworski et al. (2000) landmark study of democracy and development. To identify the impact of regime type on the growth of, say, authoritarian Chile in 1985, one would want to observe how much a democratic Chile would have grown in that year. This is not possible. Still, they say, "There seems to be a way out: We could look for some case that was exactly like 1985 Chile in all respects other than its regime and, perhaps, its rate of growth, and we could match this country with Chile. We could then compare the growth of dictatorial Chile in 1985 with the performance of its democratic match and draw a conclusion" (8).

Following standard notation of the Rubin causal model, the causal effect is the difference in potential outcomes under treatment and control, only one of which is observed for each observation. Let Y_{i1} denote the electrification level for cell i that is under democratic rule and Y_{i0} be the electrification level for a cell under autocratic rule. Treatment is denoted T_i, equaling 1 when i is in the treatment regime and 0 otherwise. The observed outcome for i is $Y_i = T_i Y_{i1} + (1 - T_i) Y_{i0}$ and thus the treatment effect for i is $\tau_i = Y_{i1} - Y_{i0}$. In experimental settings with perfect randomization, individuals in both treatment and control groups are equally as likely to receive treatment and so estimation of the treatment effect is simply the mean difference in observed outcomes between the treatment and control groups. However, in observational settings like the one under consideration, treatment is not randomly assigned, and the treatment and control groups are likely to differ along multiple dimensions. If we assume that selection into the treated group depends only on observable covariates X_i, we can estimate the average treatment effect on the treated, or ATT:[6]

$$\tau \, |(T = 1) = E\{E(Y_i | X_i, T_i = 1) - E(Y_i | X_i, T_i = 0) | T_i = 1\} \tag{6.1}$$

In other words, I identify the effect of democratic rule as the expected difference in electrification status between a cell that is under democratic rule and the expected status of that cell had it not been under democratic governance, conditional on a set of covariates, X.

To identify matches, I use the genetic search algorithm, GenMatch (Sekhon 2011), which is particularly well suited to optimizing balance in contexts in which the dimensionality of covariates is large. The algorithm uses one-to-one matching with replacement where the estimand is the average treatment effect on the treated (ATT).

---

[6] The model assumes strong ignorability in which, conditional on X, treatment assignment is unconfounded, $Y_0, Y_1 \perp T \, |X$. Overlap is also assumed, $0 < Pr(T = 1|X) < 1$ (Rosenbaum and Rubin 1983).

(a)

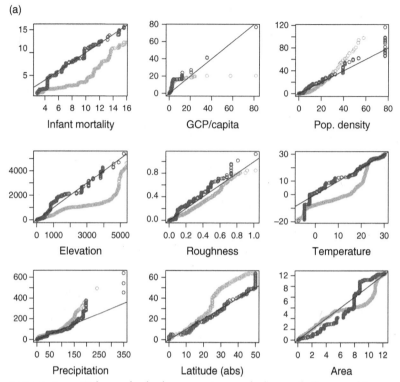

FIGURE 6.10. Balance checks for poorest areas, before and after matching.

I matched on the following nine cell-level variables: infant mortality rate, per capita income, population density, roughness, elevation, precipitation, temperate, latitude, and area. I attempted to match on additional country-level variables as well, but because the number of developing countries is small (for the purposes of matching), this proved intractable. As a result the estimates here need to be interpreted with some caution: the matched samples look very similar across cell-level characteristics but do not reflect national-level differences.

To evaluate balance, I present quantile–quantile plots comparing the distribution of variables among democracies and autocracies. The plots show the distribution before and after matching, where balance is better when observations lie closer to the 45-degree line. Balance plots for the highest infant mortality quartile are shown in Figure 6.10a and for the lowest income quartile in Figure 6.10b. Before matching, there are significant differences between regime types, most notably in infant mortality rates, which are lower in poor areas of democracies. There are geographic differences as well: average temperatures are lower in poor areas of democracies, while elevation is also generally lower

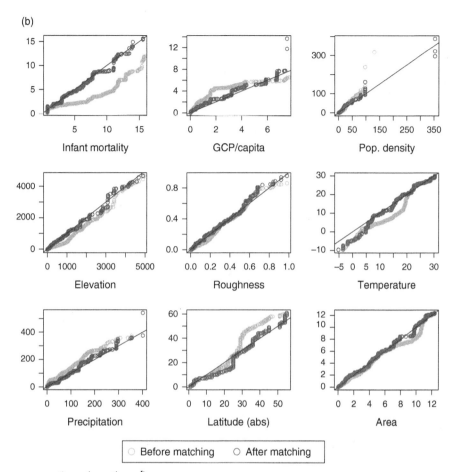

FIGURE 6.10. (*continued*)

and precipitation higher in democracies in Figure 6.10a. For both sets of samples, balance has improved substantially after matching.

Based on the matched samples, I compare differences in electrification rates to estimate the effect of democracy in Table 6.2. The analysis of matched samples confirms the powerful effect of democracy on increasing electricity provision to the poor. In the poorest areas as defined by infant mortality rates, 14 percent more of the population live in electrified areas in democracies. In the lowest per capita income areas, 8 percent more benefit from electricity. These effects are large, affecting millions of people, and statistically significant. The results are also consistent with the full sample regression analysis presented earlier, demonstrating that electricity is provided to more of the poor in democracies than in nondemocracies.

TABLE 6.2. *ATT estimates for effect of democracy on electricity provision in the poorest quartile*

	Highest Infant Mortality Quartile	Lowest Per Capita Income Quartile	Most Poor (Highest Mortality and Lowest Income)
ATT estimate	0.140	0.078	0.045
Standard error	0.062	0.030	0.035
p-value	0.026	0.009	0.21
Observations	1,558	1,080	402

Elections and the Targeting of Voters

The evidence in the preceding text suggests that developing democracies do indeed provide more electricity to their poorest citizens. Why do they do this? I have argued it is because democratic politicians have unique incentives that drive them to distribute public goods more broadly than in autocracies. In the presence of elections, politicians seek out electoral benefits that accrue from directing public goods and services to those who value them the most, particularly among the poor.

One way of validating this expectation is to look more closely for differences in how public goods are distributed *within* the poorest areas of both regime types. If democratic leaders are conditioned to seek out votes, then all else equal, we should see that democracies pay more attention to areas with larger numbers of citizens (i.e., voters), because the aggregation of per capita benefits flowing from electrification will be higher in dense areas. Meanwhile, in autocracies, no consistent relationship is expected between population density and public goods access.

Figure 6.11 provides a first test of this expectation across regime types. Each panel compares rates of electricity access as a function of population density, looking only at cells that comprise the poorest areas of developing states, measured by infant mortality on top and by income on the bottom. Overall, there is a negative correlation between electrification and population density in both regime types. Part of this pattern reflects the increased technical complexity and economic costs associated with electrifying densely populated areas. Given that each cell corresponds roughly to a 100 km × 100 km area, providing full electrification to a cell in which there are only a few villages is far less challenging than doing the same for a cell with more than 10 million residents such as the cell encompassing the industrial city of Kanpur and its impoverished environs in northern India.

In addition, the negative trend is partially an artifact of pooling observations from very diverse countries, resulting in a comparison of cases between low-density and high-density countries. Although cells from 71 countries are represented in the top panel, only 11 countries contribute observations with

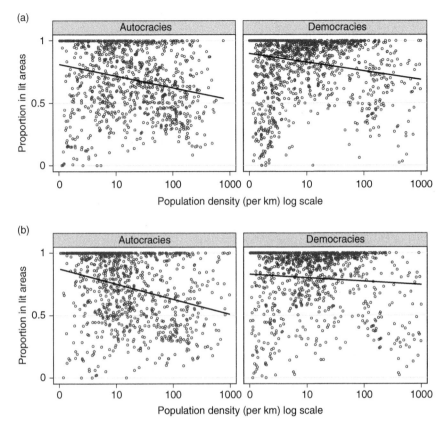

FIGURE 6.11. Democracies respond to population density in the poorest regions of developing states. Top panel shows poorest quartile cells identified by highest infant mortality rates, bottom panel by lowest per capita incomes.

population densities higher than 400 people per square kilometer, including countries such as India, Brazil, and Indonesia.

Nevertheless, the figures show that in democracies, the provision of public goods to poor areas with more people is systematically higher than in autocracies where targeting the poor offers few immediate political payoffs. Still, these visual patterns do not reveal whether it is actually democracy that is causing the apparent differences in electrification across regime types. Democracies and autocracies differ on nonpolitical dimensions that may be important drivers of electrification. In 2002, the average developing democracy was wealthier, more populous, geographically larger, and less mountainous than the typical autocracy, and so the correlations documented previously could be caused by other confounding factors. To examine more rigorously how patterns of distribution vary within countries, I conduct regressions to account for other factors that might affect the apparent relationship observed in the scatterplots.

Country fixed effects are included to help account for country-specific factors that can influence the provision of electrification. The fixed effects absorb
all *between*-country variation and enable a focus on factors that shape
within-country variation in access to electricity. This allows for a more direct
evaluation of the claim that within poor areas of their countries, democracies
are likely to target areas with more voters while no such pattern is expected to
exist among autocracies.

Since country fixed effects are correlated with whether a country is a democracy or not, I conduct subsample analysis, presenting results for developing
democracies in models 1 to 3 of Table 6.3 and developing autocracies in models 4 to 6. Direct comparison of coefficients across different subsamples can
be misleading. Yet, the results affirm the overall expectation that population
density is a significant and positive determinant of electricity provision within
democracies, but seemingly has no consistent effect in autocracies. This shows
that democratic leaders respond to electoral incentives, directing electricity
provision to areas with the greatest voter densities, even among the poorest
regions of their countries. An increase of one standard deviation in population density, from 8 to 43 people/km^2, is associated with a 3.1 percent increase
in electricity access. Interestingly, differences in the level of economic output
across poor areas seem to have little effect, except in model 1. If a strategy of
poverty alleviation were at work, we might expect a more consistent relationship between economic output and public goods provision.

Meanwhile, in autocracies, population density is an insignificant predictor
of electricity provision as expected, given the lack of electoral incentives that
compel leaders to provide public goods broadly to their citizenry. Meanwhile,
there is some evidence that within the poorest regions, autocratic governments
provide less access to electricity in areas with higher economic output (models
5 and 6). Overall, the inconsistent effects of population and economic measures on electricity provision within autocratic regimes reflect the idiosyncratic
preferences and priorities that vary across such states.

Conclusion

The findings of this chapter show that democracies provide broader levels of
electricity provision to their poorest citizens. These results are consistent with
the expectations of institutional theories in which electoral incentives motivate
democratic leaders to provide more public services to their citizens. However,
the finding that democracies are effective at serving the poorest quartile of their
citizenry is surprising given the many concerns about the lackluster performance of democratic governments in low income settings.

The results also challenge the expectations of clientelism theory, in which
the influence of the poor on public policy is discounted because their votes are
so easily swayed by promises and threats or by token gifts or handouts. When
poor voters are fearful that politicians will withdraw even these small benefits,

TABLE 6.3. *Electricity provision in poor areas: Fractional logit analysis of electrification rates with country fixed effects*

	Poorest Quartile by Infant Mortality	Poorest Quartile by Per Capita Income	Most Poor (Highest Mortality and Lowest Income)	Poorest Quartile by Infant Mortality	Poorest Quartile by Per Capita Income	Most Poor (Highest Mortality and Lowest Income)
	(1)	(2)	(3)	(4)	(5)	(6)
Population density[a]	0.1611+	0.2610**	0.2851**	−0.0843+	−0.0522	0.0231
	(0.083)	(0.087)	(0.107)	(0.047)	(0.076)	(0.069)
Gross cell product[a,b]	0.5078**	−0.0501	−0.2935*	−0.0237	−0.4778+	−1.2524**
	(0.133)	(0.134)	(0.147)	(0.115)	(0.271)	(0.209)
Roughness	0.4526	0.0326	0.1101	−0.9273**	0.3843	−0.5238+
	(0.433)	(0.293)	(0.755)	(0.207)	(0.320)	(0.298)
Elevation, avg.	−0.0001	0.0005**	0.0004**	0.0003+	0.0000	0.0004*
	(0.000)	(0.000)	(0.000)	(0.000)	(0.000)	(0.000)
Precipitation, avg.	−0.0004	−0.0009	−0.0012	−0.0036	−0.0047**	−0.0009
	(0.002)	(0.001)	(0.002)	(0.003)	(0.002)	(0.003)
Temperature, avg.	0.0096	0.0697**	0.0772**	0.0470	0.0327	0.0412
	(0.048)	(0.016)	(0.022)	(0.031)	(0.024)	(0.048)
Absolute latitude	0.0709*	0.0580**	0.1033*	0.0199	0.0385*	0.0422
	(0.032)	(0.015)	(0.045)	(0.035)	(0.019)	(0.048)
Area	0.0037	0.0019	−0.0150	−0.0299	−0.0457**	−0.0005
	(0.017)	(0.016)	(0.023)	(0.020)	(0.011)	(0.031)
Country fixed effects	Yes	Yes	Yes	Yes	Yes	Yes
Constant	−1.9502	−3.9640**	−4.2173**	−0.2159	3.1126**	−2.1632
	(1.205)	(0.538)	(1.152)	(1.802)	(1.003)	(2.207)
Observations	1,558	1,142	402	999	949	287

The dependent variable is the share of cell population in lit areas, 2003. Huber–White robust standard errors, clustered by country, in parentheses.

** p-value ≤ 0.01; * p-value ≤ 0.05; + p-value ≤ 0.10.

[a] Logged values, 2000.

[b] In 1995 purchasing power parity (PPP) US dollars.

a perverse accountability arises in which voters are accountable to their elected leaders and are not willing to vote according to their true preferences (Stokes 2005). Yet, I find evidence of higher rates of electricity provision even in areas where clientelism may be most pernicious.

My explanation is that irrespective of the extent of clientelistic practice in the developing world, competitive elections in democracies generate powerful institutional incentives for public service provision. For democratic leaders, the delivery of a broad-based public service such as electricity is a cost-effective means of garnering political support, especially in areas where the poor have few outside alternatives and thus place a high value on provision by the state.

Inductively, patterns of broader electricity provision in poor democratic areas can also be interpreted as evidence of an equilibrium in which democratic leaders steer public services toward poor areas exactly because poor voters are receptive to these investments. The way elections induce a correspondence between political demand and supply is an important mechanism in electorally competitive settings that does not apply in nondemocratic settings.

The evidence in this chapter and the previous one shows that democracies provide greater levels and broader distributions of electricity to their citizens than in autocracies. But how does this happen? To pursue this question, the next chapter explores how electoral competition shapes the distribution of scarce electrical power within the context of democratic India.

7

Electrifying India

Introduction

In the developing world, whether or not one has access to public goods such as electricity, clean water, or education is largely determined first, by the decision of governments to provide them, and second, by the strategies employed by political actors in delivering them. Chapters 5 and 6 have underscored the broader provision of public goods to the less advantaged in democratic settings, showing that democracies provide broader access to electricity, even among the poorest segments of their countries. This chapter seeks to better illuminate the process by which public goods, which are often wrapped in a universalist veneer when they are proposed, are manipulated by political actors who shape their delivery in the pursuit of electoral payoffs.

More people in India lack electricity than in any other country in the world, and nowhere more so than in the state of Uttar Pradesh (UP), where an estimated 60 million people have no electrical connection at home. Electricity is desired everywhere because it improves quality of life and enables economic development. Yet Uttar Pradesh lacks the electricity supply to provide to all who need or want it, and thus its distribution must be heavily rationed through ubiquitous power cuts that impose steep costs on both citizens and businesses.

Using evidence from satellite imagery over time, I demonstrate that governments in India are motivated by political incentives to manipulate the distribution of electricity. In a context where access to electricity is fundamentally supply constrained, I use detailed local-level evidence collected over nearly two decades to show that electricity provision follows a cycle in which more villages enjoy stable access to electricity in periods around elections than during nonelection periods.[1]

---

[1] In closely related work, Baskaran, Min, and Uppal (2015) use data from across India to show that constituencies are brighter due to elections, looking specifically at special elections whose

These election period effects are highest in areas represented by parties whose platforms and ideological commitments are credibly served by targeting public services to poor and rural areas.

The analysis draws on annual composite imagery of the earth at night that enable detection of electricity availability to all 98,000 villages in UP in each year from 1992 to 2010. The timeframe captures a period of dramatic political change in UP, particularly due to the emergence of the low-caste Bahujan Samaj Party (BSP), whose core support lies primarily among poor and rural Scheduled Caste (SC) voters. Drawing on the full set of village observations and controlling for village- and constituency-level factors using multilevel models, I show that villages were significantly more likely to benefit from stable electricity service in election periods than in non-election periods, and that these effects were strongest among constituencies represented by the BSP.

Although the observational data reveal important electoral patterns, these do not necessarily imply a causal effect, as that requires the evaluation of a counterfactual. Would a village's electrification status have been different if it had been represented by a party other than the BSP? I attempt to uncover the causal effect of BSP representation by focusing on a subset of villages around the pivotal 2002 state election in which political power shifted from the right-wing Bharatiya Janata Party (BJP) to the low-caste BSP. Exploiting the abundance of data, I use matching techniques to identify similar villages that differ only on whether they were to be represented by the BSP or the BJP in the state legislature. Based on the matched samples, I show a strong positive treatment effect of BSP representation on the probability of new village electrification.

The data provide an unusually fine-grained perspective on how universal public goods schemes are transformed into vehicles that deliver discrete benefits to electorally critical regions and voters. Unlike official government data sources and survey-based studies, the satellite data provide complete geographical coverage with no missing data, and are measured repeatedly over time enabling the tracking of light signatures over individual villages across multiple election cycles. Moreover, the satellite-derived data are tracked using a consistent and automated process and thus are not impacted by potential biases imparted by human record collectors. As a result, the data avoid some common empirical challenges that constrain research on service delivery in the developing world.

---

timings are exogenous to economic conditions because they are held following the death of incumbent legislators. Min and Golden (2014) show that rates of electricity line loss – power that is distributed but not paid for presumably due to theft and other irregularities – also increase in election years, benefiting incumbents who are more likely to win re-election in areas with higher line losses.

Electoral Competition and Distribution in Uttar Pradesh

Uttar Pradesh (UP) is the most populous state in India. Home to some 200 million people in an area about half the size of California, it has more people than every country in the world except China, India itself, the United States, and Indonesia. Spanning the fertile plains of the Ganges River, the densely populated state remains predominantly rural, with 80 percent of the people living in the countryside in some 98,000 villages. With tens of millions of farmers plowing fields of cereal crops like wheat, rice, and millet, agriculture is the largest economic activity in UP, accounting for nearly half of the state product in 1991 and employing nearly three-quarters of the workers.

Many of India's eminent political leaders have their roots in UP, including 8 of its 15 prime ministers. The state controls 80 out of 543 seats in the national parliament, nearly double the contingent of the next largest state. Yet despite its size and progeny, UP remains among India's poorest states. It ranks at or near the bottom across a range of socioeconomic indicators, including per capita income, infant mortality rates, literacy levels, and access to electricity (Uttar Pradesh Planning Department 2006). The World Bank estimates that 8 percent of the world's poor live in UP alone (World Bank 2002).

In the first four decades after independence, the Indian National Congress party enjoyed nearly uninterrupted control of UP's parliamentary seats as well as its *Vidhan Sabha* (Legislative Assembly). Congress often used pro-poor slogans to mobilize its supporters, especially in the rural villages where 70 percent of Indians live. Indira Gandhi's rallying cry of "Garibi Hatao" [abolish poverty] was a rhetorical success but a practical failure (Rath 1985). According to Kohli, "While socialist rhetoric was used to try to build political capital, policies in favor of the poor were seldom pursued vigorously" (Kohli 2004, 258). By the late 1980s, frustrations among the poor cracked Congress's base of popular support, and its hegemony in Uttar Pradesh deteriorated (Brass 1994; Hasan 2002).

The decline of Congress was hastened by the emergence of new political parties with more targeted bases of support. In UP, the significant size of both low- and high-caste groups – 21 percent of the population are Scheduled Castes and 10 percent are Brahmin, high proportions relative to those of other Indian states – made them electorally significant voting blocs that the new parties have courted. Among the entrants were two lower-caste parties, the BSP, drawing on the support of Scheduled Castes, and the Samajwadi Party (SP), supported by many Other Backward Class (OBC) and Muslim voters (Duncan 1999; Varshney 2000; Pai 2002; Jaffrelot 2003; Chandra 2004). In addition, the BJP, a conservative Hindu nationalist party, popular among upper-caste and middle-class voters, emerged as a powerful force (Hansen 1999; Thachil 2014). After Congress lost control of the UP state assembly in the 1989 elections, the BJP, BSP, and SP emerged as the most powerful parties in the state, jockeying for power amidst intense competition and fragile power-sharing coalitions. As the parties increasingly targeted their platforms to social groups, citizens aligned their votes accordingly, reinforcing the polarization of politics along caste lines (Banerjee and Pande 2007).

In her rich and nuanced account, Chandra (2004) describes UP as a patronage democracy in which access to public services such as water, roads, and electricity, is monopolized by elected officials. As a consequence, citizens cast their votes according to beliefs about which parties are most likely to deliver benefits to them and their communities. Responding to and nourishing the mobilization of the rural poor, the BSP and its leader, Mayawati Kumari, launched efforts to expand welfare programs and improve public services in historically underprivileged communities. Several projects targeted predominantly SC villages and Dalit *bastis* (neighborhoods). As Chief Minister in the late-1990s, Mayawati initiated the Ambedkar Village Programme, promising to provide more than 11,000 of the poorest villages with electrification, roads, and irrigation.

The BSP enjoyed increasing electoral success in the 1990s. Its share of assembly seats rose from 12 out of 425 seats in the 1991 elections to 67, 66, and 98 seats in the 1993, 1996, and 2002 elections, respectively.[2] In the 1996 state elections, the BSP won 62 percent of the Dalit vote, increasing to 69 percent in the 2002 election.[3] The landmark 2002 election was an inflection point in UP politics as the BSP secured more seats than the incumbent BJP, which had governed both UP and the national government in Delhi. In 2007, the BSP secured an outright majority of seats, the first time a party had achieved that feat since Congress won a majority in 1985.

Electricity and Party Politics

Although electoral competition has been vibrant in UP, this has not resulted in notable improvements in access to public services relative to the rest of India (Kohli 1987; Varshney 1995; Chandra 2004; Chhibber and Nooruddin 2004). As Drèze and Gazdar (1996) observe, "Whether we look at health care provisions, or at educational facilities, or at the public distribution system, or indeed at almost any essential public services for which relevant data are available, Uttar Pradesh stands out as a case of resilient government inertia as far as public provisioning is concerned" (53). The disparity is especially severe in terms of access to electricity, a critical public service that is primarily a state-level responsibility within India's federal structure (Modi 2005; Kale 2014). According to official Ministry of Power data, fewer than 60 percent of UP's villages were electrified in 2005 compared with well over 90 percent of villages in the neighboring states of Rajasthan and Madhya Pradesh (see Figure 7.1).

---

[2] The number of assembly seats in UP was reduced to 403 after the state was partitioned in 2000.
[3] Data from 2002 Uttar Pradesh Assembly Election Study, Center for the Study of Developing Societies.

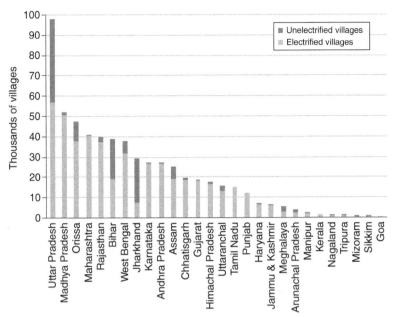

FIGURE 7.1. Village electrification rates in Indian states, 2005.
Source: Government of India, Ministry of Power.

All electricity transmission, distribution, and supply within the state is managed by the government-owned and government-operated Uttar Pradesh Power Corporation Limited (UPPCL). Against a typical available supply of 6 gigawatts (GW) in 2008, the baseline demand for power in UP hovered around 7.5 GW, peaking at 9 GW during the hottest months or around major festivals. This chronic supply shortage means that roughly a quarter of demand must go unmet, requiring massive and relentless power cuts that black out swaths of the state every day of the year. To protect the grid from catastrophic failures, cuts are scheduled following formal load-shedding guidelines as well as informal daily exceptions and adjustments. Critical decisions regarding how, when, and where power is delivered across the state are centrally made and executed from within a single UPPCL office, the Central Load Dispatching Station (CLDS). The CLDS monitors the grid and coordinates the allocation of electricity via directives to four regional Area Load Dispatch Stations (ALDS) located in Sarnath, Panki, Moradabad, and Meerut. The ALDS, in turn, make allocations from their limited supply to regional and local electric utilities. Local utilities can make further allocation decisions as necessary: for example, they may begin or end power cuts to neighborhoods or villages within their jurisdiction.

Load shedding affects almost everyone in the state. Official policy dictates anywhere from 4 hours of daily power cuts in the largest cities to 12 hours of cuts for rural villages. In Kanpur, the state's largest industrial center, daily cuts from 9 AM to 1 PM choke production, shut down businesses, and leave schools without light and homes without fans or refrigeration. Power cuts are often more frequent or last longer than scheduled, especially during the hot months. Those who can afford it run diesel generators and use power inverters that store up battery power, but these alternatives are expensive and unavailable to most poor rural residents.

A few privileged areas are designated by the government as load shed-free zones and enjoy uninterrupted power supply. These include the capital city of Lucknow, where power is deemed necessary for the government to function; the important tourist destination of Agra; the campuses of prestigious universities; the railways; and specially designated industrial zones. Occasionally, "VIP" districts are declared exempt from power cuts, with announcements often occurring right after elections, like the Noida district containing Mayawati's hometown in 2007, and the SP strongholds of Etawah and Mainpuri following the SP's victory in the 2012 election.[4] Temporary exceptions to the standard load-shedding schedule are made daily. Special allowances are often made for local holidays and festivals, typically as a result of petitions from local leaders. Protection from power cuts is also granted to the chief minister, whose travel schedule is communicated to the CLDS. A common joke says one can tell when the chief minister is in town because the power will be working.

Given that electricity is a key input to economic activity, access to electrical power is an important issue for voters. In a 2007 preelection survey in UP, nearly four in ten voters noted that development issues including electricity, road, and water concerns were their most important considerations in deciding for whom to vote.[5] Indeed, it is often said that Indian politics centers around *bijli, sadak, paani* (electricity, roads, water). In the World Bank Enterprise Survey of Indian businesses in 2006, more firms cited access to reliable electricity as the number one obstacle facing their business (35 percent) than any other concern, including taxes (25 percent) and corruption (11 percent). Firms estimated losing 6.6 percent of sales as a result of power outages.

Engineers at CLDS describe an intricate balancing act in which they must manage competing requests from elected leaders across the state. In one memorable account, a state assemblyman who had negotiated power cut exemptions from the chief minister threatened to shoot the engineer who had turned off the power to his constituency. Anecdotal evidence suggests that politicians routinely interfere in the operation of the state electricity board through patronage transfers of employees; interventions in the selection of villages for electrification projects; and the assertion of influence on when, where, and how, power cuts are timed and distributed. In a government audit of the Ambedkar Village Programme, numerous villages were found to have been electrified despite

4 "24-hour power to VIP districts in Uttar Pradesh upsets court." NDTV.com, September 11, 2012.
5 Lokniti, *Uttar Pradesh Pre-poll 2007*.

failing to meet qualification guidelines. Others were electrified following the intervention of the energy minister, contrary to the required procedure. Overall, a third of program spending, or $US 50 million, could not be accounted for, presumably lost to kickbacks and fraud.[6]

In another investigation, the Kaul Committee diagnosed a culture of political interference in the day-to-day operations of the power company. It found that the board was heavily packed by "political bosses" and that "the State Government appears to be exercising unbridled power of interference in the day to day working of the Electricity Board. This interference in transfers and postings with political patronage has totally destroyed the autonomous nature of the electricity board."[7] Bureaucrats must be responsive to politicians because their careers depend on the favor of their political bosses. Bardhan explains, "Headships of public sector units, particularly under the State Governments, are indiscriminately used as political sinecures. Efficient managers who fail to satisfy the Minister's political clients are often arbitrarily transferred" (Bardhan 1984, 69–70). In his study of corruption in India, Das concludes, "From the evidence available, it is clear that the present bureaucracy in India is used as the personal instrument of ruling politicians" (Das 2001, 219).

Because the provision of electrical power is mediated by public officials whose careers depend on the support of elected state leaders, I argue that the allocation of scarce electrical power across the state reflects the influence of competing political interests. This claim implies that the distribution of electricity should vary across time and space as a function of changes in the political environment. Media reports provide plenty of corroborating evidence of how this occurs. Saifai, the home village of SP leader Mulayam Singh Yadav, has benefited from numerous public works projects, including new highways, a stadium, and a dedicated power substation. According to one account, the village of 4,500 has enjoyed protection against load shedding: "While all districts in the state, including Lucknow, face severe power cuts, Saifai has been spared. 'We thank the chief minister for uninterrupted power supply,' says Amar Yadav."[8] A similar story emerged in Badalpur, the home village of BSP leader Mayawati (often referred to as Behenji by her followers). Following the BSP's majority victory in 2007, the village chief declared, "We get just 7 to 8 hours electricity. All of it will change now," while the area's newly elected BSP MLA announced, "We will give 24-hour electricity supply to the village as in the previous Behenji regime. All projects announced by Behenji earlier for the village will be revived."[9]

The ability of politicians to pressure power company officials to redirect power supply can also be discerned from space. In October 1997, Naresh

[6] Comptroller and Auditor General of India, *Report on Uttar Pradesh*, 2002, p. 46.
[7] Suresh Chandra Sharma vs Chairman, UPSEB & Ors. RD-SC 20 (January 13, 1998).
[8] Chakraborty, Tapas, "Air and star power for CM village." *The Telegraph*, September 5, 2004.
[9] Sharma, Aman, "Maya magic sweeps Noida." *Indian Express*, May 13, 2007.

Agarwal defected from the Congress party and transferred his support and that of his followers to the BJP, enabling it to take over the reins of UP's state government. In return, Agarwal was granted the plum position of Energy Minister. Figure 7.2 reveals the effects of his ascendancy in his constituency, Hardoi. From 1998 onwards, lights in Hardoi increased in intensity and extent as "blackout-free electricity reached even the most rustic areas of [Agarwal's] constituency."[10] Then in August 2001, Agarwal was removed from his cabinet post for disloyalty. With no further influence on UP's electricity supply, Hardoi experienced a massive decline in power provision, as revealed by satellite imagery, with the 2002 image showing a reversion almost back to the levels before Agarwal's promotion.

Less prominent legislators can also influence the provision of electricity. As part of the Ambedkar Village Programme, MLAs and upper state house members were each entitled to recommend up to five villages per year for new electrification.[11] Elected MLAs also have access to roughly $US 400,000 per year in local area development funds (Keefer and Khemani 2009), which can be directed toward electrification projects. MLAs can use their local clout to aid their constituents in many other ways, including by pressuring the utility company to speed up electrification projects or defer power outages.

These anecdotes support the claim that politicians can distort access to basic public services such as electricity down to the local level. Given this expectation, we should observe that the distribution of electricity varies across time and space, with the most notable improvements in periods when access to electricity is most politically salient, in places where citizens have few alternatives to public provision, and by elected leaders who can most effectively use improved electricity provision as a credible signal of their commitment to their supporters. In the remainder of the chapter, I examine satellite data from the last two decades to show that, consistent with these expectations, improvements in electricity access are most notable during election periods, especially in areas represented by the BSP as compared to those represented by other parties with less credible commitments to the poor.

Research Design and Data

To evaluate how the delivery of electricity varies as a function of electoral politics, I construct a dataset of all 98,000 villages in UP, structured in village-constituency-year format, with annual indicators of electricity service availability from 1992 to 2010. Villages are located within 403 state assembly constituencies, and state elections were held in 1993, 1996, 2002,

---

[10] "Caste Adrift in India." *The Economist*, February 7, 2002.
[11] Comptroller and Auditor General of India, *Report on Uttar Pradesh*, 2002, p. 45.

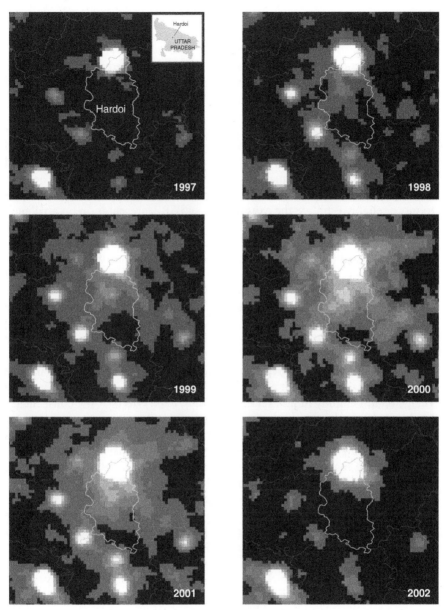

FIGURE 7.2. Nighttime light output in Hardoi constituency, 1997–2002.
Source: NOAA National Geophysical Data Center and US Air Force Weather Agency.

and 2007. I conduct two broad sets of analyses. The first evaluates party effects using time-series cross-sectional data of nearly two million observations tracking all villages over 19 years to see whether electricity service is higher in election years than non-election years. Moreover, I estimate the conditional probability that a village will be lit in constituencies that voted for the BSP versus in those that did not elect the BSP. However, observational data will not necessarily identify a causal effect of BSP representation. To estimate the causal effect of party treatment requires the evaluation of a counterfactual: Would a village's access to electricity have been different had it been represented by another party? If villages could be randomly assigned to BSP treatment, then estimating the causal effect of BSP rule would be easy. Because that is not possible, in the second analysis, I use matching techniques to more reliably estimate the causal effect of BSP representation on a village's access to electricity.

It is important to note that while the unit of analysis is the village, the key treatment regarding election of state legislators occurs at the assembly constituency level. The data are therefore structured as hierarchical or multilevel data in which individual observations are clustered within groups and the key treatment is applied at the group level. An alternative design could aggregate the village observations into constituency-level totals and means (which I do as a robustness check). However, using village-level data efficiently uses all the available data, enables the detection of heterogeneous effects within constituencies, and helps avoid aggregation problems of ecological inference and the related modifiable areal unit problem. To account for the grouped nature of the village data, I employ multilevel models using fixed effects at the constituency level and cluster the standard errors by constituency.

An additional form of nonindependence may also exist among geographically proximate villages. Because electrification is a networked phenomenon, a village may be more likely to be electrified where the grid is dense and other nearby villages have power. If there is spatial autocorrelation, it needs to be taken into account to derive correct standard errors. However, standard methods for controlling for spatial dependence are not tractable for networks as large as those observed here. Spatial lag models with binary dependent variables do not have closed-form solutions and are difficult to estimate (Ward and Gleditsch 2002). A more primitive strategy adopted here is to include controls that relate directly to the extent and density of the electrical grid, namely a village's distance from the nearest town (because all towns are connected to the grid). The inclusion of fixed effects will also help account for unmeasured regional variations in the power grid by allowing the intercepts to vary across constituencies. A shortcoming of these approaches is that unlike spatial lag models, which allow the degree of similarity to be measured continuously across all villages, varying-intercept models can only control for fixed spatial autocorrelation across constituencies and not within each constituency.

Dependent Variable: Lit Villages

To estimate the availability of electricity in individual villages, I rely on satellite imagery of the earth at night. As described in Chapter 4, the imagery comes from the Defense Meteorological Satellite Program's Operational Linescan System (DMSP-OLS), a set of US military weather satellites that have been flying in polar orbit since 1970 recording high-resolution images of the earth each night, typically between 7PM and 10PM local time. Captured at an altitude of 830 km, these images reveal concentrations of outdoor lights, fires, and gas flares at a fine resolution of 0.56 km and a smoothed resolution of 2.7 km. Beginning in 1992, all DMSP-OLS images were digitized, facilitating their analysis and use by the scientific community. Annual composite images are created by overlaying all images captured during a calendar year, dropping images where lights are shrouded by cloud cover or overpowered by the aurora or solar glare (near the poles), and removing ephemeral lights such as fires and other noise. The result is a series of images of time-stable night lights covering the globe for each year from 1992 to 2010 (Elvidge et al. 1997a; Imhoff et al. 1997; Elvidge et al. 2001). Images are scaled onto a georeferenced 30-arcsecond grid (approximately 1 km²). Each pixel is encoded with a measure of its annual average brightness on a 6-bit scale from 0 to 63. Figure 7.3a shows an image of 2002 time-stable night lights in UP. The state's largest cities are brightly lit, including the capital Lucknow, and the manufacturing center Kanpur. But given that 80 percent of UP's population is rural, the image also reveals vast areas of darkness. This is not simply because the satellite cannot detect very low levels of light: in fact, thousands of small villages emit discernible levels of light. The fact that some villages appear lit while many otherwise similar villages are dark suggests instead that access to electricity varies widely across the state.

Compared with traditional data on energy production and consumption, the satellite images explicitly reveal the geographic distribution of electrical power, providing a clearer and more dynamic picture of who benefits from electricity than could be gained from maps of static electrical infrastructure.

By comparing composite images from different years, trends in light output can be visualized. The two maps in Figure 7.3b contrast light output from satellite images in 1992/1993 against those from 2009/2010. On the left, the dark grey areas identify pixels that have become newly lit over that timespan. Many newly lit areas correspond to zones of urban expansion and grid extensions, including around the Agra area, which has benefited from many infrastructure improvements. On the right, dark grey pixels show areas that have gone *dark* over this timespan: these are areas where lights were once visible in 1992 and 1993 but are no longer consistently detectable by satellite sensors. These newly dark areas are heavily concentrated in the impoverished eastern region. These patterns reflect the decay of infrastructure, lack of maintenance including the replacement of streetlight bulbs, and increasingly frequent power outages. The

(a)

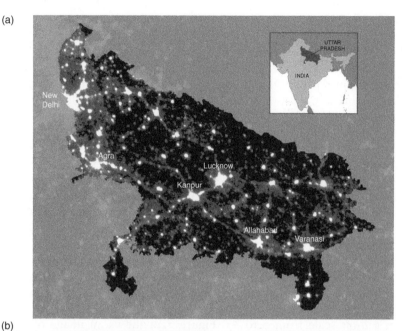

(b)

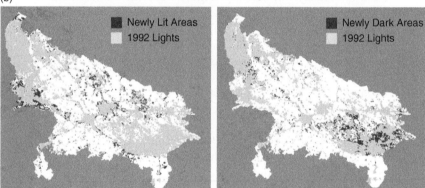

FIGURE 7.3. Nighttime lights in Uttar Pradesh. (a) Average annual stable lights, 2002, (b) Change detection, 1992/93 versus 2009/2010.
Source: Satellite data from NOAA National Geophysical Data Center and US Air Force Weather Agency.

change detection image illustrates the dynamic nature of electrical service and the reality that its provision can both improve and worsen over time.

The primary dependent variable is a dichotomous measure of whether a village benefits from stable electricity supply or not in each year, by which I mean whether a village center appears lit in the relevant annual composite stable lights image. The data extractions are performed using GIS software to spatially match village locations to the satellite imagery.[12] The emission of light at night reveals both the presence of electrical infrastructure *and* the regular flow of electrical power converted into outdoor lighting at night. Outdoor lighting is meaningful because it is a useful application of electricity with broad public benefits and suggests wider availability of electricity to residences and businesses. Indeed, electric poles and wires are irrelevant if the supply of power is inconsistent or unreliable. As one upset villager in a newly "electrified" village reported, "We have only had a few hours of power since the men came to install the poles. It is worse now. Now we get a bill even though there is still no electricity!"

Independent Variables

The primary independent variables of interest are an indicator variable for election years, indicators for the party of the MLA representing each constituency, and the set of interaction terms between these variables. Several control variables account for factors that might make a village more likely to be electrified for nonpolitical reasons that might nevertheless be confounded with the party variables. *Village population* identifies the number of potential consumers of electricity, with larger villages more likely to be targeted. The presence of complementary infrastructure such as a *School, Medical facility*, or a *Paved approach road* may induce a higher local demand for electricity. A village's *Literacy rate* may reflect a latent factor associated with the ability of local residents to secure government projects in their village. *Distance to nearest town* is measured in kilometers and provides an upper bound on distance to the electrical grid, since all towns are electrified.

Data at the assembly constituency level include *Constituency population* and *Number of villages*. The variable *Scheduled Caste population* codes the proportion of the population classified as Scheduled Caste according to the 2001 Indian Census. Given the very high rates of support for the BSP among SC voters, this variable serves as a proxy for BSP core voters. I create an interaction term *BSP × SC population share* to explore heterogeneous effects of BSP MLA representation depending on the proportion of core voters within a village. Some assembly constituency seats are *Reserved* for Scheduled Caste candidates.

To account for variations in the level of industrialization and development across the state, *Income index* is calculated based on adjusted district per capita income, scaled on an index between 0 and 1 (Uttar Pradesh Planning Department 2006). District-level income data are available for 1991, 2001, and 2005 for all 70 districts and are the most disaggregated estimates of income of which I am aware.

---

[12] The village location data are from ML Infomap.

The UPPCL reports the *Total available power supply* in the state in each year. This is important because it is easier to distribute electricity more broadly when greater supply is available. Reflecting the greater priority the state's leaders have put on managing the *distribution* of electricity rather than making more costly and less visible investments in increasing its supply, UP's power generation totaled 21 terawatt-hours in 2010, a figure no higher than it was in 1995. Meanwhile, UP has artfully increased the availability of electricity by importing from the central grid, which now accounts for up to two-thirds of total power in the state. The flexibility to import more power from its neighbors when needed, despite the generally high cost, is what enables temporary increases in electricity provision in critical periods such as those around elections.

Over the timespan of the study, night lights data were recorded from six distinct DMSP satellites: F10, F12, F14, F15, F16, and F18. To account for differences in the characteristics of each sensor, I code separate satellite dummy variables, which function in the models as satellite fixed effects. Moreover, sensors are known to degrade over time. To account for these effects, I create sensor-specific variables that count the number of years for which that sensor has provided DMSP-OLS data. For example, F10, which provided data in the first two years of the series, is coded as 1 in 1992, 2 in 1993, and 0 in all other years. Finally, I include a year counter variable that tracks the progression of calendar time. The inclusion of these sensor age and year counter variables helps account for period-specific factors that affect all villages.

Results and Analysis

Descriptive Trends

Figure 7.4 plots the proportion of villages appearing lit in satellite imagery with thin lines depicting smoothed trends in individual constituencies and the dark line showing the overall state average (see also Tables 7.6–7.9 in the chapter's Appendix). The noisy figure reveals high variation, both across constituencies and over time. Only in a few constituencies around large cities are villages fully lit in each year. In the rest of the state, there has been little improvement in the rate of lit villages over the last two decades, with just over half of the state's villages appearing lit at both the starting and ending points. This slow pace of change is consistent with expert observations. According to one report, "Power is the most critical bottleneck the state is currently facing. There has been practically no addition to generation capacity in the state since 1990, while the demand has been increasing. The distribution network is obsolete and overloaded resulting in frequent breakdowns" (Singh 2009, 6). Nevertheless, the overall statewide pattern reveals a cyclical pattern in which more villages are generally lit around elections than in nonelection periods.

Table 7.1 presents logit regressions to more formally evaluate the impact of elections. The results show consistently that villages are more likely to be lit in years when an election is held. Model 1 shows the impact of election

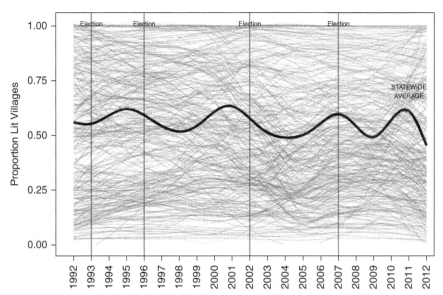

FIGURE 7.4. Proportion of villages lit by constituency, 1992–2010. Individual lines represent smoothed averages for each of Uttar Pradesh's 403 assembly constituencies.

years versus nonelection years on all pooled village observations with a control accounting for the total power supply available in the state in each year. Models 2 and 3 add additional dummies to estimate the effect in years immediately prior to and following election years. In all cases, the election year effect is large and significant. Models 4 to 6 add village fixed effects, estimating a separate intercept for each individual village to help account for fixed characteristics that may make it more or less likely that a village will be electrified, such as size, level of economic activity, or proximity to larger towns. These results show an even larger effect of elections. Although one cannot make causal claims based on these results, it is important to note that the effect is substantively large: based on model 4, the probability that a village is lit is 51 percent in election years versus 40 percent for the same village in nonelection years.

Focusing on some key constituencies further reveals the influence of individual politicians and the significance of elections when it comes to the distribution of electricity. The first plot in Figure 7.5 shows the proportion of villages lit in Hardoi constituency, tracking the rise and fall of Naresh Aggarwal discussed previously and shown in Figure 7.2. Amethi is the seat of power of India's Nehru–Gandhi clan. Its close association with the Congress party has been both a blessing and curse to its residents. The steep decline in electricity provision following the 2002 election reflects a shifting of the political winds toward the BSP and SP, with Congress declining to historic lows, winning only 25 and 22 seats in 2002 and 2007, respectively.

TABLE 7.1. *Election year effects on village lit or not, 1992–2010 logit regressions*

Dependent Variable: Village lit	(1)	(2)	(3)	(4)	(5)	(6)
Years since election: −2			0.2741**			0.5770**
			(0.004)			(0.008)
Years since election: −1		−0.0950**	−0.0023		−0.2002**	−0.0106
		(0.003)	(0.003)		(0.006)	(0.007)
Years since election: 0	0.2244**	0.2904**	0.4691**	0.4485**	0.5977**	0.9893**
	(0.002)	(0.003)	(0.004)	(0.005)	(0.006)	(0.009)
Years since election: +1		0.3519**	0.4153**		0.7238**	0.8735**
		(0.003)	(0.004)		(0.007)	(0.008)
Years since election: +2			0.1976**			0.4210**
			(0.004)			(0.008)
Total power supply	−0.0049**	−0.0147**	−0.0054**	−0.0099**	−0.0309**	−0.0117**
	(0.000)	(0.000)	(0.000)	(0.000)	(0.000)	(0.000)
Village fixed effects	No	No	No	Yes	Yes	Yes
Constant	0.1750**	0.4805**	−0.0314*			
	(0.009)	(0.011)	(0.015)			
Observations	1,874,065	1,676,795	1,479,525	1,333,629	1,161,185	984,480

Robust standard errors clustered on villages in parentheses.

**p ≤ 0.01, *p ≤ 0.05.

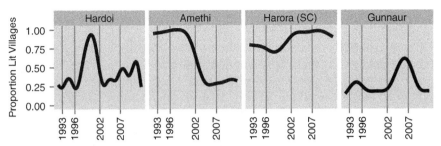

FIGURE 7.5. Villages lit in politically significant constituencies, 1992–2010.
Source: Satellite data from NOAA National Geophysical Data Center and US Air Force Weather Agency.

Yet the Gandhi clan continues to retain influence: media reports in summer 2012 reported that Sonia Gandhi had secured a promise of uninterrupted power supply to Amethi from the new incoming chief minister.[13]

Mayawati, on her rise to leadership of the BSP, first served as MLA of Harora constituency from October 1996 to October 1998, a period when the BSP was a weak player in state politics. When the BSP won enough seats in 2002 for Mayawati to secure the chief minister's post, access to electricity in Harora reflected her growing political power and influence. Following the collapse of her coalition government in 2003, Mulayam Singh Yadav became chief minister in September 2003. Following constitutional requirements that the chief minister also hold a seat in the state legislature, Yadav was elected MLA of Gunnaur constituency in a February 2004 by-election. The constituency benefited immediately from its new and powerful representative. In the village of Chhabilpur, a schoolmaster marveled, "We get electricity for almost 20 hours a day, a distant dream three years ago when this village didn't even have electricity poles."[14] Yet when Yadav lost his post as CM in 2007 (to Mayawati), many villages in Gunnaur, including Chhabilpur, were once again plunged into darkness.

Because the satellite data represent averages over the calendar year, there is no straightforward way to use this data to investigate whether light output peaks in the weeks and months prior to an election or in the period afterward. The cases above suggest, however, that both can occur, as some leaders persuade power company officials to increase power leading up to elections when voters are most attuned to their performance, while later, newly elected leaders shake up the status quo by advocating for new distributional allocations favoring their critical constituents. In the next subsection, I examine whether the impact of elections on electricity provision can be generalized beyond these anecdotal cases in a statistical framework that accounts for confounding factors.

[13] "A word from Sonia Gandhi ensures uninterrupted power supply in Rae Bareli, Amethi." *Times of India*, August 29, 2012.
[14] "Mulayam as MLA changes face of Gunnaur." *Indian Express*, March 18, 2007.

Time-Series Cross-Sectional Analysis

Table 7.2 shows a set of logit regressions to evaluate election and party effects on the likelihood that a village will be lit in the satellite imagery. The models include fixed effects for all 403 constituencies to help account for unobserved factors that may be associated with patterns of electrification such as geography or economic potential. To help account for nonindependence of village observations within the same constituency, standard errors are clustered at the constituency level.

Across all models, the coefficient on election year is positive and significant, indicating that a village's probability of being lit is higher in those years than in nonelection years. To evaluate whether the election year effects vary by party, model 1 includes party dummies, interactions of each party dummy with the election year dummy, and the measure of total available electrical power in the state. The upper-caste BJP is the omitted reference category. None of the main party effects are significant, suggesting that the party of the MLA makes no difference to the likelihood that a village will be lit in nonelection years. But in election years, parties matter. The interaction term (Election year × BSP MLA) is positive and significant, meaning that villages in BSP constituencies are more likely to be lit in election years than those in BJP constituencies. Controlling for differences in district-level income and a wide range of village-level covariates in model 2 does not change the positive effect of election years and the (Election year × BSP MLA) interaction term.

One possible explanation for the BSP-election year effects is that they are actually driven by differences in political participation and competitiveness. In model 3, I add political variables that control for the win margin, the turnout rate, and the number of registered voters, and whether the incumbent party won in the most recent election. The results show that the likelihood of villages being lit is lower in areas with lower turnout and with reelected incumbents. This may suggest that elected representatives are more likely to be complacent when voter participation is lower. Yet these effects do not meaningfully change the coefficients on election years or the (Election year × BSP) interaction.

Models 4 and 5 add variables identifying the party of the chief minister, and interaction terms between the chief minister's party and the MLA party. The results show interestingly that compared to years with a BJP chief minister (1992, 1998–2001), electricity provision was significantly worse under all other chief ministers and in periods of *President's rule* (in which no ruling coalition emerged, necessitating direct federal rule). Moreover, the (BSP CM × BSP MLA) interaction term shows that electricity provision in BSP-represented constituencies was even worse when there was a co-partisan BSP chief minister than it was in the omitted category of BJP-represented constituencies. Although this result is somewhat unexpected, it affirms how strategic senior political leaders can be in their allocation of political resources. The result suggests in particular that the BSP chief minister may have been more focused on directing

TABLE 7.2. *Fixed effects logit regressions on village lit or not, 1992–2010*

Dependent variable: Village lit	(1)	(2)	(3)	(4)	(5)
Election year	0.1630**	0.1747**	0.2533**	0.4441**	0.4673**
	(0.054)	(0.058)	(0.065)	(0.069)	(0.103)
BSP MLA	−0.0582	−0.0626	−0.0835	0.0039	0.1556
	(0.068)	(0.074)	(0.075)	(0.075)	(0.095)
INC MLA	−0.0609	−0.0658	−0.0927	−0.1047	0.0463
	(0.084)	(0.091)	(0.092)	(0.090)	(0.126)
Other MLA	−0.1487	−0.1640	−0.1940	−0.1774	−0.3152*
	(0.095)	(0.104)	(0.106)	(0.107)	(0.134)
SP MLA	−0.0237	−0.0263	−0.0333	0.0276	−0.0027
	(0.062)	(0.068)	(0.069)	(0.069)	(0.097)
Election year × BSP MLA	0.3423**	0.3722**	0.3061**	0.1751*	0.1677
	(0.076)	(0.083)	(0.083)	(0.084)	(0.117)
Election year × INC MLA	−0.0473	−0.0537	−0.0809	−0.1108	−0.0996
	(0.108)	(0.118)	(0.120)	(0.118)	(0.167)
Election year × Other MLA	0.2292*	0.2504*	0.2204*	0.1664	0.1138
	(0.095)	(0.102)	(0.104)	(0.104)	(0.161)
Election year × SP MLA	0.0686	0.0753	0.0379	−0.0263	−0.0457
	(0.062)	(0.067)	(0.067)	(0.067)	(0.121)
BSP CM				−0.5922**	−0.4835**
				(0.055)	(0.087)
President's rule				−1.2944**	−1.4442**
				(0.120)	(0.154)
SP CM				−0.7759**	−0.8279**
				(0.065)	(0.109)
BSP MLA × BSP CM					−0.3712**
					(0.134)
(All other MLA party × CM party interactions)					Yes
Win margin			0.0061	0.0057	0.0061
			(0.003)	(0.003)	(0.003)
Turnout			−0.0212**	−0.0006	0.0007
			(0.005)	(0.006)	(0.006)
Electors			−0.0038	0.0002	0.0008
			(0.002)	(0.002)	(0.002)
Incumbent wins			−0.1087*	−0.0801	−0.0772
			(0.054)	(0.053)	(0.052)
Income (district level)		0.4208	0.1998	2.2540*	2.2371*
		(0.648)	(0.741)	(1.003)	(0.994)

(*continued*)

TABLE 7.2. (*continued*)

Dependent variable: Village lit	(1)	(2)	(3)	(4)	(5)
Total power supply in state	0.0088 (0.005)	0.0096 (0.005)	0.0014 (0.006)	−0.0082 (0.007)	−0.0067 (0.007)
Constituency fixed effects	Yes	Yes	Yes	Yes	Yes
Village controls[a]	No	Yes	Yes	Yes	Yes
Satellite sensor-age	Yes	Yes	Yes	Yes	Yes
Year trend	Yes	Yes	Yes	Yes	Yes
Constant	0.7588** (0.111)	0.6670** (0.235)	3.2318** (0.657)	0.5116 (0.785)	0.2479 (0.769)
Observations	1,865,667	1,852,690	1,849,081	1,849,081	1,849,081

Robust standard errors clustered on assembly constituency in parentheses. BSP, Bahujan Samaj Party; CM, chief minister; INC, Indian National Congress Party; MLA, member of the legislative assembly; SP, Samajwadi Party.

** $p \leq 0.01$, * $p \leq 0.05$.

[a] Village controls include population; proportion Scheduled Caste; proportion literate; presence of a school, a medical facility, a paved road; and distance to nearest town (km).

electricity supply toward constituencies of marginal support than to areas of core support. Still, even after accounting for these effects, the main finding on the election year variable remains robust and positive, and the (Election year × BSP MLA) coefficient remains positive though it now just misses standard levels of statistical significance.

These results are notable given the claims in India that, on the one hand, access to state resources depends entirely on who you vote for, and on the other hand, that all parties are equally ineffective in addressing the needs of the poor. When it comes to village electrification, the differences across parties are substantial but only in election years, with the largest effects occurring in villages located in BSP constituencies.

These findings are robust to different estimation strategies and codings of the dependent variable. The chapter's appendix reports models that include a lagged dependent variable rather than a fixed effects specification (Appendix Table 7.7). The same positive effect of election years and interactions between election years and BSP legislators persists. The findings are also unchanged when recoding the dependent variable to look for light output in a larger area than just the village center (using bilinear interpolation of the 2 × 2 pixel area) (Appendix Table 7.8). Finally, to be sure that the results are not artificially driven by the large number of observations in the multilevel dataset, I collapse the data into a constituency-level dataset where the dependent variable is the fraction of villages in a constituency that are lit. Using fractional logit (Papke and Wooldridge 1996) and regressing a comparable set of explanatory variables on this outcome, I find again the same positive effect of election years and their interaction with BSP representation (Appendix Table 7.9).

That said, we cannot easily conclude that these patterns reflect a true causal effect of BSP representation, as these findings could be biased by unobserved factors associated with both BSP electoral success *and* higher electrification rates. Although the inclusion of constituency fixed effects should absorb time-invariant factors that matter within constituencies, and the satellite sensor-age variables should account for broad temporal trends affecting the whole state, these statistical adjustments provide only a partial response to such concerns. In the next section, I focus on a smaller subset of villages and use matching techniques to derive a more compelling estimate of the causal effect of BSP representation.

Deriving Causal Estimates of BSP Representation on Village Electrification

The 2002 election marked an inflection point in the ascendancy of the BSP when it secured 98 seats to surpass the upper caste BJP whose seat share dropped from 157 to 88. For the BSP, the election was an impressive and surprising achievement. Replacing the BJP leader Rajnath Singh, the BSP's Mayawati was named chief minister and served in that post for 16 months from May 2002 through August 2003. Given the dramatic transition in power from BJP to BSP rule during this timeframe, I focus on the period immediately prior to and following the 2002 election to evaluate party effects on changes in village electrification rates.

To define my sphere of analysis, I begin with the 157 assembly constituencies that were represented by the BJP prior to the 2002 election. In the election, 37 switched their support to the BSP while 52 retained BJP representation. Based on this study sample, I ask whether unlit villages in constituencies that switched to BSP representation (the "treatment" group) were more likely to become lit than if they had retained the BJP (the "control" group). Constituencies that have no unlit villages (mostly urban areas) are excluded from the analysis. This results in a sample that comprises a treatment group of 2,679 villages in 29 constituencies that switched from BJP to the BSP, and a control group of 3,223 villages in 29 seats that retained the BJP. The contingency table in Table 7.3 presents a first comparison of the data. Within the treatment group, 10 percent of unlit villages that switched to BSP representation now appeared lit in 2003. That rate is more than twice as high as the rate for unlit villages that retained their BJP representatives.

To address selection bias further and reduce the dependence of results on model specification and parametric assumptions, I use matching in an effort to achieve a higher level of balance across covariates between the treatment and control groups. Matching seeks to make the characteristics of the treated group look similar to those of the control group, allowing analysis that is less sensitive to choices of functional form and model selection (see discussion in Chapter 6).

TABLE 7.3. *Comparing changes in village electrification, 2001–2003*

	Retains BJP BJP, 2001 → BJP, 2003	Switches To BSP BJP, 2001 → BSP, 2003	Total
Unlit 2001 → Lit 2003	4.8%	10.1%	7.2%
	154 villages	272 villages	426 villages
Unlit 2001 → Unlit	95.2%	89.8%	92.8%
2003	3,069	2,407	5,476
Total	100%	100%	100%
	3,223	2,679	5,902

By improving balance, matching reduces model dependence and reduces bias and variance (Ho et al. 2007). Using GenMatch to conduct one-to-one matching with replacement, I match on the seven village and four constituency-level covariates listed in Table 7.4. Empirical-QQ plots of all continuous variables in Figure 7.6 show improvement in balance after matching, especially on the village-level covariates.

If matching achieved perfect balance across all covariates, the treatment effect could be estimated by comparing the mean outcomes across treatment and control groups. However, some differences remain even after matching. As a result, I continue the analysis on the matched sample, conditioning on covariates by estimating multilevel models using random effects logistic regression. The multilevel approach for dealing with grouped data is preferable to the clustering of standard errors used in the preceding text and allows us to estimate the effects of constituency-level factors that are not possible in a fixed effects framework. Specifically, the model estimates

$$\Pr(y_i = 1) = \text{logit}^{-1}(X_i\beta + \alpha_{j[i]}), \text{ for } i = 1, ..., n \tag{7.1}$$

$$\alpha^j \sim N(U_j\gamma, \sigma_\alpha^2), \text{ for } j = 1,..., 403, \tag{7.2}$$

where X is a matrix of village-level covariates and $j[i]$ is an index indicating the constituency in which village i is located. At the constituency level, U is a matrix of constituency-level predictors, γ is the vector of coefficients for the predictors, and σ_α^2 is the variance of the constituency-level errors. An important assumption of the model is that the random effects and errors are assumed to be normally distributed with constant mean and variance in each constituency, j (Gelman and Hill 2007). The multilevel model estimates both equations at the same time, thus avoiding collinearity problems, while accounting for both village- and constituency-level variations in estimating the key constituency-level coefficient of BSP representation.

Table 7.5 presents the main results on the matched sample and evaluates whether unlit villages that switched to BSP representation were more likely to

TABLE 7.4. *Characteristics of unlit villages in study group, 2001*

	Retains BJP In 2002 Election BJP 2001 → BJP 2003 3,223 Villages in 29 Assembly Constituencies				Switches To BSP In 2002 Election BJP 2001 → BSP 2003 2,679 Villages in 29 Assembly Constituencies			
	Mean	SD	Min	Max	Mean	SD	Min	Max
Village-level variables								
Proportion Scheduled Caste	0.23	0.19	0	1	0.29	0.22	0	1
Population (thousands)	1.31	1.26	0.001	11.61	1.39	1.51	0.001	15.54
Literacy rate	0.35	0.13	0	1	0.40	0.13	0	1
School	0.71	0.45	0	1	0.75	0.43	0	1
Medical facility	0.27	0.44	0	1	0.25	0.44	0	1
Paved approach road	0.52	0.50	0	1	0.51	0.50	0	1
Dist. to town (km)	11.90	9.31	0	105	12.14	10.26	0	99
Assembly constituency-level variables								
Income index (district)	0.40	0.04	0.35	0.50	0.43	0.04	0.37	0.65
2001 total light output (log)	7.17	0.71	5.44	8.65	7.54	0.54	6.56	9.09
Reserved seat	0.23	0.42	0	1	0.20	0.40	0	1
Proportion Scheduled Caste	0.22	0.07	0.10	0.40	0.26	0.05	0.14	0.34

be lit than those that stayed with the BJP.[15] The coefficient on the BSP treatment indicator is positive and statistically significant in both the reduced (model 1) and full specifications (model 2). The fact that BSP legislators are effective at improving access to electricity to villages is notable because electrification is a targeted action that requires active coordination on the part of numerous officials. Against the backdrop of endemic power blackouts, the emergence of new lights is a noteworthy and visible signal of political effort to court voters. The positive BSP coefficient suggests that new BSP legislators have more aggressively pursued efforts to improve village electrification than their BJP counterparts, consistent with differences in the respective parties' ideological commitments to the rural poor.

---

[15] Appendix Table 7.10 shows results of the analysis on the unmatched samples.

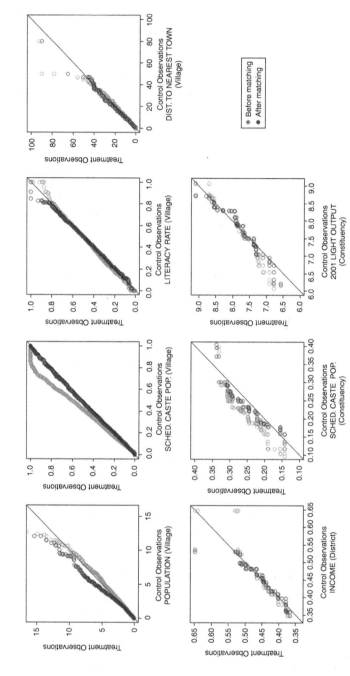

FIGURE 7.6. Empirical-QQ plots of key covariates, before and after matching.

TABLE 7.5. *Evaluating BSP treatment effects on village electrification random effects logistic regressions on matched sample*

	Outcome: Newly Lit in 2003	
	(1)	(2)
BSP treatment	1.6680*	1.9314*
	(0.7663)	(0.7910)
Scheduled Caste population share		1.3190**
		(0.4435)
BSP treatment × SC population share		−1.7844**
		(0.5930)
Village-level controls		
Village population (thousands)		−0.0527
		(0.0477)
Literacy rate in village		2.3317**
		(0.5875)
School in village		−0.3617*
		(0.1663)
Medical facility in village		0.0299
		(0.1295)
Paved approach road to village		0.5063**
		(0.1203)
Distance to nearest town (km)		−0.0368**
		(0.0090)
Constituency-level controls		
Income index	12.0242*	6.4064
	(5.7739)	(6.1200)
2001 Nighttime light output (log)		1.0654
		(0.6189)
Reserved constituency		−0.2551
		(0.9561)
Scheduled Caste population share		−0.5918
		(6.8396)
Constant	−9.3191**	−15.5634**
	(2.4363)	(4.6062)
Observations	5358	5358
Constituencies in sample	56	56

Standard errors in parentheses.
**p-value ≤ 0.01; *p-value ≤ 0.05.

Although the positive impact of BSP representation is validated here, it is also the case that the overall number of impacted villages remains small. Absent any meaningful increase in the overall supply of electrical power, any improvement in electricity provision to one constituency is difficult to sustain over time. Visual analysis of these BSP constituencies suggests that even the limited improvements dissipated rapidly in the years that followed, as outcomes reverted to the status quo. Although empowered legislators may use their influence to impel the power company to enhance electricity delivery at critical moments, such deviations cannot be sustained in the face of the state's chronic power shortages. Overall, these results support and strengthen the descriptive and time-series findings given earlier. Electricity access can indeed be shaped by opportunistic legislators and parties, but given resource constraints and awareness that such manipulations will only have short-term effects, such efforts will be concentrated during only the most politically important junctures.

Conclusion

This chapter uses satellite imagery of the earth at night to study variations in the provision of electrical power across Uttar Pradesh. By examining a period of substantial political change in one of India's poorest states, I show that many villages have benefited from the rise of the lower caste BSP over the last two decades. Using annual data on village electrification from 1992 to 2010, I show that the probability of receiving electricity is substantially and significantly higher in constituencies represented by the BSP, especially in election years. Using matching techniques to evaluate similar villages that differ only on whether they switched to BSP representation in the critical 2002 elections, I also show a positive BSP treatment effect.

This chapter shows that while the electrical grid is often conceived of as a public good imparting nonrival and nonexcludable benefits, in practice, the actual service that it delivers – the flow of useful electrical power – is far from static. Because the distribution of electricity is controlled by political actors, its benefits can be provided and taken away in accordance with political priorities and strategic considerations. The results illustrate the dangers of conflating the provision of infrastructure with service delivery, a problem that afflicts the study of many public goods such as education and health services, given that the presence of buildings or the expenditure of budgets do not necessarily imply the actual delivery of services (Chaudhury et al. 2006). Moreover, the account of UP shows that although many politicians campaign to improve access to public goods, whether or not they can do so depends on the credibility of their parties to such commitments and their ability to persuade officials to respond to their demands.

Appendix

TABLE 7.6. *Summary statistics*

Outcome Variables	Observations	Mean	Std. Dev.	Min.	Max.
All Villages, 1992–2010					
Lit in annual composite satellite image	1,860,898	0.503	0.500	0	1
Average annual light output (0–63 scale)	1,860,898	2.986	5.057	0	63
Village-level characteristics[a]					
Population of village	97,942	1.344	1.475	0.001	99.51
Proportion Scheduled Caste (SC) in village	97,942	0.244	0.208	0	1
Proportion literate in village	97,942	0.422	0.132	0	1
School in village	97,926	0.703	0.457	0	1
Clinic in village	97,926	0.265	0.441	0	1
Paved road to village	97,926	0.594	0.491	0	1
Distance to nearest town (km)	97,942	8.725	4.865	0.003	49.6
Assembly constituency-level characteristics[b]					
Population (thousands)	403	412.401	251.390	0.634	2731
Number of villages	403	242.993	150.799	3	1190
Average proportion of SC	403	0.233	0.071	0.034	0.572
Proportion of villages with school	403	0.755	0.138	0.333	1
Proportion of villages with paved road	403	0.633	0.152	0.326	1
Proportion of villages with clinic	403	0.317	0.169	0.041	1
Reserved constituency	403	0.221	0.415	0	1
District-level characteristics[c]					
Income index, 1991	70	0.321	0.056	0.208	0.517
Income index, 2001	70	0.440	0.058	0.349	0.648
Income index, 2005	70	0.439	0.061	0.326	0.643

(continued)

TABLE 7.6. (*continued*)

Outcome Variables	Observations	Mean	Std. Dev.	Min.	Max.
Education index, 1991	70	0.403	0.089	0.227	0.640
Education index, 2001	70	0.560	0.091	0.338	0.744
Education index, 2005	70	0.596	0.098	0.344	0.775
Health index, 1991	70	0.560	0.128	0.284	0.853
Health index, 2001	70	0.592	0.052	0.483	0.750
Health index, 2005	70	0.643	0.046	0.545	0.783
State-level characteristic					
Annual total power supply (TWh)[d]	19	40.223	9.149	28.563	61.121
State assembly election results[e]					
Seats won by					
Bahujan Samaj Party (BSP)		67	66	98	206
Samajwadi Party (SP)		135	114	143	97
Bharatiya Janata Party (BJP)		164	157	88	51
Indian National Congress Party (INC)		22	33	25	22
Other party		15	33	49	27
Total seats		403	403	403	403
Average win margin (%)		10.1	9.6	8.1	7.3
Turnout (%)		57.4	56.3	54.5	46.5
Incumbent party reelected (%)		33.5	35.1	37.2	32.5
Registered voters (thousands)		213.1	238.9	247.5	281.8

[a] Data from 2001 Census of India.
[b] Estimates based on 2001 Census data and spatial joins of village locations to constituencies.
[c] Data from *Uttar Pradesh Human Development Report 2006*, background tables.
[d] Available electrical power at all station busbars in terawatt-hours. Data from UPPCL Annual Reports.
[e] Excludes constituencies in the northwestern districts that were separated into the new state of Uttaranchal in 2000.

TABLE 7.7. *Logit regressions on villages lit or not, 1992–2010 with lagged dependent variable*

Dependent Variable (DV): Village Lit	(1)	(2)	(3)	(4)	(5)
L.lit (lagged DV)	2.9474**	2.7043**	2.6491**	2.7607**	2.7569**
	(0.061)	(0.055)	(0.054)	(0.052)	(0.052)
Election year	-0.1368*	-0.1138	-0.1983**	0.2351**	0.2837*
	(0.068)	(0.071)	(0.072)	(0.078)	(0.130)
BSP MLA	-0.1591*	-0.1599*	-0.1700*	-0.0866	-0.0833
	(0.075)	(0.072)	(0.069)	(0.064)	(0.115)
INC MLA	-0.1811	-0.1185	-0.1910*	-0.1779	-0.2394
	(0.098)	(0.098)	(0.088)	(0.091)	(0.147)
Other MLA	0.1138	0.0499	-0.0253	0.0689	-0.2234
	(0.109)	(0.098)	(0.101)	(0.102)	(0.164)
SP MLA	-0.1780*	-0.1406*	-0.1168	-0.0377	-0.1607
	(0.071)	(0.071)	(0.066)	(0.066)	(0.099)
Election year × BSP MLA	0.4597**	0.4645**	0.4038**	0.1089	0.0236
	(0.085)	(0.089)	(0.090)	(0.087)	(0.158)
Election year × INC MLA	0.1603	0.1353	0.1171	0.0929	0.1146
	(0.136)	(0.140)	(0.144)	(0.124)	(0.222)
Election year × Other MLA	0.3065**	0.3180**	0.3298**	0.1936	0.1234
	(0.101)	(0.108)	(0.109)	(0.105)	(0.203)
Election year × SP MLA	0.1333	0.1264	0.1086	-0.0223	-0.0476
	(0.070)	(0.072)	(0.073)	(0.072)	(0.156)
BSP CM				-0.9984**	-1.0634**
				(0.059)	(0.089)
Pres Rule CM				-3.6040**	-3.8106**
				(0.133)	(0.197)

(continued)

TABLE 7.7. (*continued*)

Dependent Variable (DV): Village Lit	(1)	(2)	(3)	(4)	(5)
SP CM				-1.5294**	-1.7013**
				(0.089)	(0.124)
BSP MLA × BSP CM					-0.0563
					(0.136)
Win margin			0.0088**	0.0080**	0.0081**
			(0.002)	(0.002)	(0.002)
Turnout			-0.0193**	-0.0158**	-0.0153**
			(0.005)	(0.005)	(0.005)
Electors			0.0064**	0.0065**	0.0066**
			(0.001)	(0.001)	(0.001)
Incumbent wins			-0.0648	-0.0285	-0.0229
			(0.049)	(0.048)	(0.048)
Income (district level)		1.1902*	2.1692**	3.2102**	3.2824**
		(0.528)	(0.645)	(0.739)	(0.730)
Total power supply in state	-0.0293**	-0.0264**	-0.0443**	-0.0778**	-0.0780**
	(0.004)	(0.004)	(0.005)	(0.007)	(0.007)
Constituency fixed effects	No	No	No	No	No
Village controls	No	Yes	Yes	Yes	Yes
Satellite sensor-age	Yes	Yes	Yes	Yes	Yes
Year trend	Yes	Yes	Yes	Yes	Yes
Constant	-0.8616**	-1.2339**	-1.2108*	-0.6520	-0.6533
	(0.128)	(0.239)	(0.539)	(0.552)	(0.549)
Observations	1,775,430	1,762,668	1,760,157	1,760,157	1,760,157

Robust standard errors clustered on assembly constituency in parentheses. BSP, Bahujan Samaj Party; CM, chief minister; INC, Indian National Congress Party; MLA, member of the legislative assembly; SP, Samajwadi Party.

** $p \le 0.01$; * $p \le 0.05$.

TABLE 7.8. *Logit regressions on villages lit or not, 1992–2010 using interpolated light values*

Dependent Variable: Village Lit (Using Bilinear Interpolation)	(1)	(2)	(3)	(4)	(5)
Election year	0.1999** (0.053)	0.2170** (0.057)	0.3035** (0.065)	0.5238** (0.069)	0.5292** (0.102)
BSP MLA	-0.0713 (0.068)	-0.0788 (0.073)	-0.0992 (0.074)	-0.0132 (0.073)	0.1588 (0.095)
INC MLA	-0.0580 (0.080)	-0.0620 (0.087)	-0.0876 (0.088)	-0.1036 (0.088)	0.0328 (0.124)
Other MLA	-0.1700 (0.096)	-0.1851 (0.105)	-0.2140* (0.108)	-0.2027 (0.108)	-0.3399* (0.135)
SP MLA	-0.0239 (0.062)	-0.0267 (0.067)	-0.0317 (0.068)	0.0283 (0.068)	-0.0109 (0.096)
Election year × BSP MLA	0.3433** (0.075)	0.3749** (0.082)	0.3070** (0.082)	0.1776* (0.084)	0.1940 (0.118)
Election year × INC MLA	-0.0500 (0.108)	-0.0555 (0.118)	-0.0846 (0.120)	-0.1126 (0.117)	-0.0534 (0.179)
Election year × Other MLA	0.2341* (0.101)	0.2574* (0.109)	0.2273* (0.110)	0.1758 (0.110)	0.1251 (0.167)
Election year × SP MLA	0.0639 (0.061)	0.0703 (0.066)	0.0306 (0.067)	-0.0354 (0.066)	-0.0386 (0.122)
BSP CM				-0.6456** (0.055)	-0.5400** (0.085)
Pres Rule CM				-1.3188** (0.118)	-1.4416** (0.153)
SP CM				-0.7566** (0.066)	-0.8101** (0.110)

(continued)

TABLE 7.8. (continued)

Dependent Variable: Village Lit (Using Bilinear Interpolation)	(1)	(2)	(3)	(4)	(5)
BSP MLA × BSP CM					−0.3880**
					(0.133)
All other MLA × CM interactions					Yes
Win margin			0.0061	0.0055	0.0059
			(0.003)	(0.003)	(0.003)
Turnout			−0.0216**	−0.0013	−0.0001
			(0.005)	(0.006)	(0.006)
Electors			−0.0043*	0.0002	0.0007
			(0.002)	(0.002)	(0.002)
Incumbent wins			−0.1120*	−0.0842	−0.0813
			(0.053)	(0.052)	(0.051)
Income (district level)		−0.0781	−0.3490	1.3928	1.3714
		(0.644)	(0.743)	(1.000)	(0.994)
Total power supply in state	0.0136**	0.0149**	0.0070	0.0019	0.0035
	(0.005)	(0.005)	(0.006)	(0.007)	(0.007)
Constituency fixed effects	Yes	Yes	Yes	Yes	Yes
Village controls	No	Yes	Yes	Yes	Yes
Satellite sensor-age	Yes	Yes	Yes	Yes	Yes
Year trend	Yes	Yes	Yes	Yes	Yes
Constant	1.0136**	1.0877**	3.7977**	1.0029	0.7522
	(0.112)	(0.234)	(0.655)	(0.784)	(0.772)
Observations	1,863,330	1,850,486	1,846,877	1,846,877	1,846,877

Robust standard errors clustered on assembly constituency in parentheses. BSP, Bahujan Samaj Party; CM, chief minister; INC, Indian National Congress Party; MLA, member of the legislative assembly; SP, Samajwadi Party.

$**p \leq 0.01$; $*p \leq 0.05$.

TABLE 7.9. *Fractional logit regressions on proportion of villages lit in constituency, 1992–2010*

Dependent Variable: Proportion Villages Lit	(1)	(2)	(3)	(4)	(5)
Election year	0.2048**	0.2029**	0.2574**	0.4676**	0.5221**
	(0.051)	(0.051)	(0.059)	(0.063)	(0.095)
BSP MLA	−0.0103	−0.0079	−0.0207	0.0559	0.1829*
	(0.066)	(0.067)	(0.068)	(0.068)	(0.093)
INC MLA	−0.0609	−0.0614	−0.0837	−0.0902	0.0734
	(0.087)	(0.087)	(0.089)	(0.087)	(0.109)
Other MLA	−0.0860	−0.0895	−0.1228	−0.0967	−0.1776
	(0.090)	(0.090)	(0.093)	(0.093)	(0.111)
SP MLA	−0.0225	−0.0227	−0.0251	0.0380	−0.0214
	(0.056)	(0.056)	(0.058)	(0.059)	(0.080)
Election year × BSP MLA	0.2998**	0.2971**	0.2410**	0.1164	0.0519
	(0.068)	(0.069)	(0.069)	(0.069)	(0.105)
Election year × INC MLA	−0.0645	−0.0659	−0.0884	−0.1202	−0.1895
	(0.108)	(0.108)	(0.109)	(0.109)	(0.145)
Election year × Other MLA	0.2318*	0.2305*	0.2080*	0.1520	0.0921
	(0.091)	(0.091)	(0.092)	(0.092)	(0.137)
Election year × SP MLA	0.0100	0.0095	−0.0193	−0.0826	−0.1326
	(0.058)	(0.058)	(0.058)	(0.058)	(0.106)
BSP CM				−0.5734**	−0.5191**
				(0.046)	(0.075)
Pres Rule CM				−1.1983**	−1.3472**
				(0.097)	(0.134)
SP CM				−0.6695**	−0.6937**
				(0.054)	(0.090)

(*continued*)

TABLE 7.9. (continued)

Dependent Variable: Proportion Villages Lit	(1)	(2)	(3)	(4)	(5)
BSP MLA × BSP CM					−0.2461*
					(0.119)
All other MLA × CM interactions					Yes
Win margin			0.0066*	0.0060*	0.0064*
			(0.003)	(0.003)	(0.003)
Turnout			−0.0173**	−0.0006	0.0006
			(0.004)	(0.005)	(0.005)
Electors			−0.0026	0.0011	0.0016
			(0.002)	(0.002)	(0.002)
Incumbent wins			−0.0461	−0.0222	−0.0251
			(0.048)	(0.048)	(0.048)
Income (district level)		0.6039	0.4864	1.9563*	1.9645*
		(0.553)	(0.611)	(0.814)	(0.811)
Total power supply in state	0.0060	0.0060	−0.0012	−0.0063	−0.0059
	(0.004)	(0.004)	(0.005)	(0.006)	(0.006)
Constituency fixed effects	Yes	Yes	Yes	Yes	Yes
Village controls	No	Yes	Yes	Yes	Yes
Satellite sensor-age	Yes	Yes	Yes	Yes	Yes
Year trend	Yes	Yes	Yes	Yes	Yes
Constant	0.7924**	9.1591**	11.3101**	8.3195**	7.9917**
	(0.098)	(0.371)	(1.017)	(1.151)	(1.146)
Observations	7,657	7,657	7,634	7,634	7,634

Robust standard errors clustered on assembly constituency in parentheses. BSP, Bahujan Samaj Party; CM, chief minister; INC, Indian National Congress Party; MLA, member of the legislative assembly; SP, Samajwadi Party.

**$p \leq 0.01$, *$p \leq 0.05$.

TABLE 7.10. *BSP effects on unmatched sample*

	Outcome: Newly Lit in 2003	
	(1)	(2)
Bahujan Samaj Party (BSP) treatment	1.0236	0.9037
	(0.6084)	(0.6305)
Scheduled Caste (SC) population share		−0.4696
		(0.6558)
BSP treatment × SC population share		−0.0997
		(0.7565)
Village-level controls		
Village population (thousands)		2.5873**
		(0.5593)
Literacy rate in village		0.0705
		(0.1628)
School in village		−0.2326
		(0.1460)
Medical facility in village		0.2097
		(0.1306)
Paved approach road to village		−0.0287**
		(0.0091)
Distance to nearest town (km)		12.8120*
		(5.4762)
Constituency-level controls		
Income index	16.6825**	0.0140
	(5.2632)	(0.5251)
Nighttime light output, 2001 (log)		0.7046
		(0.4454)
Reserved constituency		0.0527
		(0.0477)
SC population share		−2.5379
		(5.4108)
Constant	−10.7466	−14.5531**
	(2.2399)	(3.3334)
Observations	5902	5902
Assembly constituencies in sample	58	58

Standard errors in parentheses. **p-value ≤ 0.01; *p-value ≤ 0.05.

8

Conclusion

On April 27, 1994, 20 million South Africans cast ballots in the first free election in the country's history, electing Nelson Mandela and the African National Congress (ANC) party to power. Mandela inherited a country broken by the legacy of apartheid, with low levels of access to even the most basic goods for large swaths of the newly enfranchised population. Access to electricity was especially abysmal, reaching only a third of South African households, with four in five homes relying on the burning of wood for their energy needs.

As part of a sweeping initiative to reshape the country, the new ANC government announced an ambitious National Electrification Program (NEP), proposing rapid increases in electrification to black townships and rural areas, with the goal of universal electrification by 2012. By 2001, 2 million new households had been connected to the power grid, a faster rate of progress than during the first years of Franklin Roosevelt's Rural Electrification Administration (Dinkelman 2011). By 2007, South Africa's electrification rate had soared to 75 percent (Bekker et al. 2008), a seeming testament to the power of democracy in inducing governments to serve their citizens.

But as 2008 began, what had initially been sporadic power outages had become a full-scale pandemic. Widespread blackouts darkened the countryside, shut down commerce in Johannesburg and Cape Town, and even forced closures of the country's lucrative gold and diamond mines. Three months into the power crisis, analysts estimated that blackouts had cost the economy some $US 6.5 billion and stalled growth to its lowest quarterly rate in six years.[1] Long proud of their status as Africa's most modern and stable economy, South Africans responded to the power crisis with widespread anger against their government and its failed management of the state-owned power utility, Eskom.

---

[1] "South Africa's economy." *The Economist*, June 4, 2008.

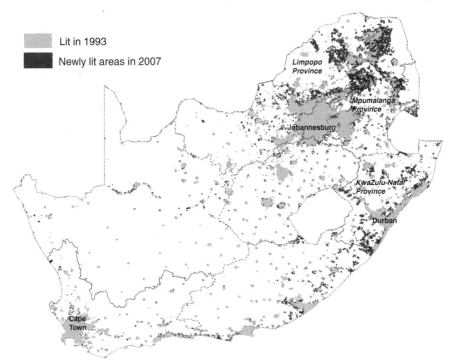

FIGURE 8.1. Expansion of electrified areas in South Africa, 1993 versus 2007.
Sources: NOAA-NGDC DMSP-OLS F101993 and F162007.

Speaking to the country during his state of the nation address that February, President Thabo Mbeki spent nearly 10 minutes of his hour-long speech discussing the electricity crisis, acknowledging that the government had failed its citizens and accepting responsibility for Eskom's inability to meet the nation's power demands. Having lost much of his legitimacy and amidst a bruising power struggle for leadership of the ANC, Mbeki resigned only some months later.

What had gone so terribly wrong? At least three factors contributed to South Africa's power crisis, all of which reflect the importance of political externalities in shaping how the ANC pursued its aim to deliver the basic public good of electricity to its citizens.

First, the government prioritized extension of the grid into impoverished rural areas and black townships that had long been overlooked by apartheid-era governments (Gaunt 2005). Given the racialized nature of elections in South Africa (Ferree 2006), the prioritization of these areas also served a compelling political purpose, allowing the ANC to strengthen its base and win new supporters in electorally important regions (Knoesen 2009; Kroth, Larcinese, and Wehner 2013). Figure 8.1 shows a change detection image comparing night light output at the end of apartheid in 1993 with output in 2007, just prior to the power crisis. The light gray zones represent previously lit areas, while the dark gray zones show newly lit areas that had successfully been electrified by 2007. Many of these newly electrified areas were concentrated in the northeast in ANC stronghold areas such as Limpopo and Mpumalenga provinces, where it was regularly winning more than 80 percent of the vote.

Motivated by political objectives, the ANC not only influenced which rural areas to electrify, but it also enacted policies delivering further benefits to its constituents, including a costly commitment in 2003 to provide free electricity by eliminating rates for poor households. Reflecting the political payoffs from its efforts, the ANC watched its national vote totals increase from 63 percent in 1994, to 66 percent in 1999, to a peak of 70 percent in the 2004 elections. Meanwhile, these policy choices added millions of low-profit consumers to Eskom's customer rolls, aggravating its financial difficulties.

Second, the ANC had failed to invest in the construction of new power plants, even as millions of consumers were added to the grid and demand for electricity climbed. For years, Eskom had expressed concern about electricity supply and demand trends in its strategic planning reports. But few of Eskom's costly power plant proposals were approved while the ANC prioritized more visible initiatives to deliver social services to black townships and rural areas where newly enfranchised voters were concentrated. Even power plant projects that were approved found themselves mired in political controversy. The massive Medupi power plant in Limpopo province promised to supply 4.8 gigawatts of desperately needed power in what would be the largest coal-burning power plant in the world. The World Bank, acknowledging the importance of energy for African development, committed $US 3.75 billion to support the project, the largest single project loan in the bank's history. However, protests regarding environmental impacts from the combustion of massive volumes of coal nearly derailed the project, a reminder that public goods schemes can have *negative* political externalities as well.

Third, increased difficulties in securing coal were forcing many of South Africa's power plants to operate at less than full capacity. Here too, political considerations were at work. In the awarding of coal supply contracts, the ANC had given preferential terms to black-owned firms as part of its broader commitment to empower black enterprises. Many of these new suppliers were small, lacking the economies of scale of larger firms. The shift toward smaller suppliers resulted in both higher coal prices for Eskom and increased supply chain problems, as small firms tended to rely on trucks for coal delivery, which further increased wear and tear on the supply roads leading to power plants (Eberhard 2011). Moreover, many small suppliers could not quickly ramp up supply as demand patterns shifted. At the peak of the power crisis, observers would note that coal problems contributed to breakdowns at some 20 power plants.[2]

---

[2] Myburgh, James. "Eskom: The Real Cause of the Crisis." PoliticsWeb, February 2008. http://www.politicsweb.co.za/politicsweb/view/politicsweb/en/page71627?oid=85789&sn=Detail

From the extension of the grid to the rural poor, to the prioritization of visible electrification efforts over the construction of costly and less alluring power plants, to the awarding of preferential contract terms, political externalities were critical in shaping the implementation of South Africa's national electrification efforts. Without a doubt, these political factors contributed to a historic improvement in electricity access for its citizens. At the same time, they shaped the conditions for crisis in the power sector that the country continues to struggle with today.

The South African experience illustrates the powerful role of political externalities in shaping how governments carry out their efforts to deliver public goods. Across the developing world, citizens look to their governments to provide basic goods and services such as education, roads, clean water, and electricity. Such goods undergird social welfare and enable economic development, and so demand for them is widespread, even when the ability of governments to supply them is not. How do governments decide how to provide these basic necessities? The answer to this question is fundamentally shaped by political externalities. From the timing and siting of projects, to the selection of contractors, to decisions about service delivery mechanisms and policies, every choice in the implementation of a public goods scheme has benefits and costs that accrue in the political arena, and not just on financial ledger sheets and in technical feasibility assessment reports. Political externalities shape the decisions that transform nebulous policy objectives into concrete activities and programs.

As I have shown in the previous chapters, the impacts of these political externalities are especially profound in democratic settings. As politicians seek to stay in office, public goods schemes are a compelling mechanism to win and sustain political support. Promises of better schools, improved electricity, and more roads are widely appealing and reflect a universalist veneer. Yet even the most transparent programmatic policy schemes require a multitude of scoping and ordering decisions to support their implementation. From the nitty-gritty details of how a service will be delivered to difficult questions about what areas to focus on first, every decision node generates political benefits and costs that are often as critical as the technical and economic factors that dominate project plans and official discourse. In electoral settings, these political externalities map tightly onto the reelection incentives that motivate politicians.

As a result of the added political motivation democratic leaders have to deliver public goods, they are provided at higher levels in democracies than in states without competitive elections. Using new data on electrification access derived from satellite imagery of the earth at night, I showed in Chapter 5 that democracies provide electricity to 10 percent more of their citizens than non-democratic states. For an average-size developing country in the post–World War II era, a consistent history of democratic rule could mean an additional 3.5 million more residents with electricity.

Not only does democracy induce broader levels of electricity provision, but it also affects who benefits from the efforts by office-seeking politicians, as they exert influence over where the grid goes and who receives its power. The political payoffs to electrification are especially high in the rural periphery, among the poor who are easily overlooked on economic grounds but command electoral significance given their numbers and receptiveness to the delivery of public goods. In Chapter 6, in a systematic comparison of the poorest regions of developing countries, I showed that democratic states consistently provide higher levels of electricity access to their poorest citizens than nondemocratic states, even after accounting for potential differences in economic, geographic, and demographic factors. These findings challenge the view that democracy is a luxury of the rich. In fact, *especially* among the world's poor, competitive elections have a large impact in inducing governments to target the poor with valuable public goods.

The importance of electoral considerations in shaping the provision of electricity is especially evident in India, where more people lack access to electricity than anywhere else in the world. In my evaluation of power politics in Uttar Pradesh, I showed that those who benefit from electricity can change over time. In a context of chronic shortages of electricity supply, systematic rolling blackouts and load shedding are used to protect the creaky grid. As Chapter 7 demonstrated, the incidence of these blackouts is far from random, following instead the electoral cycle and having less impact on areas represented by pro-poor parties.

As indicated by the struggles facing both India and South Africa's power sector, political externalities can have other effects beyond broader provision to the poor. One clear implication is that political considerations create a premium on activities that are most likely to result in immediate electoral payoffs, and a disincentive to focus on efforts that do not help win elections. Partly, this is a reminder of the well-known time inconsistency problem facing democratic politicians in pursuing investments whose benefits will not accrue until far into the future. But this also highlights that among the myriad activities that are required for the successful implementation of a public goods scheme, democratic politicians are more likely to champion those activities associated with visible outcomes and credit claiming opportunities, rather than those whose benefits are largely hidden from the public eye. Thus in both the Indian and South African cases, politicians advocated vigorously for efforts to extend the grid and provide electricity to new villages even as they ignored the obvious need to build more power plants to accommodate growing demand for electricity.

The argument of this book also provides perspective on a commonly raised question among policy analysts and scholars: How can we get governments to invest more in public goods and less in targetable goods and services that are susceptible to distortion and manipulation? Broad literatures on clientelism and distributive politics regularly observe that governments prefer targetable goods over public goods because of the greater ease by which they can be manipulated and withdrawn. As Keefer and Khemani (2005) state,

There is ample evidence that governments, particularly in poorer countries, prefer to spend more on targeted programs, such as government jobs or infrastructure investment, than on improvements in broad social services... The problem for development is that many governments have exaggerated preferences for targeted expenditures. (3)

Implicit in such observations is the belief that greater investments in public goods would be preferable and less subject to distortion. Lamenting the large fraction of government budgets "not devoted to genuinely useful public projects, but rather to redistribution and pork-barrel projects," Lizzeri and Persico (2001) argue, "it would be desirable to reduce the money tied up in redistribution, and increase the fraction devoted to public goods" (225).

Yet these arguments assume that activities of the state can be neatly classified as private goods or as public goods. This book has shown that this is a false dichotomy. Even the most broad public goods scheme has not only components that provide nonrival and nonexcludable benefits but also private goods components that can be shaped, targeted, and delivered in politically consequential ways. The political externalities associated with public goods schemes are critical factors that motivate politicians to pursue their provision. To assume that there is a sphere of state goods and services that do not generate political externalities and that can be produced in a politically neutral way would contradict the evidence presented in this book's chapters.

Energy Politics and Climate Change

The findings of this book also point to some daunting implications regarding climate change. In 1990, the Intergovernmental Panel on Climate Change (IPCC) released its landmark report identifying human activities as the primary cause of a greenhouse effect that was raising global mean temperatures. Of all these human activities, none is responsible for more greenhouse gas emissions than electricity generation. Yet, since 1990, global electricity consumption has nearly doubled, a rate faster than global population growth or global economic growth. Human demand for electricity appears to show no signs of slowing down, and political institutions are what shape the responsiveness of governments to meet the demand of their citizens. Simply put, politics determines who gets electricity, and how much electricity is provided shapes the trajectory of climate change.

Figure 8.2 shows the relationship between income level and electricity consumption for countries around the world in 2009. The figure depicts a strong and positive relationship: people in richer countries use more electricity per person than those in poorer countries. At first glance, this pattern would seem intuitive. Yet, there are at least two striking features worth worrying about. First, there is no evidence that energy demands are satiated with increasing

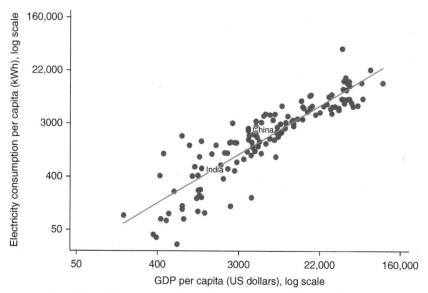

FIGURE 8.2. Electricity consumption and income around the world, 2009.
Source: World Bank Development Indicators.

wealth. This is quite different from many other indicators of human welfare that tend to approach some natural limit. Life expectancy, infant mortality rates, literacy rates, and calorie consumption, all improve rapidly as societies move up the development ladder, but progress eventually slows down or reaches a bound set by human biology or by the achievement of some goal. Energy consumption appears to exhibit no such willingness to slow down at higher levels of development (Asafu-Adjaye 2000, Chontanawat et al. 2009).

Second, there is no indication that energy efficiency improves with wealth. This is not to imply that efficiency gains are not possible with wealth, but rather that the current global trajectory does not indicate such a trend. Richer countries do not seem to put more effort into becoming more energy efficient. Put another way, as countries become richer, it does not appear that wealth enables the production of increased economic output with lower levels of energy inputs. Rather, in an example of the Jevons Paradox, increases in income seem to lead to increased electricity use, even though wealth should make it possible to use energy more efficiently (Sorell 2009, Alcott 2005).

Combined, these two features reflect an agonizingly inconvenient fact about development: as countries develop and lift their populations out of poverty, this is likely to entail a parallel increase in the consumption of electricity. Because there is little evidence that increases in wealth will be accompanied by a decline in energy consumption or increased efficiency in its use, the pressures on the climate induced by development are likely to be intense.

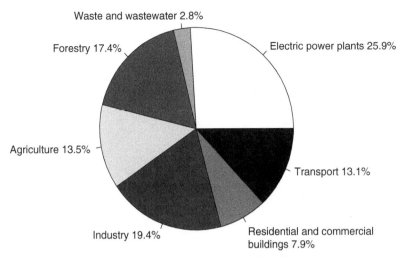

FIGURE 8.3. Anthropogenic greenhouse gas emissions by source, 2004.
Source: Intergovernmental Panel on Climate Change (2007).

According to the IPCC, electricity generation is the single most important source of anthropogenic greenhouse gas emissions. Emissions from power plants produce 26 percent of greenhouse gases, twice as much as is generated by cars, planes, trains, and all other transportation sources combined (Figure 8.3). By 2008, carbon dioxide (CO_2) emissions from power generation represented more than 27 percent of the total anthropogenic CO_2 emissions. Total CO_2 emissions from electricity plants generation have tripled since 1970, outpacing even the rise in emissions from automobiles and trucks (Figure 8.4).

What do the findings of this book mean for the trajectory of energy consumption and climate change? First, they suggest that not all governments will respond in the same way to the growing energy demands of their citizens. Electoral pressures induce democracies to prioritize the delivery of electricity because of its valuable political externalities. Although this dynamic has contributed to significant increases in access to electricity, especially among the rural poor in democratic states in the short run, it may mean added strain on the environment in the long run.

Second, acknowledging the constraints imposed by the domestic political environment can also help in understanding why achieving a global consensus around mitigating climate change is so difficult. The unwillingness of the US Congress to consider the Kyoto Protocol, which committed industrialized states to reducing their overall greenhouse gas emissions, and the eventual withdrawal of Canada from the pact to which it was an original signatory, reflect political calculations as much as they do economic and environmental ones.

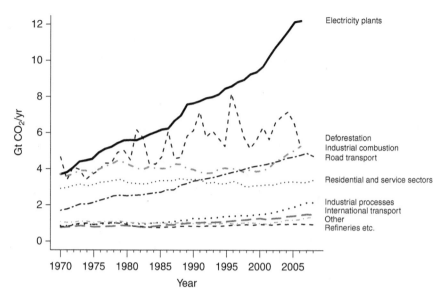

FIGURE 8.4. Carbon dioxide emissions by source, 1970–2008.
Source: Adapted from European Commission, Joint Research Centre (JRC)/Netherlands Environmental Assessment Agency (PBL). Emission Database for Global Atmospheric Research (EDGAR), release version 4.2. http://edgar.jrc.ec.europa.eu, 2011.

Third, it is imperative to acknowledge that the political externalities associated with energy access vary dramatically across regime types and political settings. As a result, the viability of any specific policy proposal to address impacts of energy use on the climate will vary accordingly. The key sources of domestic opposition and support will differ across countries with different political systems such as India and China. Recognizing this implies that one-size-fits-all solutions are unlikely to succeed and that more innovative proposals that recognize the political constraints and opportunities that exist across different regime types are needed.

New technologies will surely help. Solar panels, wind turbines, and other renewable energy solutions offer an exciting vista of opportunity for the billions who still have limited access to electrical power. Solar energy in particular offers far more promise than we have yet tapped. The total energy consumed by humans in 2008 is equivalent to the energy from the sun hitting the earth in a little more than one hour. Yet substantial technical hurdles remain. Historically, electricity has been generated most efficiently at large centralized power plants and the loss of economies of scale implied by a transition to small off-grid solutions would be substantial. Moreover, large cost improvements in energy storage remain necessary to overcome the problems of intermittency associated with wind and solar power.

In any case, technological innovation alone is no panacea. Beyond the economic and technical obstacles that will need to be overcome, this book has shown that all efforts to deliver public goods, whether these be electricity generated from dirty coal-burning plants or green energy from renewable sources, are accompanied by political externalities. These political considerations motivate state leaders to pursue the provision of public goods, because politicians are motivated by political payoffs at least as much as they are by economic and technical factors. All of this implies the need to incorporate a deeply political perspective in the ongoing dialogue on the world's energy needs. As economies grow, so too will the thirst for energy. The ways in which that thirst is quenched, and the attendant impacts on our climate, will be shaped by political institutions in ways that cannot be ignored.

Appendix

Satellite-Derived Estimates of Electrification

Electrification rates in 2003. Derived from analysis of night lights imagery from DMSP-OLS 2003 (F15 time stable annual composite) and population data from LandScan 2006. See Chapter 5 for details.

Rank	Country	Electrification rate as observed by satellite (%)	Population in unlit areas (millions)	Total population (millions)
1	Burundi	12.0	7.20	8.19
2	Rwanda	17.0	8.00	9.64
3	Cambodia	20.6	11.06	13.92
4	Myanmar (Burma)	30.2	32.11	46.00
5	Laos	30.6	4.42	6.37
6	Papua New Guinea	31.6	3.47	5.06
7	Afghanistan	33.1	20.78	31.08
8	Zaire	33.4	41.51	62.35
9	Ethiopia	36.3	47.61	74.79
10	Haiti	36.4	5.05	7.94
11	Burkina Faso	40.6	8.26	13.90
12	Madagascar	40.9	11.05	18.70
13	Kenya	41.0	20.80	35.24
14	Guinea	41.9	5.65	9.72
15	Eritrea	42.6	2.73	4.75
16	Sierra Leone	43.5	3.33	5.89
17	Cameroon	45.1	9.63	17.54
18	Uganda	45.8	15.90	29.34
19	Nepal	45.9	15.47	28.61
20	Angola	47.0	6.35	11.96
21	Malawi	47.9	6.93	13.29

(*continued*)

Rank	Country	Electrification rate as observed by satellite (%)	Population in unlit areas (millions)	Total population (millions)
22	Tanzania	49.5	18.49	36.65
23	Mozambique	51.3	9.87	20.25
24	Korea, North	51.4	11.09	22.81
25	Mali	52.2	5.59	11.70
26	Swaziland	53.7	0.53	1.14
27	Niger	56.2	5.48	12.51
28	Chad	57.6	4.24	9.99
29	Guinea-Bissau	57.8	0.50	1.18
30	Zimbabwe	58.4	5.08	12.20
31	Namibia	59.4	0.83	2.05
32	Mauritania	60.8	1.25	3.18
33	Central African Republic	60.9	1.66	4.24
34	Yemen	61.4	8.17	21.17
35	Zambia	62.3	4.27	11.34
36	Ivory Coast	62.8	6.31	16.98
37	Senegal	63.6	4.35	11.93
38	Gambia, The	63.8	0.57	1.57
39	Ghana	65.7	7.52	21.92
40	Benin	65.9	2.71	7.95
41	Nigeria	65.9	44.65	131.09
42	Congo	66.4	1.26	3.76
43	Honduras	66.5	2.39	7.14
44	Bangladesh	66.8	48.04	144.69
45	Nicaragua	67.0	1.82	5.52
46	Sudan	67.5	13.40	41.22
47	Lesotho	67.6	0.65	2.00
48	Togo	68.4	1.75	5.54
49	Thailand	71.0	18.61	64.22
50	Botswana	71.7	0.45	1.61
51	China	71.8	367.00	1300.81
52	Somalia	72.1	2.46	8.82
53	Georgia	72.2	1.25	4.52
54	Peru	73.6	7.45	28.27
55	Liberia	74.0	0.69	2.64
56	India	75.2	275.00	1107.75
57	Philippines	76.6	19.87	84.89
58	Moldova	77.1	0.96	4.18
59	Bolivia	77.5	2.02	8.95
60	Morocco	78.0	7.22	32.86
61	South Africa	78.7	9.37	44.01
62	Gabon	79.6	0.27	1.33
63	Belarus	79.6	1.99	9.76

Rank	Country	Electrification rate as observed by satellite (%)	Population in unlit areas (millions)	Total population (millions)
64	Guatemala	80.1	2.47	12.44
65	Albania	80.2	0.70	3.56
66	Latvia	80.3	0.44	2.24
67	Ecuador	80.4	2.53	12.90
68	Lithuania	80.6	0.88	4.51
69	Vietnam	81.0	15.70	82.87
70	Paraguay	82.6	1.13	6.50
71	Panama	82.7	0.53	3.06
72	Indonesia	83.4	36.82	221.87
73	Azerbaijan	83.7	1.28	7.90
74	Colombia	85.2	6.41	43.32
75	Cuba	85.5	1.57	10.84
76	Bosnia and Herzegovina	85.9	0.64	4.50
77	Turkey	85.9	9.72	68.85
78	Armenia	86.1	0.41	2.98
79	Kazakhstan	86.3	2.10	15.33
80	Brazil	86.5	24.89	184.23
81	Ukraine	87.3	5.93	46.67
82	Estonia	88.0	0.16	1.30
83	Mongolia	88.4	0.33	2.83
84	Tajikistan	90.7	0.65	6.95
85	El Salvador	91.0	0.61	6.79
86	Kyrgyzstan	91.2	0.45	5.13
87	Romania	91.8	1.83	22.34
88	Sri Lanka	92.1	1.58	19.99
89	Dominican Republic	92.2	0.71	9.10
90	Russia	92.3	10.86	140.89
91	New Zealand	92.5	0.28	3.68
92	Tunisia	92.6	0.72	9.71
93	Chile	92.6	1.18	15.87
94	Costa Rica	92.6	0.30	4.07
95	Argentina	93.0	2.79	39.61
96	Algeria	93.1	2.26	32.68
97	Malaysia	93.2	1.53	22.37
98	Pakistan	93.5	10.82	165.60
99	Turkmenistan	93.6	0.32	5.05
100	Bulgaria	93.6	0.47	7.32
101	Yugoslavia	93.6	0.69	10.80
102	Iraq	93.8	1.66	26.78
103	Mexico	94.8	5.53	106.77
104	Macedonia	95.4	0.10	2.05
105	Iran	95.9	2.68	64.80

(*continued*)

Rank	Country	Electrification rate as observed by satellite (%)	Population in unlit areas (millions)	Total population (millions)
106	Syria	96.0	0.74	18.53
107	Venezuela	96.4	0.90	25.10
108	Uzbekistan	96.5	0.96	27.23
109	Uruguay	96.8	0.11	3.31
110	Australia	96.9	0.61	19.87
111	Croatia	97.0	0.12	4.16
112	Poland	97.0	1.15	38.48
113	Norway	97.2	0.11	3.90
114	Ireland	97.5	0.14	5.58
115	Slovenia	97.6	0.05	1.96
116	France	97.8	1.31	59.62
117	Oman	98.0	0.06	2.79
118	Spain	98.0	0.78	39.04
119	Portugal	98.0	0.20	10.21
120	Denmark	98.1	0.09	5.08
121	Hungary	98.2	0.18	9.99
122	Greece	98.4	0.16	9.89
123	Slovakia	98.6	0.07	5.43
124	Jordan	99.0	0.08	8.25
125	Saudi Arabia	99.1	0.25	26.61
126	Germany	99.2	0.65	82.27
127	Canada	99.2	0.25	32.48
128	Libya	99.3	0.04	5.85
129	United Kingdom	99.4	0.35	57.71
130	United States	99.4	1.77	294.02
131	Sweden	99.5	0.04	8.42
132	Austria	99.6	0.03	8.19
133	Lebanon	99.6	0.01	3.77
134	Finland	99.7	0.01	5.06
135	Italy	99.7	0.16	56.82
136	Trinidad and Tobago	99.7	0.00	1.00
137	Japan	99.7	0.32	123.69
138	Switzerland	99.8	0.01	7.61
139	Jamaica	99.9	0.00	2.57
140	Israel	99.9	0.01	7.85
141	Czech Republic	99.9	0.01	10.23
142	Egypt	100.0	0.03	78.02
143	Taiwan	100.0	0.01	22.37
144	Netherlands	100.0	0.00	16.35
145	United Arab Emirates	100.0	0.00	2.24
146	Belgium	100.0	0.00	10.49
147	Korea, South	100.0	0.00	46.44
148	Kuwait	100.0	0.00	2.36

References

Aaron, Henry, and Martin McGuire. 1970. "Public goods and income distribution." *Econometrica: Journal of the Econometric Society* 38(6): 907–920.

Abbott, Malcolm. 2001. "Is the security of electricity supply a public good?" *The Electricity Journal* 14(7): 31–33.

Acemoglu, Daron, and James A. Robinson. 2006a. "Economic backwardness in political perspective." *American Political Science Review* 100(01): 115–131.

2006b. *Economic origins of dictatorship and democracy*. New York: Cambridge University Press.

Ades, Alberto F., and Edward L Glaeser. 1995. "Trade and circuses: Explaining urban giants." *The Quarterly Journal of Economics* 110(1): 195–227.

Agnew, John, Thomas Gillespie, Jorge Gonzalez, and Brian Min. 2008. "Baghdad nights: Evaluating the US military surge using night light signatures." *Environment and Planning A* 40(10): 2285–2295.

Aidt, Toke S., and Bianca Dallal. 2008. "Female voting power: The contribution of women's suffrage to the growth of social spending in Western Europe (1869–1960)." *Public Choice* 134(3–4): 391–417.

Aidt, Toke S., and Dalibor S. Eterovic. 2011. "Political competition, electoral participation and public finance in 20th century Latin America." *European Journal of Political Economy* 27(1): 181–200.

Aidt, Toke S., and Peter S. Jensen. 2013. "Democratization and the size of government: Evidence from the long 19th century." *Public Choice* 157(3–4): 511–542.

Ake, Claude. 2000. *Feasibility of democracy in Africa*. Dakar, Senegal: Council for the Development of Social Science Research in Africa.

Alcott, Blake. 2005. "Jevons' paradox." *Ecological Economics* 54(1):9–21.

Alesina, Alberto, Reza Baqir, and William Easterly. 1999. "Public goods and ethnic divisions." *Quarterly Journal of Economics* 114(4): 1243–1284.

Allcott, Hunt, Allan Collard-Wexler, and Stephen D. O'Connell. 2014. "How do electricity shortages affect productivity? Evidence from India." Working Paper No. 19977. Cambridge, MA: National Bureau of Economic Research.

Ansell, Ben W. 2010. *From the ballot to the blackboard: The redistributive political economy of education*. Cambridge and New York: Cambridge University Press.

Asafu-Adjaye, John. 2000. "The relationship between energy consumption, energy prices and economic growth: time series evidence from Asian developing countries." *Energy Economics* 22(6):615–625.

Asher, Sam, and Paul Novosad. 2013. "Politics and local economic growth: Evidence from India." Unpublished manuscript.

Azam, Jean-Paul. 2001. "The redistributive state and conflicts in Africa." *Journal of Peace Research* 38(4): 429–444.

Bairoch, Paul. 1988. *Cities and economic development: From the dawn of history to the present.* Los Angeles and Berkeley: University of California Press.

Banerjee, Abhijit V., and Rohini Pande. 2007. "Parochial politics: Ethnic preferences and politician corruption." KSG Working Paper No. RWP07-031. Available at http://dx.doi.org/10.2139/ssrn.976548

Banerjee, Abhijit, and Rohini Somanathan. 2007. "The political economy of public goods: Some evidence from India." *Journal of Development Economics* 82(2): 287–314.

Banerjee, Abhijit, Rohini Somanathan, and Lakshmi Iyer. 2005. "History, social divisions and public goods in rural India." *Journal of the European Economic Association* 3(2–3): 639–647.

Bardhan, Pranab. 1984. *The political economy of development in India.* Oxford and New York: Basil Blackwell.

Bardhan, Pranab, and Dilip Mookherjee. 2000. "Capture and governance at local and national levels." *The American Economic Review* 90(2): 135–139.

Barkan, Joel D., M. L. McNulty, and M. A. O. Ayeni. 1991. "'Hometown' voluntary associations, local development, and the emergence of civil society in western Nigeria." *The Journal of Modern African Studies* 29(3): 457–480.

Barnes, Douglas F., and Willem M. Floor. 1996. "Rural energy in developing countries: A challenge for economic development." *Annual Review of Energy and the Environment* 21: 497–530.

Barro, Robert J. 1996. "Democracy and growth." *Journal of Economic Growth* 1(1): 1–27.

Baskaran, Thushyanthan, Brian Min, and Yogesh Uppal. 2015. "Election cycles and electricity provision: Evidence from a quasi-experiment with Indian special elections." *Journal of Public Economics.* In press.

Bates, Robert. 1981. *Markets and states in tropical Africa: The political basis of agricultural policies.* Berkeley and Los Angeles: University of California Press.

2008. *When things fell apart: State failure in late-century Africa.* Cambridge and New York: Cambridge University Press.

Bekker, Bernard, Anton Eberhard, Trevor Gaunt, and Andrew Marquard. 2008. "South Africa's rapid electrification programme: Policy, institutional, planning, financing and technical innovations." *Energy Policy* 36(8): 3125–3137.

Berenschot, Ward. 2010. "Everyday mediation: The politics of public service delivery in Gujarat, India." *Development and Change* 41(5): 883–905.

Berry, William D. 1979. "Utility regulation in the states: The policy effects of professionalism and salience to the consumer." *American Journal of Political Science* 23(2): 263–277.

Bertrand, Elodie. 2006. "The Coasean analysis of lighthouse financing: Myths and realities." *Cambridge Journal of Economics* 30(3): 389–402.

Besley, Timothy. 2006. *Principled agents?: The political economy of good government.* New York: Oxford University Press.

Besley, Timothy, and Robin Burgess. 2002. "The political economy of government responsiveness: Theory and evidence from India." *Quarterly Journal of Economics* 117(4): 1415–1451.

Besley, Timothy, and Stephen Coate. 1998. "Sources of inefficiency in a representative democracy: A dynamic analysis." *American Economic Review* 88(1): 139–156.

Besley, Timothy, and Maitreesh Ghatak. 2006. "Public goods and economic development." In *Understanding poverty*, ed. Abhijit V. Banerjee, Roland Bénabou, and Dilip Mookherjee, pp. 285–302. Oxford and New York: Oxford University Press.

Besley, Timothy, and Masayuki Kudamatsu. 2006. "Health and democracy." *The American Economic Review* 96(2): 313–318.

Besley, Timothy, and Torsten Persson. 2009. "The origins of state capacity: Property rights, taxation, and politics." *American Economic Review* 99(4): 1218–1244.

Blaydes, Lisa. 2013. *Elections and distributive politics in Mubarak's Egypt.* Cambridge and New York: Cambridge University Press.

Blaydes, Lisa, and Mark Andreas Kayser. 2011. "Counting calories: Democracy and distribution in the developing world." *International Studies Quarterly* 55(4): 887–908.

Blimpo, Moussa P., Robin Harding, and Leonard Wantchekon. 2013. "Public investment in rural infrastructure: Some political economy considerations." *Journal of African Economies* 22(Suppl 2): 57–83.

Boix, Carles. 2001. "Democracy, development, and the public sector." *American Journal of Political Science* 45(1): 1–17.

2003. *Democracy and redistribution.* New York: Cambridge University Press.

Brass, Paul R. 1994. *The politics of India since independence.* New York: Cambridge University Press.

Bratton, Michael, and Nicholas van de Walle. 1994. "Neopatrimonial regimes and political transitions in Africa." *World Politics* 46(4): 453–489.

Brautigam, Deborah, Odd Helge Fjeldstad, and Mick Moore, ed. 2008. *Taxation and state-building in developing countries: Capacity and consent.* New York: Cambridge University Press.

Briggs, Ryan C. 2012. "Electrifying the base? Aid and incumbent advantage in Ghana." *The Journal of Modern African Studies* 50(4): 603–624.

Brown, David S., and Ahmed M. Mobarak. 2009. "The transforming power of democracy: Regime type and the distribution of electricity." *American Political Science Review* 103(2): 193–213.

Brownlee, W. Elliot. 2004. *Federal taxation in America: A short history*, 2nd ed. Cambridge and New York: Cambridge University Press.

Broz, J. Lawrence, and Daniel Maliniak. 2011. "Malapportionment, gasoline taxes, and climate change." Typescript. University of California, San Diego.

Buchanan, James M. 1965. "An economic theory of clubs." *Economica 32(125): 1–14.*

Bueno de Mesquita, Bruce, Alastair Smith, Randolph M. Siverson, and James D. Morrow. 2003. *The logic of political survival.* Cambridge, MA: MIT Press.

Calvo, Ernesto, and Maria Victoria Murillo. 2004. "Who delivers? Partisan clients in the Argentine electoral market." *American Journal of Political Science* 48(4): 742–757.

Campbell, David. 2000. "When the lights came on." *Rural Cooperatives* 67(4): 6–9.

Canning, David. 1998. "A database of world stocks of infrastructure, 1950–95." *World Bank Economic Review* 12(3): 529.

Chandra, Kanchan. 2004. *Why ethnic parties succeed.* Cambridge and New York: Cambridge University Press.

Chaudhury, Nazmul, Jeffrey Hammer, Michael Kremer, Karthik Muralidharan, and F. Halsey Rogers. 2006. "Missing in action: Teacher and health worker absence in developing countries." *The Journal of Economic Perspectives* 20(1): 91–116.

Cheibub, José A., and Jennifer Gandhi. 2004. "Classifying political regimes: A six-fold measure of democracies and dictatorships." Typescript. Presented at annual meeting of the American Political Science Association, Chicago.

Cheibub, José Antonio, Jennifer Gandhi, and James Raymond Vreeland. 2010. "Democracy and dictatorship revisited." *Public Choice* 143(1–2): 67–101.

Chen, Jowei, and Jonathan Rodden. 2013. "Unintentional gerrymandering: Political geography and electoral bias in legislatures." *The Quarterly Journal of Political Science* 8(3): 239–269.

Chen, Xi, and William D. Nordhaus. 2011. "Using luminosity data as a proxy for economic statistics." *Proceedings of the National Academy of Sciences* 108(21) 8589–8594.

Chhibber, Pradeep, and Irfan Nooruddin. 2004. "Do party systems count? The number of parties and government performance in the Indian states." *Comparative Political Studies* 37(2): 152–187.

Chhibber, Pradeep, Sandeep Shastri, and Richard Sisson. 2004. "Federal arrangements and the provision of public goods in India." *Asian Survey* 44(3): 339–352.

Chontanawat, Jaruwan, Lester C. Hunt, and Richard Pierse. 2008. "Does energy consumption cause economic growth?: Evidence from a systematic study of over 100 countries." *Journal of Policy Modeling* 30(2):209–220.

Coase, Ronald H. 1974. "The lighthouse in economics." *Journal of Law and Economics* 17(2): 357–376.

Collie, Melissa P. 1988. "Universalism and the parties in the US House of Representatives, 1921–80." *American Journal of Political Science* 32(4): 865–883.

Cornes, Richard. 1996. *The theory of externalities, public goods, and club goods.* Cambridge and New York: Cambridge University Press.

Cox, Gary, and Matthew McCubbins. 2001. "The Institutional determinants of economic policy outcomes." In *Structure and policy in presidential democracies,* ed. Stephan Haggard and Matthew McCubbins, pp. 21–63. New York: Cambridge University Press.

Dahl, Robert A. 1971. *Polyarchy: Participation and opposition.* New Haven: Yale University Press.

Das, S.K. 2001. *Public office, private interest: Bureaucracy and corruption in India.* New Delhi: Oxford University Press.

Davis, James C., and J Vernon Henderson. 2003. "Evidence on the political economy of the urbanization process." *Journal of Urban Economics* 53(1): 98–125.

Deaton, Angus, and Jean Drèze. 2002. "Poverty and inequality in India: A reexamination." *Economic and Political Weekly* 37(36): 3729–3748.

de Mesquita, Bruce Bueno, and Alastair Smith. 2011. *The dictator's handbook: Why bad behavior is almost always good politics.* New York: PublicAffairs.

Démurger, Sylvie, Jeffrey D. Sachs, Wing Thye Woo, Shuming Bao, Gene Chang, and Andrew Mellinger. 2002. "Geography, economic policy, and regional development in China." *Asian Economic Papers* 1(1): 146–197.

Di Bella, Gabriel, Lawrence Norton, Joseph Ntamatungiro, Sumiko Ogawa, Issouf Samaké, Marika Santoro. 2015. "Energy subsidies in Latin America and the Caribbean: Stocktaking and policy challenges." Technical report. Working Paper 15/30, International Monetary Fund.

Diamond, Larry Jay. 1990. "Three paradoxes of democracy." *Journal of Democracy* 1(3): 48–60.

Diaz-Cayeros, Alberto. 2008. "Electoral risk and redistributive politics in Mexico and the United States." *Studies in Comparative International Development* 43(2): 129–150.

Diaz-Cayeros, Alberto, Beatriz Magaloni, and Federico Estévez. Forthcoming. *Strategies of Vote Buying: Democracy, Clientelism, and Poverty Relief in Mexico*. New York: Cambridge University Press.

Dinkelman, Taryn. 2011. "The effects of rural electrification on employment: New evidence from South Africa." *The American Economic Review* 101(7): 3078–3108.

Dixit, Avinash, and John Londregan. 1996. "The determinants of success of special interests in redistributive politics." *The Journal of Politics* 58(4): 1132–1155.

Dobson, Jerome E., Edward A. Bright, Phillip R. Coleman, Richard C. Durfee, and Brian A. Worley. 2000. "LandScan: a global population database for estimating populations at risk." *Photogrammetric Engineering and Remote Sensing* 66(7):849–857.

Doll, Christopher N. H., Jan-Peter Muller, and Christopher D. Elvidge. 2000. "Night-time imagery as a tool for global mapping of socioeconomic parameters and greenhouse gas emissions." *AMBIO: A Journal of the Human Environment* 29(3): 157–162.

Doll, C. N. H., J. P. Muller, and J. G. Morley. 2006. "Mapping regional economic activity from night-time light satellite imagery." *Ecological Economics* 57(1): 75–92.

Doucouliagos, Hristos, and Mehmet Ali Ulubasoglu. 2008. "Democracy and economic growth: A meta-analysis." *American Journal of Political Science* 52(1): 61–83.

Drèze, Jean, and Haris Gazdar. 1996. "Uttar Pradesh: The burden of inertia." In *Indian development: Selected regional perspectives*, ed. Jean Drèze, and Amartya Sen, pp. 33–128. New Delhi: Oxford University Press.

Dubash, Navroz K., and Sudhir C. Rajan. 2002. "Electricity reform under political constraints." In *Power politics: Equity and environment in electricity reform*, ed. Navroz K. Dubash, pp. 51–73. Washington, DC: World Resources Institute.

Duncan, Ian. 1999. "Dalits and politics in rural north India: The Bahujan Samaj Party in Uttar Pradesh." *Journal of Peasant Studies* 27(1): 35–60.

Dunning, Thad, and Janhavi Nilekani. 2013. "Ethnic quotas and political mobilization: caste, parties, and distribution in Indian village councils." *American Political Science Review* 107(1): 35–56.

Eberhard, Anton. 2011. The future of South African Coal: Market, investment, and policy challenges. Technical Report. PESD Working Paper 100, Stanford.

Eberhard, Anton, Orvika Rosnes, Maria Shkaratan, and Haakon Vennemo. 2011. *Africa's power infrastructure: Investment, integration, efficiency*. Washington, DC: The World Bank.

Elvidge, Christopher D., Daniel Ziskin, Kimberly E. Baugh, Benjamin T. Tuttle, Tilottama Ghosh, Dee W. Pack, Edward H. Erwin, and Mikhail Zhizhin. 2009. "A fifteen year record of global natural gas flaring derived from satellite data." *Energies* 2(3): 595–622.

Elvidge, Christopher D., Kimberly E. Baugh, Eric A. Kihn, Herbert W. Kroehl, and Ethan R. Davis. 1997a. "Mapping city lights with nighttime data from the DMSP

Operational Linescan System." *Photogrammetric Engineering & Remote Sensing* 63(6): 727–734.

Elvidge, Christopher D., Kimberley E. Baugh, Eric A. Kihn, Herbert W. Kroehl, Ethan R. Davis, and Chris W. Davis. 1997b. "Relation between satellite observed visible-near infrared emissions, population, economic activity, and power consumption." *International Journal of Remote Sensing* 18(6): 1373–1379.

Elvidge, Christopher D., Marc L. Imhoff, Kimberly E. Baugh, Vinita Ruth Hobson, Ingrid Nelson, Jeff Safran, John B. Dietz, and Benjamin T. Tuttle. 2001. "Night-time lights of the world: 1994–1995." *ISPRS Journal of Photogrammetry & Remote Sensing* 56: 81–99.

Erikson, Robert S. 1972. "Malapportionment, gerrymandering, and party fortunes in Congressional elections." *The American Political Science Review* 66(4): 1234–1245.

Fearon, James D. 2011. "Self-enforcing democracy." *Quarterly Journal of Economics* 126(4): 1661–1708.

Fearon, James D., and David D. Laitin. 2003. "Ethnicity, insurgency, and civil war." *American Political Science Review* 97(1): 75–90.

Fehr, Ernst, and Simon Gächter. 2000. "Cooperation and punishment in public goods experiments." *American Economic Review* 90(4): 980–994.

Ferree, Karen E. 2006. "Explaining South Africa's racial census." *Journal of Politics* 68(4): 803–815.

Fox, Jonathan. 1996. "How does civil society thicken? The political construction of social capital in rural Mexico." *World Development* 24(6): 1089–1103.

Fox, William F., and Tim R. Smith. 1990. "Public infrastructure policy and economic development." *Economic Review* 75: 49–59.

Franco, Álvaro, Carlos Álvarez-Dardet, and Maria Teresa Ruiz. 2004. "Effect of democracy on health: Ecological study." *BNJ* 329(7480): 1421–1423.

Friedman, Thomas L. 2008. *Hot, flat, and crowded: Why we need a green revolution – and how it can renew America.* New York: Macmillan.

Fuller, Wayne Edison. 1964. *RFD: The changing face of rural America.* Bloomington: Indiana University Press.

Fund for Peace. 2008. "The failed states index." *Foreign Policy* 197: 64–68.

Gallagher, Michael, and Paul Mitchell. 2005. *The politics of electoral systems.* Cambridge and New York: Cambridge University Press.

Gandhi, Jennifer. 2008. *Political institutions under dictatorship.* Cambridge and New York: Cambridge University Press.

Gandhi, Jennifer, and Adam Przeworski. 2006. "Cooperation, cooptation, and rebellion under dictatorships." *Economics and Politics* 18(1): 1–26.

Gaunt, C. T. 2005. "Meeting electrification's social objectives in South Africa, and implications for developing countries." *Energy Policy* 33(10): 1309–1317.

Geddes, Barbara. 1996. *Politician's dilemma: Building state capacity in Latin America.* Berkeley: University of California Press.

Gehlbach, Scott, and Philip Keefer. 2011. "Investment without democracy: Ruling-party institutionalization and credible commitment in autocracies." *Journal of Comparative Economics* 39(2): 123–139.

Gelman, Andrew, and Jennifer Hill. 2007. *Data analysis using regression and multilevel/hierarchical models.* New York: Cambridge University Press.

Gillespie, Thomas W., Elizabeth Frankenberg, Kai Fung Chum, and Duncan Thomas. 2014. "Night-time lights time series of tsunami damage, recovery, and economic metrics in Sumatra, Indonesia." *Remote Sensing Letters* 5(3): 286–294.

Gleditsch, Kristian. 2003. "Distance between capital cities dataset." University of Essex. http://privatewww.essex.ac.uk/~ksg/data-5.html

Golden, Miriam, and Brian Min. 2013. "Distributive politics around the world." *Annual Review of Political Science* 16: 73–99.

Golden, Miriam, and Lucio Picci. 2005. "Proposal for a new measure of corruption, illustrated with Italian data." *Economics and Politics* 17(1): 37–75.

Golder, Matt. 2005. "Democratic electoral systems around the world, 1946–2000." *Electoral Studies* 24(1): 103–121.

Gradstein, Mark. 1993. "Rent seeking and the provision of public goods." *Economic Journal* 103(420): 1236–1243.

Graham, Stephen, and Nigel Thrift. 2007. "Out of order: Understanding repair and maintenance." *Theory, Culture & Society* 24(3): 1–25.

Groseclose, Timothy, and James M. Snyder. 1996. "Buying supermajorities." *American Political Science Review* 90(2): 303–315.

Grossman, Gene M., and Elhanan Helpman. 1996. "Electoral competition and special interest politics." *The Review of Economic Studies* 63(2): 265–286.

Groves, Robert M. 2006. "Nonresponse rates and nonresponse bias in household surveys." *Public Opinion Quarterly* 70(5): 646–675.

Guinier, Lani. 1994. *The tyranny of the majority: Fundamental fairness in representative democracy.* New York: Free Press.

Haber, Stephen, and Victor Menaldo. 2011. "Do natural resources fuel authoritarianism? A reappraisal of the resource curse." *American Political Science Review* 105(1): 1–26.

Hajnal, Zoltan L. 2009. "Who loses In American democracy? A count of votes demonstrates the limited representation of African Americans." *American Political Science Review* 103(1): 37–57.

Hansen, Thomas Blom. 1999. *The saffron wave: Democracy and Hindu nationalism in modern India.* Princeton, NJ: Princeton University Press.

Harding, Robin, and David Stasavage. 2014. "What democracy does (and doesn't do) for basic services: School fees, school inputs, and African elections." *The Journal of Politics* 76(01): 229–245.

Hasan, Zoya, ed. 2002. *Parties and party politics in India.* New Delhi: Oxford University Press.

Head, John G., and Carl S. Shoup. 1969. "Public goods, private goods, and ambiguous goods." *The Economic Journal* 79(315): 567–572.

Hegre, Håvard, and Nicholas Sambanis. 2006. "Sensitivity analysis of empirical results on civil war onset." *Journal of Conflict Resolution* 50(4): 508–535.

Helliwell, John F. 1994. "Empirical linkages between democracy and economic growth." *British Journal of Political Science* 24(2): 225–248.

Henderson, J. Vernon, Adam Storeygard, and David N. Weil. 2012. "Measuring economic growth from outer space." *American Economic Review* 102(2): 994–1028.

Hendrix, Cullen S. 2010. "Measuring state capacity: Theoretical and empirical implications for the study of civil conflict." *Journal of Peace Research* 47(3): 273–285.

Henninger, N., and M. Snel. 2002. *Where are the poor? Experiences with the development and use of poverty maps*. Washington, DC: World Resources Institute.

Hentschel, J., J. Lanjouw, P. Lanjouw, and J. Poggi. 2000. "Combining census and survey data to trace the spatial dimensions of poverty: A case study of Ecuador." *World Bank Economic Review* 14: 147–165.

Herbst, Jeffrey. 2000. *States and power in Africa*. Princeton, NJ: Princeton University Press.

Hicken, Allen. 2011. "Clientelism." *Annual Review of Political Science* 14: 289–310.

Hicken, Allen, and Joel W. Simmons. 2008. "The personal vote and the efficacy of education spending." *American Journal of Political Science* 52(1): 109–124.

Ho, Daniel E., Kosuke Imai, Gary King, and Elizabeth A. Stuart. 2007. "Matching as nonparametric preprocessing for reducing model dependence in parametric causal inference." *Political Analysis* 15(3): 199–236.

Holland, Alisha C. 2015. "The distributive politics of enforcement." *American Journal of Political Science* 59(2): 357–371.

Holz, Carsten A. 2006. "China's reform period economic growth: How reliable are Angus Maddison's estimates?" *Review of Income and Wealth* 52(1): 85–119.

Hood, Kyle K. 2005. "Description of environmental variables accompanying the G-Econ dataset." Yale University. http://gecon.yale.edu/data-and-documentation-g-econ-project

Hoxby, Caroline M. 1999. "The productivity of schools and other local public goods producers." *Journal of Public Economics* 74(1): 1–30.

Hughes, Thomas P. 1983. *Networks of power: Electrification in Western society, 1880–1930*. Baltimore, MD: Johns Hopkins University Press.

Humphreys, Macartan. 2005. "Natural resources, conflict, and conflict resolution: Uncovering the mechanisms." *Journal of Conflict Resolution* 49(4): 508–537.

Huntington, Samuel P. 1968. *Political order in changing societies*. New Haven, CT: Yale University Press.

Imhoff, Mark L., William T. Lawrence, David C. Stutzer, and Christopher D. Elvidge. 1997. "A technique for using composite DMSP/OLS 'city lights' satellite data to map urban area." *Remote Sensing of Environment* 61(3): 361–370.

Intergovernmental Panel on Climate Change. 2007. *Climate change 2007: Working group III report on mitigation of climate change*. Technical Report. Cambridge and New York: Cambridge University Press.

International Energy Agency. 2002. *World energy outlook 2002*. Paris: Organisation for Economic Co-operation and Development (OECD)/IEA.

2011. *World energy outlook 2011*. Paris: Organisation for Economic Co-operation and Development (OECD)/IEA.

2012. *World energy outlook 2012*. Paris: Organisation for Economic Co-operation and Development (OECD)/IEA.

2013. *World energy outlook 2013*. Paris: Organisation for Economic Co-operation and Development (OECD)/IEA.

Jaffrelot, Christophe. 2003. *India's silent revolution: The rise of the low castes in North Indian politics*. New Delhi: Permanent Black.

Jerven, Morten. 2013. *Poor numbers: How we are misled by African development statistics and what to do about it*. Ithaca, NY: Cornell University Press.

Kale, Sunila. 2014. *Electrifying India: Regional political economies of development*. Stanford, CA: Stanford University Press.

Karekezi, Stephen, and Lugard Majoro. 2002. "Improving modern energy services for Africa's urban poor." *Energy Policy* 30(11): 1015–1028.

Kaufmann, Daniel, Aart Kraay, and Massimo Mastruzzi. 2005. "Governance matters IV: Governance indicators for 1996–2004." *World Bank Policy Research Working Paper* 3630. Washington, DC: World Bank.

Keefer, Philip, and Stuti Khemani. 2005. "Democracy, public expenditures, and the poor: Understanding political incentives for providing public services." *World Bank Research Observer* 20(1): 1–27.

2009. "When do legislators pass on pork? The role of political parties in determining legislator effort." *American Political Science Review* 103(1): 99–112.

Kernell, Samuel, and Michael P. McDonald. 1999. "Congress and America's political development: The transformation of the post office from patronage to service." *American Journal of Political Science* 43(3): 792–811.

Kerner, Andrew, Morten Jerven, and Alison Beatty. 2014. "Are Development Statistics Manipulable?" Simons Papers in Security and Development, No. 37/2014, School for International Studies, Simon Fraser University, Vancouver.

Kinder, Donald R., and D. Roderick Kiewiet. 1979. "Economic discontent and political behavior: The role of personal grievances and collective economic judgments in congressional voting." *American Journal of Political Science* 23(3): 495–527.

King, Gary, James Honaker, Anne Joseph, and Kenneth Scheve. 2002. "Analyzing incomplete political science data: An alternative algorithm for multiple imputation." *American Political Science Review* 95(1): 49–69.

Kitfield, James. 1991. "Conventional wisdom revisited." *Government Executive* 23: 18–28.

Kitschelt, Herbert, and Steven Wilkinson. 2007. *Patrons, clients, and policies: Patterns of democratic accountability and political competition.* New York: Cambridge University Press.

Knoesen, Sarah Gray. 2009. "The politics of distribution in South Africa."

Kohiyama, M., H. Hayashi, N. Maki, M. Higashida, H. W. Kroehl, C. D. Elvidge, and V. R. Hobson. 2004. "Early damaged area estimation system using DMSP-OLS night-time imagery." *International Journal of Remote Sensing* 25(11): 2015–2036.

Kohli, Atul. 1987. *The state and poverty in India: The politics of reform.* New York: Cambridge University Press.

2004. *State-directed development: Political power and industrialization in the global periphery.* New York: Cambridge University Press.

Kramer, Gerald H. 1971. "Short-term fluctuations in US voting behavior, 1896–1964." *American Political Science Review* 65(1): 131–143.

Krishna, Anirudh. 2008. "Introduction: Poor people and democracy." In *Poverty, participation, and democracy: A global perspective,* ed. Anirudh Krishna, pp. 1–27. Cambridge and New York: Cambridge University Press.

Kromm, David E. 1970. "Soviet planning for increases in electric power production and capacity." *Transactions of the Kansas Academy of Science* 73(3): 281–291.

Kroth, Verena, Valentino Larcinese, and Joachim Wehner. 2013. "A better life for all? Democratization and electrification in post-Apartheid South Africa." Typescript. London School of Economics and Political Science.

Kudamatsu, Masayuki. 2012. "Has democratization reduced infant mortality in Sub-Saharan Africa? Evidence from micro data." *Journal of the European Economic Association* 10(6): 1294–1317.

Kudamatsu, Masayuki, and Timothy Besley. 2008. "Making autocracy work." In *Institutions and economic performance*, ed. Elhanan Helpman, pp. 452–510. Cambridge, MA: Harvard University Press.

Kuenzi, Michelle, and Gina M. S. Lambright. 2007. "Voter turnout in Africa's multiparty regimes." *Comparative Political Studies* 40(6): 665–690.

Kuran, Timur. 2001. "The provision of public goods under Islamic law: Origins, impact, and limitations of the waqf system." *Law and Society Review* 35(4): 841–898.

Lai, Hongyi Harry. 2002. "China's western development program: Its rationale, implementation, and prospects." *Modern China* 28(4): 432–466.

Lake, David A., and Matt Baum. 2001. "The invisible hand of democracy: Political control and the provision of public services." *Comparative Political Studies* 34(6): 587–621.

Lee, Kuan Yew. 2000. *From third world to first: The Singapore story: 1965–2000.* New York: HarperCollins.

Levi-Faur, David. 2003. "The politics of liberalisation: Privatisation and regulation-for-competition in Europe's and Latin America's telecoms and electricity industries." *European Journal of Political Research* 42(5): 705–740.

Levinson, Robert, Sopen Shah, and Paige K. Connor. 2011. Impact of defense spending: A state-by-state analysis. Technical Report. Bloomberg Government. Washington, DC.

Li, Xi, and Deren Li. 2014. "Can night-time light images play a role in evaluating the Syrian crisis?" *International Journal of Remote Sensing* 35(18): 6648–6661.

Lichbach, Mark I. 1994. "What makes rational peasants revolutionary? Dilemma, paradox, and irony in peasant collective action." *World Politics* 46(3): 383–418.

Lieberman, Evan S. 2002. "Taxation data as indicators of state-society relations: Possibilities and pitfalls in cross-national research." *Studies in Comparative International Development* 36(4): 89–115.

Lindert, Peter H. 2004. *Growing public: Social spending and economic growth since the eighteenth century.* New York: Cambridge University Press.

Lipset, Seymour Martin. 1959. "Some social requisites of democracy: Economic development and political legitimacy." *American Political Science Review* 53(1): 69–105.

Lipton, Michael. 1977. *Why poor people stay poor: A study of urban bias in world development.* Cambridge, MA: Harvard University Press.

Lizzeri, Alessandro, and Nicola Persico. 2001. "The provision of public goods under alternative electoral incentives." *American Economic Review* 91(1): 225–239.

    2004. "Why did the elites extend the suffrage? Democracy and the scope of government, with an application to Britain's age of reform." *The Quarterly Journal of Economics* 119(2): 707–765.

Lo, C. P. 2001. "Modeling the population of China using DMSP operational linescan system nighttime data." *Photogrammetric Engineering and Remote Sensing* 67(9): 1037–1047.

Maddison, Angus. 1998. *Chinese economic performance in the long run.* Paris: Organisation for Economic Co-operation and Development.

Magaloni, Beatriz. 2006. *Voting for autocracy: Hegemonic party survival and its demise in Mexico.* Cambridge and New York: Cambridge University Press.

Mani, Anandi, and Sharun Mukand. 2007. "Democracy, visibility and public good provision." *Journal of Development Economics* 83(2): 506–529.

Manin, Bernard, Adam Przeworski, and Susan C. Stokes. 1999. "Introduction." In *Democracy, accountability, and representation*, ed. Adam Przeworski, Susan C. Stokes, and Bernard Manin, pp. 1–26. New York: Cambridge University Press.

Mayhew, David R. 1974. *Congress: The electoral connection.* New Haven, CT: Yale University Press.

McGuire, James W. 2010. *Wealth, health, and democracy in East Asia and Latin America.* New York and Cambridge: Cambridge University Press.

Meltzer, Allan H., and Scott F. Richard. 1981. "A rational theory of the size of government." *Journal of Political Economy* 89(5): 914–927.

Mertha, Andrew. 2008. *China's water warriors: Citizen action and policy change.* Ithaca, NY: Cornell University Press.

Miguel, Edward. 2004. "Tribe or nation? Nation-building and public goods in Kenya versus Tanzania." *World Politics* 56(3): 327–362.

Miguel, Edward, and Mary Kay Gugerty. 2005. "Ethnic diversity, social sanctions, and public goods in Kenya." *Journal of Public Economics* 89(11–12): 2325–2368.

Milesi-Ferretti, Gian Maria, Roberto Perotti, and Massimo Rostagno. 2002. "Electoral systems and public spending." *Quarterly Journal of Economics* 117(May): 609–657.

Min, Brian, and Kwawu Mensan Gaba. 2014. "Tracking electrification in Vietnam using nighttime lights." *Remote Sensing* 6(10): 9511–9529.

Min, Brian, and Miriam Golden. 2014. "Electoral cycles in electricity losses in India." *Energy Policy* 65: 619–625.

Min, Brian, Kwawu Mensan Gaba, Ousmane Fall Sarr, and Alassane Agalassou. 2013. "Detection of rural electrification in Africa using DMSP-OLS night lights imagery." *International Journal of Remote Sensing* 34(22): 8118–8141.

Minot, Nicholas. 2007. "Are poor, remote areas left behind in agricultural development: The case of Tanzania." *Journal of African Economies* 17(2): 239–276.

Modi, Vijay. 2005. Improving electricity services in rural India. Working Paper 30. Earth Institute at Columbia University, New York.

Murillo, Maria Victoria. 2009. *Political competition, partisanship, and policy making in Latin American public utilities.* New York and Cambridge: Cambridge University Press.

Myrdal, Gunnar. 1957. *Economic theory and underdeveloped regions.* London: Duckworth.

Nakayama, Mikiyasu, and Christopher D. Elvidge. 1999. "Applying newly developed calibrated radiance DMSP/OLS data for estimation of population." *20th Asian Conference on Remote Sensing.* Hong Kong: Joint Laboratory for GeoInformation Science of The Chinese Academy of Sciences and The Chinese University of Hong Kong.

Naughton, Barry. 2007. *The Chinese economy: transitions and growth.* Cambridge, MA: MIT Press.

Neumayer, Eric. 2003. "Good policy can lower violent crime: Evidence from a cross-national panel of homicide rates, 1980–97." *Journal of Peace Research* 40(6): 619.

New, M., D. Lister, M. Hulme, and I. Makin. 2002. "A high-resolution data set of surface climate over global land areas." *Climate Research* 21(1): 1–25.

Nichol, Jim. 2009. Central Asia: Regional development and implications for US Interests. Technical Report 7-5700. Congressional Research Service.

Nordhaus, William D., Quazi Azam, David Corderi, Kyle Hood, N. Makarova Victor, Mukhtar Mohammed, Alexandra Miltner, and Jyldyz Weiss. 2006. "The G-Econ database on gridded output: Methods and data." Yale University. http://gecon.yale.edu/

Nye, David E. 1992. *Electrifying America: Social meanings of a new technology, 1880–1940*. Cambridge, MA: MIT Press.

2010. *When the lights went out: A history of blackouts in America*. Cambridge, MA: MIT Press.

Oi, Jean C. 1985. "Communism and clientelism: Rural politics in China." *World Politics* 37(2): 238–266.

Olson, Mancur. 1965. *The logic of collective action: Public goods and the theory of groups*. Cambridge, MA: Harvard University Press.

1993. "Dictatorship, democracy, and development." *American Political Science Review* 87(3): 567–576.

Padrói Miquel, Gerard. 2007. "The control of politicians in divided societies: The politics of fear." *Review of Economic Studies* 74(4): 1259–1274.

Pai, Sudha. 2002. *Dalit assertion and the unfinished democratic revolution: The Bahujan Samaj Party in Uttar Pradesh*. New Delhi: SAGE.

Palfrey, Thomas R., and Jeffrey E. Prisbrey. 1997. "Anomalous behavior in public goods experiments: How much and why?" *The American Economic Review* 87(5): 829–846.

Pan, Jiahua, Peng Wuyuan, Li Meng, Wu Xiangyang, Wan Lishuang, Hisham Zerriffi, David Victor, Becca Elias, and Chi Zhang. 2006. "Rural electrification in China 1950–2004: Historical processes and key driving forces." Working Paper 60. Program on Energy and Sustainable Development at Stanford University.

Papke, Leslie E., and Jeffrey M. Wooldridge. 1996. "Econometric methods for fractional response variables with an application to 401 (k) plan participation rates." *Journal of Applied Econometrics* 11(6): 619–632.

Paxson, Christina, and Norbert R. Schady. 2002. "The allocation and impact of social funds: Spending on school infrastructure in Peru." *The World Bank Economic Review* 16(2): 297–319.

Perotti, Roberto. 1996. "Growth, income distribution, and democracy: What the data say." *Journal of Economic Growth* 1(2): 149–187.

Posner, Daniel N. 2004. "The political salience of cultural difference: Why Chewas and Tumbukas are allies in Zambia and adversaries in Malawi." *American Political Science Review* 98(4): 529–545.

2005. *Institutions and ethnic politics in Africa*. Cambridge and New York: Cambridge University Press.

Powell, G. Bingham, Jr. 1986. "American voter turnout in comparative perspective." *The American Political Science Review* 80(1): 17–43.

Powell, G. Bingham, Jr., and Georg S. Vanberg. 2000. "Election laws, disproportionality and median correspondence: Implications for two visions of democracy." *British Journal of Political Science* 30(3): 383–411.

Przeworski, A., M. Alvarez, J. Cheibub, and F. Limongi. 2000. *Democracy and development: Political institutions and material well being in the world*. New York: Cambridge University Press.

Przeworski, Adam, and Fernando Limongi. 1993. "Political regimes and economic growth." *Journal of Economic Perspectives* 7(3): 51–69.

Ramos, Antonio Pedro. 2014. "Has democracy reduced inequalities in child mortality? An analysis of 5 million births from 50 developing countries since 1970." Typescript. University of California, Los Angeles.

Rana, Mahendra Singh. 2006. *India votes: Lok Sabha & Vidhan Sabha elections 2001–2005*. New Delhi: Sarup & Sons.

Rath, Nilakantha. 1985. "Garibi Hatao: Can IRDP do it?" *Economic and Political Weekly* 20(6): 238–246.

Rodden, Jonathan. 2010. "The geographic distribution of political preferences." *Annual Review of Political Science* 13: 321–340.

Ross, Michael I.. 2006. "Is democracy good for the poor?" *American Journal of Political Science* 50(4): 860–874.

Sachs, Jeffrey. 2006. *The end of poverty: Economic possibilities for our time*. New York: Penguin.

Samuels, David, and Richard Snyder. 2001. "The value of a vote: Malapportionment in comparative perspective." *British Journal of Political Science* 31(4): 651–671.

Samuelson, Paul A. 1954. "The pure theory of public expenditure." *The Review of Economics and Statistics* 36(4): 387–389.

   1955. "Diagrammatic exposition of a theory of public expenditure." *The Review of Economics and Statistics* 37(4): 350–356.

   1958. "Aspects of public expenditure theories." *The Review of Economics and Statistics* 40(4): 332–338.

   1964. *Economics: An introductory analysis*, 6th ed. New York: McGraw-Hill.

Schady, Norbert R. 2000. "The political economy of expenditures by the Peruvian Social Fund (FONCODES), 1991–95." *American Political Science Review* 94(2): 289–304.

Scheiner, Ethan. 2006. *Democracy without competition in Japan: Opposition failure in a one-party dominant state*. New York: Cambridge University Press.

Schlozman, Kay Lehman, and Henry E. Brady. 1995. *Voice and equality: Civic voluntarism in American politics*. Cambridge, MA: Harvard University Press.

Schmitter, Philippe C., and Terry L. Karl. 1991. "What democracy is … and is not." *Journal of Democracy* 2(3): 75–88.

Scott, James C. 1969. "Corruption, machine politics, and political change." *The American Political Science Review* 63(4): 1142–1158.

Sekhon, Jasjeet S. 2011. "Multivariate and propensity score matching software with automated balance optimization: The matching package for R." *Journal of Statistical Software* 42(7): 1–52.

Sen, Amartya. 1999. *Development as freedom*. New York: Oxford University Press.

Singh, Ajit Kumar. 2009. "The challenge of rapid development of Uttar Pradesh." Working Paper. Giri Institute of Development Studies, Lucknow, India.

Sinton, Jonathan E. 2001. "Accuracy and reliability of China's energy statistics." *China Economic Review* 12(4): 373–383.

Small, C., Francesca Pozzi, and Christopher D. Elvidge. 2005. "Spatial analysis of global urban extent from DMSP-OLS night lights." *Remote Sensing of Environment* 96(3–4): 277–291.

Smith, Alastair. 2008. "The perils of unearned income." *The Journal of Politics* 70(3): 780–793.

Sorrell, Steve. 2009. "Jevons' paradox revisited: The evidence for backfire from improved energy efficiency." *Energy Policy* 37(4): 1456-1469.

Stasavage, David. 2005. "Democracy and education spending in Africa." *American Journal of Political Science* 49(2): 343–358.

Stokes, Susan C. 2005. "Perverse accountability: A formal model of machine politics with evidence from Argentina." *American Political Science Review* 99(3): 315–325.

Stokes, Susan C., Thad Dunning, Marcelo Nazareno, and Valeria Brusco. 2013. *Brokers, voters, and clientelism: The puzzle of distributive politics.* Cambridge and New York: Cambridge University Press.

Strand, Jon. 2012. "Low-level versus high-level equilibrium in public utility services." *Journal of Public Economics* 96(1): 163–172.

Svolik, Milan W. 2012. *The politics of authoritarian rule.* Cambridge and New York: Cambridge University Press.

Thachil, Tariq. 2014. "Elite Parties and Poor Voters: Theory and Evidence from India." *American Political Science Review* 108(2): 454–477.

Thies, Michael F. 1998. "When will pork leave the farm? Institutional bias in Japan and the United States." *Legislative Studies Quarterly* 23(November): 467–492.

Tiebout, Charles M. 1956. "A pure theory of local public expenditures." *Journal of Political Economy* 64(5): 416–424.

Tilly, Charles. 1990. *Coercion, capital, and European states, AD 990–1992.* Cambridge, MA: Basil Blackwell.

Treier, Shawn, and Simon Jackman. 2008. "Democracy as a latent variable." *American Journal of Political Science* 52(1): 201–217.

Treiman, Donald J. 2007. "Growth and determinants of literacy in China." In *Education and reform in China.* ed. Emily Hannum and Albert Park, pp. 135–153. New York: Routledge.

Tsai, Lily. 2007. "Solidary groups, informal accountability, and local public goods provision in rural China." *American Political Science Review* 101(2): 355–372.

Tuttle, Benjamin T., Sharolyn Anderson, Chris Elvidge, Tilottama Ghosh, Kim Baugh, and Paul Sutton. 2014. "Aladdin's magic lamp: Active target calibration of the DMSP OLS." *Remote Sensing* 6(12): 12708–12722.

US Census Bureau. 1975. *Historical statistics of the United States: Colonial times to 1970.* Washington, DC: US Census Bureau.

Uttar Pradesh Planning Department. 2006. Uttar Pradesh Human Development Report 2006. Technical Report. Government of Uttar Pradesh.

Van Zandt, David E. 1993. "The lessons of the lighthouse: 'Government' or 'private' provision of goods." *The Journal of Legal Studies* 22(1): 47–72.

Varshney, Ashutosh. 1995. *Democracy, development, and the countryside: Urban-rural struggles in India.* Cambridge and New York: Cambridge University Press.

2000. "Is India becoming more democratic?" *The Journal of Asian Studies* 59(1): 3–25.

Ward, Michael D., and Kristian Skrede Gleditsch. 2002. "Location, location, location: An MCMC approach to modeling the spatial context of war and peace." *Political Analysis* 10(3): 244–260.

Weghorst, Keith R., and Staffan I Lindberg. 2013. "What drives the swing voter in Africa?" *American Journal of Political Science* 57(3): 717–734.

Weiner, Myron. 1962. *The politics of scarcity: Public pressure and political response in India.* Chicago: University of Chicago Press.

Weingast, Barry R., Kenneth A. Shepsle, and Christopher Johnsen. 1981. "The political economy of benefits and costs: A neoclassical approach to distributive politics." *Journal of Political Economy* 89(4): 642–664.

Weitz-Shapiro, Rebecca. 2012. "What wins votes: Why some politicians opt out of clientelism." *American Journal of Political Science* 56(3): 568–583.

Wengle, Susanne A. 2015. *Post-Soviet power: State-led development and Russia's marketization*. Cambridge and New York: Cambridge University Press.

Wibbels, Erik. 2006. "Dependency revisited: International markets, business cycles, and social spending in the developing world." *International Organization* 60(2): 433–468.

Wilkinson, Steven I. 2004. *Votes and violence: Electoral competition and ethnic riots in India*. New York: Cambridge University Press.

2006. "The politics of infrastructural spending in India." Typescript. University of Chicago.

Wimmer, Andreas, Lars-Erik Cederman, and Brian Min. 2009. "Ethnic politics and armed conflict: A configurational analysis." *American Sociological Review* 74(2): 316–337.

Wintrobe, Ronald. 1998. *The political economy of dictatorship*. Cambridge and New York: Cambridge University Press.

Wittman, Donald. 1989. "Why democracies produce efficient results." *Journal of Political Economy* 97(6): 1395–1424.

Wooldridge, Jeffrey M. 2002. *Econometric analysis of cross section and panel data*. Cambridge, MA: MIT Press.

World Bank. 1994. *World development report 1994: Infrastructure for development*. Washington, DC: World Bank.

2002. Poverty in India: The challenge of Uttar Pradesh. Report No. 22323-IN. Poverty Reduction and Economic Management Sector Unit, South Asia Region.

Wright, Joseph. 2008. "Do authoritarian institutions constrain? How legislatures affect economic growth and investment." *American Journal of Political Science* 52(2): 322–343.

Yadav, Yogendra. 2000. "Understanding the second democratic upsurge: Trends of Bahujan participation in electoral politics in the 1990s." In *Transforming India: Social and political dynamics of democracy*, ed. Francine R. Frankel, Zoya Hasan, Rajeev Bhargava, and Arora Balveer, pp. 120–145. New Delhi: Oxford University Press.

Zhang, Xiaobo, Shenggen Fan, Linxiu Zhang, and Jikun Huang. 2004. "Local governance and public goods provision in rural China." *Journal of Public Economics* 88(12): 2857–2871.

Zweifel, Thomas D., and Patricio Navia. 2000. "Democracy, dictatorship, and infant mortality." *Journal of Democracy* 11(2): 99–114.

Index